The *Wunderkammer*
of Lady Charlotte Guest

The *Wunderkammer* of Lady Charlotte Guest

Erica Obey

Lehigh
University
Press

Bethlehem: Lehigh University Press

Associated University Presses
2010 Eastpark Boulevard
Cranbury, NJ 08512

The paper used in this publication meets the requirements of the American National Standard for Permanence of Paper for Printed Library Materials Z39.48–1984.

Library of Congress Cataloging-in-Publication Data

Obey, Erica, 1959-
  The wunderkammer of Lady Charlotte Guest / Erica Obey.
    p. cm.
  Includes bibliographical references and index.
  ISBN-13: 978-0-934223-88-1 (alk. paper)
  ISBN-10: 0-934223-88-2 (alk. paper)
  1. Schreiber, Charlotte, Lady, 1812-1895. 2. Great Britain—History—Victoria, 1837–1901—Biography. 3. Industrialists—Great Britain—Biography. 5. Nobility—Great Britain—Biography. I. Title.
  DA565.S34O24 2007
  941.08092—dc22
  [B]
                          2006020204

To the memories
of the Rev. Robert F. Obey and Jane Landon Baird,
who both loved books as much as life.

Contents

Acknowledgments

I WOULD LIKE TO THANK JOSHUA WILNER FOR HIS INTELLECTUAL generosity as a dissertation advisor on an earlier version of this project. William Coleman and Catherine McKenna also provided valuable critical readings of the manuscript. In addition, I would like to thank Judith Mayer at Lehigh University Press. There are no words to express the debt of gratitude I owe George Baird, exemplary academic husband, whose talents run the gamut from writing permissions letters to sizing digital images.

Anderson, Charles R. Sidney Lanier: Centennial Edition, pp. x, 20, 121–22, 249–50, 324. ©1945 [Copyright Holder]. Reprinted with permission of The Johns Hopkins University Press.

Images from the Schreiber Collection are ©V&A Images/Victoria and Albert Museum.

Excerpts from Lady Charlotte Guest's Papers are by permission of Viscount Wimborne and Llyfrgell Genedlaethol Cymru/The National Library of Wales. I would also like to express my appreciation of the unfailing cheerfulness and helpfulness of the library's staff—especially that of the South Reading Room.

Excerpts from *Lady Charlotte: A Biography of the Nineteenth Century* (forthcoming from Tempus Publishing, Stroud, Gloucestire, England, 2007) by kind permission of Revel Guest and Angela V. John.

The *Wunderkammer*
of Lady Charlotte Guest

Introduction:
The Despotism of Fact

LADY CHARLOTTE GUEST (LADY CHARLOTTE SCHREIBER), 1812–95, was a figure to strike fear into the hearts of workingmen, museum curators, and ne'er-do-well nephews. A vortex of Victorian industry, she faced down striking colliers while she ran her first husband's ironmongery single-handedly; learned Welsh in order to translate the *Mabinogion*; established schools for her workers; and assembled exhaustive collections of ceramics, fans, and playing cards, which were presented to the Victoria and Albert and British Museums—all the while selling embroidery for the relief of Turkish refugees and knitting a bright red scarf a day for London's hansom cab drivers. In contrast to these exemplary accomplishments, however, she also managed to create a minor scandal when she married her son's penniless tutor, fourteen years her junior, with what many saw as inappropriate swiftness after her first husband's death. All of these adventures, and more, are described in the ten thousand pages that make up her journals, which she wrote regularly during the course of her long and eventful life.

In the length of her life, which spanned almost all the nineteenth century, as well as its details, Lady Charlotte is arguably a microcosm of the Victorian Age—as well as an apparent answer to Jean Hyppolite's question, as posed by Michel Foucault: "if philosophy really must begin as absolute discourse, then what of history, and what is this beginning which starts out with a singular individual, within a society and a social class?"[1] Lady Charlotte is at once a singular individual and a product of her social class. Her first marriage is emblematic of the socioeconomic shift that took place during the century her life spanned: Her family's aristocratic roots went back to

Elizabeth I, while John Guest was a parliamentarian and an industrialist, a member of the rising bourgeoisie. Similarly, her second marriage is emblematic of the multiple social resistances to the power structures from which both she and her first husband benefited. More interestingly, Lady Charlotte's journals can feel like a Who's Who of Victorian culture and politics: When she was reminded of a lost love while at the opera, she was watching Malibran singing *La Sonnambula*. When her husband accused her of infidelity, it was with Austen Henry Layard, the discoverer of Nineveh. When she was socially embarrassed by the age discrepancy between her second husband and herself, it was while she was being presented to the queen. Her stately home was renovated by the architect who had designed the Houses of Parliament. Tennyson sought her opinions on pronunciation. She dined with Wilde.

Most importantly, the two great intellectual works for which she is remembered, her translation of the *Mabinogion* and her china collections, are both seminal to the cultural discourse of Victorian England. Her translation of the *Mabinogion* introduced one of the great cultural symbols of the nineteenth century, the Matter of Britain; no lesser figures than Matthew Arnold and Alfred, Lord Tennyson both announced their debt to her translation. The china collections she amassed during her second marriage put her on a level with such arbiters of artistic taste as Mrs. Jameson, Lady Eastlake, Joseph Marryat, and Joseph Joel Duveen. Indeed, it is not going too far to claim that both of Lady Charlotte's major accomplishments were seminal in defining the cultural discourse of Victorian England. Yet, Lady Charlotte's own position *vis à vis* this very discourse was a significantly and sometimes multiply marginalized one.

Paradoxically, much of this marginalization can be attributed to her privileged socioeconomic status. In particular, Lady Charlotte's accomplishment in translating the *Mabinogion* has been appreciated at best grudgingly. On the one hand, contemporary professional scholars routinely dismiss her as a "gifted amateur," a peculiarly mercantile denigration that is especially ironic in the face of nineteenth-century critics such as Lady Eastlake, who bemoaned the mercantile classes replacing the eighteenth-century amateurs as collectors. Perhaps more understandably, there are also many Welsh scholars who reject Lady Charlotte's accomplishments largely because of her role in perpetuating the unequal cultural exchange between the Welsh and the English. These detractors argue that she "didn't really" translate the *Mabinogion,* but instead used her wealth and connections to publish and publicize a translation that was largely the work of her Welsh colleagues.[2] On the other hand, critics such as Judith Johnston characterize Lady Charlotte's translation as an act of cultural appropriation, arguing that "Once you name, and transcribe, you acquire."[3] Given this assumption, Johnston characterizes Lady Charlotte's translation as "both an imperialist and a feminist project, although never expressed in either of those terms."[4]

This is not to say it is not legitimate to read Lady Charlotte's translation in terms of an unequal exchange of cultural capital. Although Guest's ironworks were located in Wales, neither he nor Lady Charlotte was Welsh. Moreover, his role as parliamentary representative for Dowlais meant that the couple spent much of their time in London. And, although Guest's politics were liberal—he was a founding member of the Reform Club—the very fact Dowlais's largest employer was also its parliamentary representative is ample evidence of the unequal balance of power in their relationship.

Furthermore, Lady Charlotte's translation certainly inscribed this unequal balance of power into nineteenth-century cultural discourse. In no less a work than his reviled *On the Study of Celtic Literature,* Matthew Arnold specifically announced his intellectual debt to Lady Charlotte for having translated the *Mabinogion.* It is a connection that Lady Charlotte might well have preferred not to acknowledge. *Celtic Literature* is a post-colonial nightmare, in which Arnold infamously attempts to define the "English genius"—primarily by contrasting it to the Saxon and Celtic geniuses from which it is formed. The Saxon (or German) genius, he claims, is "steadiness with honesty," while somewhat predictably, the Celtic genius is a sentimental one.[5] Arnold then spends the remainder of his essay defining the English genius as a combination of these two strains, adding, with the careful precision of a chef, the Norman genius—which excels at rhetoric and has a "Roman talent for affairs"—to his recipe at the end.[6] This clear demarcation between the three cultural types is exactly paralleled by three separate types of linguistic principles: The scientific principle is that of prosaic, but absolutely truthful, language. The poetic principle is the "passionate, turbulent, indomitable reaction against the despotism of fact."[7] Rhetoric is the third form of language, and the only one that is not dependent on abstractions such as truth or fact. Instead, it is language situated in society: communication judged not in terms of truth value, but in terms of efficacy.

Arnold's Celts' reaction may well be "passionate, turbulent, and indomitable" because there are few facts in Arnold's argument and a great deal of despotism. Derrida has famously demonstrated the fictional nature of such postulated primal archaeologies as Arnold's, while Foucault has taken Derrida's claim a step further and argued that texts such as Arnold's are part of a larger social discourse that reinforces social power structures.[8] In contrast to this almost laughably dismissible claim about the Celts, however, Arnold's characterizing rhetoric as language situated in society is eerily prescient. Admittedly, Arnold drifts uncomfortably close to valorizing precisely the same social constructions masquerading as absolute principles that Foucault critiques; however, his locating meaning in the social context that produces language anticipates the arguments of Walter Benjamin in "Edward Fuchs: Collector and Historian."

In that essay, Benjamin argues that idealizing constructs such as "history" are an illusion. Instead, the past can only be viewed in dialectical encounter with the present, which, because it brings with it its own limitations in perspective, caused by historico-material influences, always provides an imperfect view. Furthermore, he argues forcefully against art providing any kind of escape to an idealist perspective, claiming instead that art must be seen as the product of material, economic influences. Art rather provides a locus for a dialectical encounter with its historico-material situation, which releases—albeit only momentarily and imperfectly—both the subject and object from the abstract systemization and classification that Benjamin terms Tradition.[9] This dialectical encounter can occur in circumstances as varied as translating, unveiling a cult statue, or observing "two grains of wheat in the Jewish section of the Musee Cluny 'on which a kindred soul had inscribed the complete *Shema Israel.*'"[10]

Somewhat surprisingly, Lady Charlotte's *Mabinogion* creates exactly such a dialectical encounter. For, before it is a translation, Lady Charlotte's *Mabinogion* is a collection—more than 150 pages of footnotes, illustrations, and appendices for a 275-page text. More importantly, the text now known casually as the *Mabinogion* is not a text. Rather, much like *Grimm's Fairy Tales,* the *Mabinogion* is a collection of twelve largely unrelated tales that are now perceived as a whole, simply because Lady Charlotte translated and published them together.

The importance of seeing Lady Charlotte's *Mabinogion* first and foremost as a collection becomes more evident when one considers the fact that, in conjunction with her second husband, she enjoyed a second, arguably more distinguished, career as a collector of china, fans, playing cards, and *objets d'art*. Collecting these objects is closer to collecting texts than may seem initially obvious, for several recent theorists of collecting, such as Susan Pearce and Daniel Miller, have emphasized the essentially linguistic nature of collecting. In particular, they argue that an object has a unique ability to supersede the structuralist definitions that underlie most modern discussions of meaning and interpretation. Pearce demonstrates how an artifact, such as Keppoch's sword from the Battle of Culloden, exists in a relationship that is simultaneously metonymic with respect to the actual battle in which it was used, and metaphoric with respect to present-day museum visitors, who read the sword as a symbol of the battle.[11] She then goes on to point out how the act of collecting creates a similar bridge between the metonymic relations of the actual objects and the metaphoric signification of the collector's systematization of his collection. Miller expands on this idea to make the particularly suggestive argument that this slippage between axes of interpretability lends objects a deceptive flexibility of meanings—deceptive because humans are biased toward seeing the meaning of objects as inherently more absolute than that of linguistic systems.

This same flexibility of meaning may also allow a collector to use his collection to critique the cultural discourse in which it is embedded—especially when the collector was oppressed by the prevailing cultural discourse, as a nineteenth-century female collector was. Just as, according to Benjamin, collecting objects rescued them from Tradition,[12] collecting domestic objects allowed female collectors to liberate the objects from the traditional uses to which they were put. The object's flexibility of interpretability, however, allowed such collecting to appear as appropriately feminine. Thus, early critics such as Maurice Jonas (1907) saw women's collecting domestic objects as a natural metonymic relationship, reflecting their shared delicacy or domestic functions.[13] On the other hand, in systematizing and categorizing their collections, women collectors could trespass on the conventionally masculine, idealizing territories of abstraction and categorization, which were normally considered too difficult for female minds.

Furthermore, the porcelain that Lady Charlotte collected also called tradition into question—presumably largely unintentionally

—by miniaturizing historical, allegorical, and mythic narratives into doll-like grotesques. Other objective standards of judgment were also interrogated—again, presumably unintentionally—by creating hybrid objects that were neither definably decorative nor useful, or objects, such as the "fine tureen, in the form of a RABBIT BIG AS LIFE [*sic*],"[14] which masqueraded as other objects. Interestingly, "hybridic" is exactly the term that Mieke Bal uses to characterize the impulse to collect, arguing that the impulse is "a mixture of capitalism and individualism enmeshed with alternative modes of historical and psychological existence."[15] And it is exactly this intersection between private and public, historical and psychological, capitalism and individualism that is the hallmark of Lady Charlotte's relationship to the cultural discourse of the nineteenth century.

Perhaps less obviously, this intersection is inscribed in the private discourse of her journals as well. This characteristic is directly related to the fact that her journals reflect her impulse to collect as much as her *Mabinogion* and her china collection do. Paradoxically, this impulse can be easily read in the apparently idealizing construct that opens her published diaries, in which she positions her first husband, John Guest, as her reader:

> Not now, as in the winter, can I say that the only friend I had to confide in was my journal. Now, every care and every joy, every sorrow and every delight is shared and sympathized with, and henceforth my only friend, my only confidant is my husband . . . the dates I note are, at least, of as much interest to my husband as to me, and the book in which I keep them is as much his journal as mine.[16]

It must be stressed that Guest evinced not the slightest interest in reading his wife's diaries. Instead, his imagined readership is functioning as what Sidonie Smith would term either an addressee or an Other of Lady Charlotte's autobiographical "I," an important component in what Smith terms an "autobiographical act."[17] This terminology emphasizes the constitutive and intersubjective nature of autobiography, in which she claims "personal narrators assume the role of the *bricoleur* who takes up bits and pieces of the identities and narrative forms available and, by disjoining and joining them in excessive ways, creates a history of the subject at a precise point in time and space."[18] *Bricolage* is, of course, nothing other than a form of collecting—made necessary in Smith's theory because "Whether the story is ever one's own is a question that can perhaps no longer be posed in terms of individualism and ownership in a postmodern world where concepts of self are negotiated socially and dialogically. 'Individualism' has been commodified; the personal contents of the 'personal' have been largely evacuated."[19] The narrating subject can only respond by taking ownership of her constitutive stories—in other words, collecting them.

Smith's argument establishes the private narrative as an essential locus for resistance to the public discourses that shape our lives. Indeed, writing an autobiography can be seen as writing a discourse that actively counters the discourses that reinforce the power structures in our historico-material situation. In *Assuming the Positions: Cultural Pedagogy and the Politics of Commonplace Writing*, Susan Miller takes this argument a step further by claiming that collections of private intellectual capital serve a similar function as a locus of resistance to cultural discourse—in this case that established by the textual hierarchies imposed by later state-wide mass education. Miller's discussion of "commonplace" writing derives from an item made redundant by modern printing technology—the commonplace book, in which a reader copied quotes, instructions, poems, and other forms of writing, to serve as a model for his own writing. Miller follows the lead of John Locke in describing how such commonplace books, as well as other forms of conventional writing, become a form of private intellectual or cultural capital that "opens a space for imagining an independent writer's work, not inscribed collectively held language, as a source of social identity."[20] Significantly, in addition to her journals, Lady Charlotte did keep such commonplace books. However, only two of them remain: a collection of biographies of her ancestors and a collection of Persian poetry. Despite the relative paucity of the evidence, it is clear that both collections are discourses of resistance, for they both serve as loci where Lady Charlotte asserts herself as rebellious and exotic, in contrast to the decorous role she played both actually, as well as textually in her journals.

In her later journals, the discursive role played by amassed private intellectual capital becomes even more evident. Edited by her son Montague and published as *Confidences of a Collector*, these diaries are distinguished by their combining detailed notes on her acquisitions of china with the more conventional personal experiences the rest of her diaries record.[21] Increasingly, the objects function as both the impetus and locus of experience—and eventually even narrative. A "gourd-shaped tin-glazed earthenware bottle painted with a lake scene and tulips in bright polychrome,"[22] in particular, led Lady Charlotte to write a sketch entitled "The Adventure of a Bottle," which "is a parody of the novel of sensibility with echoes of Sterne's *A Sentimental Journey*."[23]

"The Adventure of a Bottle" is not the only creative sketch Lady Charlotte ever wrote; the family had a printing press at their house at Canford and often published private periodicals. Nonetheless, at first glance it seems odd that an object inspired the one piece of creative writing of Lady Charlotte's that remains in public hands. Mieke Bal, however, argues that the acts of collecting and creating a narrative are essentially similar ones, both being a form of

> interplay between subjectivity and the cultural basis of understanding, whether you call it objectivity or intersubjectivity. Not that these two concepts are identical, of course; but they both claim to cover the status of things *outside* of the individual subject. This is, of course, the paradoxical status of all art and literature, of all cultural expression. On the one hand, both in the production and in the reception, subjectivity is the bottom line. Yet, the object produced and interpreted must be accessible, materially (objectively) and discursively (semiotically, *qua* meaning that is). Cultural objects must signify through common codes, conventions of meaning-making that both producer and reader understand.[24]

Despite their commonality, the meaning of these codes is actually created by an act of dissociation from meaning, when "The object is turned away, abducted, from itself, its inherent value, and denuded of its defining function so as to be available for use as a sign."[25] Once the object has been dissociated from the meaning established by its historico-material situation, the individual subject controls its new meaning. Such privileging private meaning over socially constructed meaning obviously creates a highly unstable signifying system. Indeed, it is this very instability that leads Jean Baudrillard to conclude his analysis of collecting with a pair of questions: "Can objects ever institute themselves as a viable language? Can they ever be fashioned into a discourse oriented otherwise than toward oneself?"[26]

It is a sign of this question's difficulty and significance that Baudrillard is forced to take recourse to notions (albeit guarded ones) of materiality and objectivity in order to answer this question, arguing that the objects themselves "prevent [the collector] from regressing toward total abstraction or psychological delirium," for they "are too concrete, too discontinuous for [the process of collecting] to be capable of articulating itself as a real dialectical structure."[27] This study will attempt to answer this question in another way, by examining how the code that Lady Charlotte created with her translation of the *Mabinogion* was reused by Sidney Lanier in his *Boy's Mabinogion*, which he took directly from her translation. As an American attempting to build an academic career in the South during Reconstruction, the discourses that shaped Lanier were very different from those that shaped Lady Charlotte. Yet the code Lady Charlotte created by collecting the *Mabinogion* provides a signifying system whose meanings are both absolute and flexible enough to be resituable to Lanier's context, allowing him to create an entirely new countering discourse using exactly the same text.

Lady Charlotte was a Great Victorian in every sense of the word. She was a triumph of individualism, boundlessly ambitious, and industrious in ways that seem impossible to the twenty-first century mind. She was also an extraordinary woman—one who was often described with the backhanded compliment, "having a masculine mind." This very individualism, arguably, makes her a classic Victorian "type." However, any notion of "type" is anti-individual and anti-subjective, depending as it does on a system of classification that is inextricably bound up in the larger cultural discourses of both the nineteenth and twenty-first centuries. Type or individual? Object of or enunciator of cultural discourse? The words that seem most likely to answer this question are the same ones Bal used to describe a collector: "mixture," "alternating," and "hybridic." And examining these admixtures in Lady Charlotte, the collector, provides deeper insights into how Lady Charlotte as both a "type" and individual functioned in the larger cultural discourse of the nineteenth century.

1

Mrs. Ellis's Wives
of England

LADY CHARLOTTE GUEST DOES NOT LEND HERSELF EASILY TO CATE-gorization: indeed, neither her biography nor her *oeuvre* presents itself as a readily graspable unity. In particular, her *oeuvre*—if she can be said to have an *oeuvre*—is a collection of disparate genres: an abortive attempt at a history of the iron trade, inspired presumably by a fit of newlywed enthusiasm; her translation of, and notes for, the *Mabinogion*; catalogues that she created for her collections of ceramics, playing cards, and fans; and finally her journal, which she kept from the time she was given her first pocket book in 1822 (ironically by her loathed stepfather Reverend Pegus[1]) until she was too blind to continue in 1891.

The fragmentary nature of Lady Charlotte's *oeuvre* lends credence to the unfairly marginalizing characterization of her as a gifted amateur who just happened to produce the first translation of a series of romances important to both English and Celtic literature. That characterization is unhappily reinforced by a contingent fact of her biography: the emphasis on modest effortlessness in all things among the English aristocracy. It is further reinforced by the way Lady Charlotte's published output is systematically conditioned by the contexts created by her biography. In Wales, among antiquarians, she translated Welsh poems; later, as an independently wealthy collector and wife, she documented the collections she amassed. Even the form of her journal changed as she transformed herself from scholar and intellectual to collector.

It is easy to read this diversity as aimlessness, a version of the problems of autobiography that Carolyn Heilbrun defines for "privileged women,"[2] a nameless malaise of which genuinely oppressed writers such as bell hooks are contemptuous. Yet, Lady Charlotte's literary production deserves more than such a simple dismissal. For, although her output may be fragmented, the act of writing was a consistent part of her life. In addition to business and scholarly documents, she wrote in her journal for an hour each day, producing ten thousand pages during the course of her lifetime.[3] Furthermore, the very diversity and contingency of her writing makes it a remarkably prescient act of literary self-construction. Like Walter Benjamin's *Arcades Project*, Lady Charlotte's journals address what is in fact the central quest of modernism: unearthing self-consciousness from the fractured elements of experience.

This prescience is particularly paradoxical, for, at first glance, Lady Charlotte seems like an exemplar of "literary" subjectivity. She was certainly not ashamed to function as a desiring subject, writing with refreshing candor in her diary, "But whatever I undertake, I must reach an eminence in"[4]—an ambition that was certainly borne on the backs of servants and her husband's income, not to mention the backs of Welsh iron workers. Yet, none of the texts she produced, including even her journals, can be easily read as a deliberate construction of—or interrogation of—self. Instead, her writings, if they can be said to be unified at all, are unified by their seeming contingency. Lady Charlotte, when we encounter her textually, is nothing so much as a series of collections: of Welsh folklore, of family biographies, of other literary excerpts. It is the dialectic between this Other-directed contingency and Lady Charlotte's inherent subjective romanticism that this chapter proposes to explore—arguing that this tension both rehearses and resolves the "irresolvable polarities of theory" that Walter Benjamin describes in "Edward Fuchs: Historian and Collector."

First, however, the contingent nature of Lady Charlotte's writing must be distinguished from the traditional Other-directedness of women's autobiography. It is a commonplace of feminist criticism that women writers from Margaret Cavendish to Gertrude Stein, rather than constructing their narrative around the romantic subject "I," instead construct their narratives in relation to an Other. Cavendish enfolds her autobiography, quite literally, in a biography of her husband; Julian of Norwich constructs her autobiography in relation to God; and Stein continues the tradition by writing her autobiography as *The Autobiography of Alice B. Toklas* by Gertrude Stein.[5]

What all these definitions have in common is that they confound the definition of autobiography that Philippe Lejeune presents in his first major discussion of the genre, *On Autobiography*. In attempting a formalist definition that avoids the obvious referential fallacy of using exterior criteria, such as the facts of the biographee's life or the author's intention to publish, Lejeune finally offers one criterion in a gesture so reductionist, it can almost seem simplistic: autobiography is a genre in which the protagonist is implicitly or directly identified with the author of the piece, by the specific fact of their having the same proper name. Cavendish's framing her autobiography as a life of her husband, as well as Stein's more obvious deflection of "her" autobiography, immediately problematize this definition, as do Lady Charlotte's diaries. In fact, in library listings, Lady Charlotte is the subject, not the author, of both published versions of her diaries. The first version, *Lady Charlotte Schreiber's Journals, Confidences of a Collector of Ceramics and Antiques,* published in 1911, is edited by her son Montague Guest, who is therefore listed in card catalogues in the place of author. The two later versions, *Lady Charlotte Guest: Extracts from her Journal 1833–52* (1950) and *Lady Charlotte Schreiber: Extracts from her Journal 1853–1891* (1952), are edited by her grandson, the Earl of Bessborough, who is credited as the author. This crediting of her editors as authors is more than a simple trick of bibliographic *legerdemain.* When one considers the fact that the only full-length biography of Lady Charlotte is done by yet another descendent, Revel Guest, as well as the fact that a large portion of Lady Charlotte's journals remain in the family's possession, it becomes obvious that, even a hundred years later, Lady Charlotte remains not so much an author as subject as an object in the family's control. Indeed, although Montague Guest contented himself with selecting extracts, the Earl of Bessborough was an editor who was interfering to the point of Bowdlerization, summarizing large passages of Lady Charlotte's life in paragraphs sometimes as long as the journal extracts he provides.

It might be immediately objected that the publication history of Lady Charlotte's diaries is indicative only of why they should not be considered as falling under Lejeune's rubric. Yet Lejeune himself considers the autobiography of Daniel Stern (Marie d'Agoult), whose publication history is almost identical to Lady Charlotte's.[6] Both Stern's *Memoires* and *Mes souvenirs* were published posthumously and, in the case of the *Memoires*, were edited extensively. As the title implies, the *Memoires* were at least begun as an autobiography and then abandoned; however, Stern's editor Olliver saw fit to embellish them with journal entries and notes, as well as journal entries by Liszt, Stern's lover.

Stern's case highlights a critical theoretical difficulty in discussing the difference between diaries and autobiography. For, if one follows Lejeune's lead, the two genres are, on the one hand, so similar as to be interchangeable, and on the other hand, radically antithetical. A diary is an interior, contingent piece of writing that could be associated on a theoretical level with both the feminine and the material in its immediacy and self-effacingness. Yet, the diary can be turned into autobiography, a romantic assertion of self as an individual or extraordinary exemplar, not by any change in writing, but simply by the act of publication. This very publication, however, calls into question the very notion of an author, for it is in fact often the work of someone other than the actual author of the text.[7]

Furthermore, the fact that Lady Charlotte is female problematizes Lejeune's ideas of autobiography from an additional perspective. For the name of the female diarist is not the static single name of the male autobiographer: Lady Charlotte, both diarist and author, was successively Lady Charlotte Bertie, Lady Charlotte Guest, and Lady Charlotte Schreiber. It is a distinction that all three of her biographers support. Montague Guest published only the diaries of Lady Charlotte Schreiber. Bessborough published two separate volumes, one devoted to Lady Charlotte Guest, the other to Lady Charlotte Schreiber. Revel Guest divides her biography in three parts: Lady Charlotte Bertie, Lady Charlotte Guest, and Lady Charlotte Schreiber. Significantly, none of Lady Charlotte's editors chose to publish the diaries of Lady Charlotte Bertie—perhaps yielding to the assumption that a woman is not a person until she is defined by a husband. Guest and John come closest, devoting twenty-one pages of a 251-page biography to Lady Charlotte Bertie.

Accepting Lejeune's definition, thus, leads to the inference that Lady Charlotte's diary consists, in fact, of three separate autobiographies of three separate lives, each defined by an external relationship to a male. Arguably, on one level, this inference is correct, for Lady Charlotte's relationships with her two husbands were so radically different that the two sets of journals can seem like two very different texts. Yet, on the other hand, these journals were all written

by a single person, whom this study will call Lady Charlotte, for that
was the single identity by which she identified herself throughout
her life. The "Lady" is as important to this identification as the
"Charlotte," for it is acutely evident throughout her writing that she
was extremely aware of her position as a daughter of the nobility
and in fact defined herself by that status.

Indeed, the title "Lady" (which consistently superseded "Mrs.")
served as a linguistic marker that functioned in dialectic tension
with her married identities, neither of which was noble. One early
indication of this tension appeared when Sir John (like many trades-
men before him) was elevated to the baronetcy, not the nobility, and
that only after their marriage. It was a distinction that Lady Charlotte considered an insult, writing on July 3, 1838:

> In to-day's [*sic*] gazette my dear Merthyr was elevated, if so I must call
> it, to the rank of Baronet. I consider it a paltry distinction and was
> much averse to his taking it, but he liked to secure something which
> would descend to Ivor . . . I shall not rest until I see something of
> more value bestowed upon him. The present change is anything but
> agreeable to me.[8]

Such obsessiveness over rank is more understandable if one real-
izes that, although Lady Charlotte was born to the nobility, that
identity was snatched away from her early in her life. She was born
Lady Charlotte Bertie, the eldest child of the Ninth Earl of Lindsey
and his second wife, Charlotte, on May 19, 1812. Lady Charlotte's father, the Earl of Lindsey, died in 1818, when she was six years old. In
1821, her mother remarried a cousin with the delightfully Dicken-
sian name of the Reverend Peter Pegus. As if inspired by the writer
himself, Lady Charlotte's life rapidly turned into a series of nineteenth-century set pieces. Her mother retreated to the couch and
delicate health, perhaps in direct reaction to Rev. Pegus's drunken
exploits such as sacking all the servants[9] and passing out pepper-
mints in church in order to disrupt a rival's sermons.[10] When laborers during the Swing Riots of 1830 burned ricks, barns, and man-
sions, the Rev. Pegus rose to the occasion in a manner that strikes
the twentieth-century reader as a music hall number, arming himself with "two swords, a double-barreled shotgun, and a brace of pis-
tols."[11] The capstone on this low farce (although probably not to the
lady in question) was Charlotte's French governess being seduced
by a cousin, Albermarle Layard, "the black sheep of the Rectory."[12]

The biographies of Lady Charlotte's two full brothers, presumably her most direct link to the entitlements the daughter of an earl might expect, could serve as nothing but a salutary story about the tenuousness of this link. The heir to the family title, referred to as Lindsey, was born two years after Charlotte in 1814. Although any kind of definitive diagnosis is impossible at this date, it is clear that Lindsey was a simpleton, who was treated, among others, by the same doctor as had treated the madness of King George III. In a series of episodes that the adolescent Charlotte could only read as indicative of how schemers were constantly attempting to snatch her hereditary identity, Lindsey was the victim of at least two mock marriages, one of them staged by his stepfather, as well as a more conventional attempt to marry him to a rich heiress.[13] The twenty-year-old Lady Charlotte, herself in the middle of marriage negotiations, was forced to intervene in the second of these mock marriages, by appealing directly and in secret to the Lord Chancellor, Lord Brougham.[14]

Lady Charlotte's other full brother, known as Bertie, was born in 1815. Like Charlotte, he was a reader and an intellectual; however, unlike his sister, he seemed incapable of turning his talents to any productive use whatsoever. According to Charlotte's son Montague, he was "a voracious reader and crammed full of information which even with his great memory," he "was totally unable to make any use of to himself or other."[15] A postmodernist could make much of this literal *aporia*. It takes only the most obvious psychological reading, however, to see the roots of Lady Charlotte's ambition and competitiveness, which often verged on caricature, in this early situation in which her identity was rendered doubly ineffectual, both by her female status and by the incapacities of her brothers. The insecurity of her position goes a long way to explaining, if not justifying, such sentiments as "my blood was of the noblest and most princely in the kingdom, and if I go into Society, it must be the very best and first. I can brook no other."[16]

The quote is also emblematic of Lady Charlotte's continuingly vexed relationship with London society. Being the daughter of an earl, Lady Charlotte was given a London season—an indulgence denied her stepsisters, who were merely daughters of a clergyman. The adolescent Charlotte was wise enough and cynical enough to understand that the purpose of the season was to obtain a husband, the wealthier and more noble the better. It was a lesson that had been drummed home when she was only fourteen and suffered her first romantic disappointment with Augustus O'Brien, the son of a neighboring squire. When they waltzed together at Lord Exeter's ball, Charlotte found herself whisked home by the Rev. Pegus to face her mother who "declared she would sooner see her daughter in her grave than married to Augustus."[17] The breach was such that the families quarreled irreparably, and a fourteen-year-old Charlotte declared "the whole object and end of my life is withdrawn."[18]

A year later, Charlotte was sufficiently recovered of her disappointment to notice Frederick Martin, Lindsey's new tutor, a "full, thin, kind-tempered man in black who used to teach me my letters and walk out with me."[19] Needless to say, if a local squire's son was not good enough for Lady Charlotte, a tutor was out of the question. Although later he managed to pull himself together to enjoy a distinguished clerical career as the author of several religious books,[20] the unfortunate Martin was destined to fade into a continuing reproach to Charlotte, "the wreck of the bright hopes of former days"[21] who, on an unwelcome visit to the married Lady Charlotte's house in Wales, exuded "a painful abandonment of hope, at the wreck of his prospects, the almost nine years expectancy of a living, and the continual disappointments."[22]

The family's sights were set on a sixty-seven-year-old politician, Robert Plumer Ward, who had already buried two wives. Ward proposed and was refused by Charlotte; however, by that time even she had accepted the impossibility of the match with Martin, perhaps encouraged by an acquaintance with the "wild, enthusiastic and very poetical" Benjamin Disraeli whose brilliance "infected [Charlotte] and [they] ran on about poetry and Venice and Baghdad and Damascus and [her] eye lit up and [her] cheek burned in the pause of the beautiful music [her] words flowed almost as rapidly as his."[23] The acquaintance with Disraeli resulted in Lady Charlotte's most traditional appearance in literature. In his 1845 novel, *Sybil*, Benjamin Disraeli refers to "'waltzing with the little Bertie' at an assembly at Lady St. Julian's."[24] He also created a character, Lady Joan Fitz Warene, who is at least partially modeled on Lady Charlotte, and who was described as

> certainly not beautiful; nobody would consider her beautiful . . . and yet she had a look, when . . . she was more than beautiful. But she was very clever, very clever, indeed, something quite extraordinary . . . languages and learned books; Arabic and Hebrew, and old manuscripts.[25]

Interestingly, this fictional character created by a man fore-grounds a central ambivalence that Lady Charlotte faced when constructing herself in her own journals. The question that continually vexed Lady Charlotte was, in the words of Nancy K. Miller, "whether the story of a woman who sees conventional female self-definition as a text to be rewritten, who refuses the inscription of her body as the ultimate truth of her self, to become, if not a man, an exceptional woman (hence like a man), is a story significantly different from that of a man who becomes an exceptional man."[26] This posited difference between constructing female and male lives is magnified by the literal act of writing the story of a woman's life, for "while a woman may fly in the face of tradition, that is, of traditional expectations for women . . . while on the face of it she is an outlaw, the real fault lies with society and its laws. To justify an unorthodox life by writing about it, however, is to *reinscribe* the original violation, to reviolate masculine turf."[27]

The double-bind created by the situation Miller describes is clear when it is considered in terms of Philippe Lejeune's discussion of nineteenth-century bourgeois autobiography. Lejeune posits three modes of autobiography, all determined by the writer's relationship to society: the exemplary autobiography, in which the writer believes in the status quo and succeeds because of this belief; the critical autobiography, in which the writer is antagonistic to the status quo; and finally the apologetic autobiography, in which the writer retains his belief in the status quo, but has been failed by it or has failed, none-theless.[28] If one accepts Miller's premises, the female autobiographer is doubly excluded from writing the first type of autobiography, the exemplary one, because the act of a woman writing to define herself as extraordinary is adversarial to both the laws and expectations of society, as well as the idealized concept of her gender.

This tension between extraordinary woman and idealized exemplar of womanhood is central to Lady Charlotte's journals. However, at this early stage, it was much more clearly expressed by an external observer, such as Disraeli. For his part, Disraeli was taken enough by Lady Charlotte (or at least by her inheritance) to write to his elder sister:

By the bye, would you like Lady [Charlotte] for a sister-in-law, very clever, £25000, and domestic? As for 'love' all my friends who married for love and beauty either beat their wives or live apart from them. This is literally the case. I may commit many follies in life, I never intend to marry for 'love,' which I am sure, is a guarantee of infelicity.[29]

Happily for Charlotte, such a romantic prospect at last fell through, and instead, she was introduced to John Guest, a forty-eight-year-old widower, still acknowledged to be handsome, who owned an iron works in Dowlais and had come to London as the first MP for Merthyr Tydfil, the Welsh district where Dowlais was located.[30] Although Guest was wealthy, he was not titled, nor was he comfortable in London society. Predictably, Lady Charlotte's mother was worried about Guest's being "in trade," but equally predictably, his enormous wealth and political future were judged to make up for the defect, and the couple were married on July 29, 1833.

Lady Charlotte—at least the Lady Charlotte created by the family editors—never pronounced anything but her undying devotion to John Guest in the diaries that cover their entire twenty-year marriage. Yet, the diaries that immediately precede her marriage to John Guest present a decidedly more reluctant Lady Charlotte. Indeed, her feelings about the marriage were apparently so ambivalent that she burned her journal entries for late September 1832 to May 1833, the eight months before her marriage to John Guest.[31] Again, it takes only rudimentary psychologizing to hypothesize that she understood the marriage as a compromise—whether with her ideals of what was due her noble blood or due her romanticism will never be known.

More interesting than the twenty-year-old aristocrat's rather predictable ambivalence about marrying a forty-eight-year old industrialist, however, is the textual construct that expresses her reluctance. For Lady Charlotte's doubts and ambivalences about the entire process of being placed on the marriage market are not expressed as direct entries in a journal. Instead, she inscribes them as an editorial act on her own writing. This editorial approach is announced in a penciled emendation on the back cover of her 1827–28 diary, which reads:

> I have been reviewing this . . . It has made me [sad?]. Nothing [strikes?] more to the heart than a journal however uninteresting it seems to [all?] but the author . . . I have made none but one or two annotations intelligible only to myself & which being in pencil can be easily effaced . . . What a reproach have some of the feelings I

have found . . . been to my present ones. In the main I am unchanged though some (many) of my impressions are less vivid—This is the Chronicle of the most miserable part (1827) of my life (except perhaps the portion at Brighton . . .)[32]

The entry is signed C. E. Bertie and dated 1829. More importantly, however, it is followed with another signed, but obliterated, entry in pen, dating from 1832. The three entries create a literally triangulated picture of Lady Charlotte during one of the most crucial periods of self-identification of her life. Interestingly, what is most characteristic about this triangle is that Lady Charlotte never obliterates or alters her original entries—only comments on them. This scholarly and evidentiary scrupulousness is reinforced by her careful dating of the comments as well as the entries. She does, however, feel free to change her comments, often scratching out entire lines of her 1829 comments during her 1832 rereading. The overall result is an explosive dialogue between three voices who argue and sometimes even override one another: A rather ordinary young girl, whose life seems to be a conventional round of visits, dances, and duties. A romantic heroine of 1828, who is given to comments such as "There was some fun that night—how better laugh at nothing than not at all." And an ironic, knowing woman of the world of 1832, who comments on the above passage, "What an odd page—It is nonsense of which I find more here than I expected."[33]

The interrelationship among these characters is particularly evident in her entry about the rupture with the O'Briens, with whose son she had had a romantic friendship:

> However <u>my pride</u> is hurt and though I laugh at these <u>reports I feel</u> and have <u>felt deeply</u> their <u>injustice and many a sorrowing hour have I preferred</u> to think that such ill nature should cause any coolings between the families.[34]

The underscores were all penciled additions from 1829 and serve to highlight the passage's original tempestuous romanticism. However, the passage's passionate effect is considerably lessened by Lady Charlotte's comment of December 3, 1832, "Is not this a grand tirade?"

Admittedly, there is something terribly lonely about all this internal dialogue, no matter how droll Lady Charlotte's retrospective perspicacity. Lady Charlotte herself acknowledges as much in her

1833 rereading of two passages from her 1829 diaries. The first is merely underscored, followed by an obliterated comment, dated 1833. The original entry read:

> When anything annoys or delights me I am accustomed to brood over it in the inmost escapes of my own bosom . . . I have never found a kindred soul to whom this whole heart may be opened being but a reflection of its own.[35]

If this picture of a lonely young woman is sad, the passage that immediately follows it is even sadder, for in it Lady Charlotte denies herself even recourse to the outlet of writing, claiming

> There are many things which I consider it dangerous to commit to paper though kept at present under lock and key. There is always the chance of the future discovering more than necessary and of erroneous notions being conveyed by the . . . often ambiguous manner in which one who keeps a journal of thoughts and sentiments . . .

Lady Charlotte herself remarked on the pathos of these passages, in a comment dated April 30, 1833, which reads, "Ah, this is very very terrible for a child of 16 and I was wiser then than now." Terrible or not, however, Lady Charlotte did find a strategy for safely inscribing these emotions she perceived as dangerous: she displaced them into discussions of literature, such as the following remarkable passage that describes her reading Virgil in 1827:

> Pater Aneas is no hero he is far too lacrymous. [Parvus Julus] is insipid and might distinguish himself, one would like to know something about him. [Turnus] is delightful especially in the last book and certainly deserved at least life. The picture of Camilla appeared to me the most perfect and spirited. On the whole her death and the burning of Troy [sounded?] the most. The battles are very fine.[36]

When Lady Charlotte returned to the text in 1829, she underlined the words "at least" preceding the word "life," then wrote, with what can only be described as romantic impetuosity:

> Better without it if beaten. For what is life without honour? Yes! I did enjoy the reading of *Virgil* more than I can express & look back to it with the more interest as it is a pleasure that may *never* recur—The first perusal of Virgil [?] explained, is a delight which surely can *never* be surpassed or equaled.

The careful addition of the word "explained" hints that Lady Charlotte's passion for Virgil may reflect her passion for her tutor, Mr. Martin, but such a conclusion is at best a surmise. Certainly, Lady Charlotte's 1832 comment offers little insight: "Here is my opinion in 1827—My pencil precis in 1829. I could write a volume upon it." Indeed, the final "it" is so ambiguous, the passage could refer to writing a volume on Virgil as easily as it might refer to writing a volume on her emotions and reactions to the situation in which she read Virgil—whatever that might be.

The dialogue on Virgil does not end with these three voices, however, or even with the voice of Virgil. For Lady Charlotte's 1829 volume also contains an entry on Virgil, written at about the same time as her penciled commentary on her 1827 diary. In 1833, Lady Charlotte remarks on the conjunction, but again offers at best an allusive evaluation of its significance: "Here is the Virgil of July 14 & 15. It had in 3 months grown a favorite—5 years have added to its value. Oh, when shall I see it again? All these notions of Virgil are curious."[37]

The overall effect of these various selves in dialogue across time can only be described as remarkable. Romantic writers—Wordsworth most famously—attempted to create a similar engagement between worldly adult self and innocent child. In such texts, however, the child's voice is necessarily filtered through the voice of the adult writer who is constructing him in order to construct himself. Lady Charlotte's diaries, for all the self-conscious anxiety that they generate (and they do generate a great deal of anxiety; indeed, at times they are genuinely painful to read), are unique in that they allow the voice of the child who is the object of observation to enter into equal dialogue with the adult writer who is observing her.

On a superficial level, at least, this juxtaposition of past and present resembles that described by Sidonie Smith in her redefinition of autobiography:

> *On a daily basis, then, personal narrators assume the role of the bricoleur who takes up bits and pieces of the identities and narrative forms available and, by disjoining and joining them in excessive ways, creates a history of the subject at a precise point in time and space* . . . Through assembling autobiographical memories one more time, personal narrators can turn an interpretation of and judgment about the past, however inflected by previous knowledge, into a countermemory. That is, they can re-

make their understanding of the "truth" of the past and reframe the present by bringing it into a new alignment of meaning with the past.[38]

However, despite the fact that Smith's definition radically challenges many other aspects of autobiography, the process she describes still privileges the status of the writer in the present examining the self in retrospect. The past and present are not simply juxtaposed; they are "interpreted" and "judged" by being brought into an alignment of meaning. Lady Charlotte creates no such alignment of meaning in her annotated diary; indeed, her later interpretations are provisional to the point of being sometimes erased. Instead, it is the "raw material" of the past that is privileged in Lady Charlotte's diaries—an act of collecting that significantly prefigures her collecting the "raw material" of the Celtic past in her notes to the *Mabinogion*.

Even more significantly, Lady Charlotte's archives contain a second collection of "raw material" that counterbalance the texts of her early diaries: two commonplace books. In *Assuming the Positions,* Susan Miller emphasizes how important such commonplace books, which contained quotes and excerpts as models of writing, were in nineteenth-century constructions of literary self-consciousness. Miller argues that commonplace books' importance in constructing self-consciousness derives from their being loci of common ideas rather than texts.[39] She goes on to claim, "The worth of these private investments . . . is verified only by their resonance with common social values. Consequently, they are pivotal spaces between the acquisition and the transmission of personal worth."[40] The paradoxical result is that such a book "opens a space for imagining an independent writer's work, not inscribed collectively held language, as a source of social identity."[41]

Although Miller is discussing antebellum writers from the American South, Lady Charlotte's literary education also depended heavily on such citation. There is sufficient textual evidence in her journals to believe she kept a separate "poetry book." Sadly, that book is not among her archives. However, two early commonplace collections, signed "CE Bertie" in her own hand, do remain. The first is a collection of excerpts from biographies of her ancestors; the second is a collection of her translations of Persian poetry. What the two have in common is a gloriously unselfconscious romanticism that

Lady Charlotte never obtained in the most unabashed effusions of her diary.

Lady Charlotte's commonplace history of her family begins in 1300 with the Siege of Carlaverock, where her ancestor, Robert de Willoughby "received a stone in the middle of his breast which ought to have been protected by his shield, if he had deigned to use it."[42] Subsequently, he was elevated to the peerage by Edward I. Her next distinguished ancestor is, in fact, a woman: the Marchioness of Dorset, "daughter of one queen [Mary Queen Dowager of France] and the mother of another."[43] The second queen in question is no less a figure than Lady Jane Grey. Nonetheless, by far the most dashing of Lady Charlotte's ancestors was Peregrine Bertie, Lord General in France for Queen Elizabeth I, who "raised [himself] by God's blessing, the Queen's favour, and [his] own deserts."[44] In an episode that might be argued to be the original of the Black Knight in *Monty Python and the Holy Grail*, when Peregrine was challenged to a duel while "he lay sick of the gout, he returned this answer, 'that although he was lame of his hands and feet, yet he would meet him with a . . . rapier in his teeth.' "[45] A last ancestor, the Earl of Lindsey, fought fearlessly for the Cavaliers (naturally) in the Civil War, and according to a poem by Mr. Abraham Cowley, "more honorably than Essex." This same Lindsey fell in battle against King Gustavus five years later, prompting Francis Wortley to write in his Elegy on the Earl of Lindsey, "What are sparrows when such falls?"[46]

The excerpt ends with a "*Hic jacet*" followed by a carefully copied ϛρατηγο. Next to it is a penciled note: "NB. Who wrote the Greek? Not I," signed CES, or Charlotte Elizabeth Schreiber. Clearly, her early diaries were not the only piece of writing to which Lady Charlotte returned to study and comment on later in life. Equally clearly, her scholarly ethos never deserted her throughout the course of her long and varied life.

The second set of excerpts is entitled "Notes on Oriental Subjects." The hallmark of these "Oriental Notes" is a fierce intellectual industry that is quintessentially High Victorian—containing, as they do, page upon page of Persian, Turkish, and Arabic vocabulary, as well as notes on Goethe, Beethoven, and Herodotus, and extracts from travel and history books about Spain and the Middle East. However, this fierce industry is offset by the highly romantic nature of the subject matter—in particular translations by Scott and Ousley of the odes of Hafiz, which routinely offer sentiments such as, "This

monkish habit which I wear shall serve as a pledge for wine."[47] Lady
Charlotte's attitude to these poems is never anything but scholarly;
nonetheless, there is a certain pleasure in imagining such an extremely proper teenager penning the prim notation on "The Casida"
by Imim Ali, the Prophet's cousin, "The author is supposed to be ad-
dressing himself after he had been abandoned by his wife who became an inmate of the Prophet's Harem."[48]

Carefully copied onto a sheaf of neat quartos, these notes are
signed C. E. Bertie and dated 1828–30. Thus, she was making these
excerpts at precisely the same time she was making her revisions to
her 1827 diaries. Consequently, the notes can be seen as an important fourth voice in the dialogue that swirls through the diaries, as
she faces what for most Victorian women would be the most important question in their lives. In her journals, Lady Charlotte's voice
ranges from impassioned romanticism to ennui, if not actual cyni-
cism, yet the overriding voice is one of correct, Victorian duty. The
highly romantic nature of these carefully preserved excerpts suggests that they offered another world, of dashing Elizabethan cour-
tiers and exotic Orientals, that Lady Charlotte accrued to herself
largely through the act of scholarship. [49] That such exoticism is inti-
mately connected with ideas of independence and freedom is made
clear by the fact that many contemporary women, such as Lady Mary
Wortley Montagu, turned to Oriental trousers as a form of dress that
allowed them freedom from the long skirts, hoops, and stays that
were fashionable at the time.[50]

At this point, one can only speculate as to why Lady Charlotte de-
cided in favor of conventionality rather than pursuing a similar free-
dom, for she burned her journal entries for late September 1832 to
May 1833, the eight months before her marriage to John Guest.[51]
Yet, it is going too far to see the "autobiography" of Lady Charlotte
Bertie as consisting largely of those burned pages. Nonetheless,
Bessborough chooses to begin his version of Lady Charlotte Guest's
journals with what is simply an epitaph for Lady Charlotte Bertie,
"To begin at the beginning:—I draw a veil over much confusion and
much arrangement and disarrangement."[52]

Despite both Lady Charlotte's and Bessborough's efforts, that
veil never stays securely drawn. Significantly, its lifting is associated
with the act of rereading and self-editing. As late as 1837, four years
after she had married, Lady Charlotte could write, after a series of
routine social visits at Uffington:

I was very low—Turning from the hurry and excitement of my London life I dwelt upon sunsets from the little garden—This is a new existence now—but I cannot help sometimes looking back upon the bright dreams of my former life. Then the victim of my heartlessness rises again in awful condemnation of my conduct and I cannot even now shake off at times a <u>conviction of retribution. But I tore myself away</u> from the calm scene and hurried back to the <u>stirring events of life.</u>[53]

The underscores are undated, but, since they are in pencil, they clearly do not date from the original writing of the passage, which was done in pen. This passage is also highlighted with penciled sidebars, as is—to the delight of any opera aficionado—the comment that follows a description of seeing Maria Malibran singing *La Sonnambula,* "Saw the same thing a few days before I married and <u>recollections were almost too much for me.</u>"[54]

After her marriage, however, there is much less evidence of such rereading. Instead, this on-going dialogue with herself is gradually replaced with another textual interlocutor: the figure of her husband, John Guest. Upon her marriage, Lady Charlotte announced her intention that her diary be fit for her husband's eyes, and it says much about Bessborough's editorial stance that he chooses to include this announcement in the first diary entry he presents:

> Not now, as in the winter, can I say that the only friend I had to confide in was my journal. Now, every care and every joy, every sorrow and every delight is shared and sympathized with, and henceforth my only friend, my only confidant is my husband . . . the dates I note are, at least, of as much interest to my husband as to me, and the book in which I keep them is as much his journal as mine.[55]

This construction of her husband is ultimately a textual, not an actual, construction, for there is no evidence that John Guest ever evinced the slightest interest in reading his wife's diaries. Many feminist critics read such a textual construction as a characteristically female strategy. For example, Celeste Schenck argues that reading such a construction is a necessary strategy for reading women's writing, claiming that women's writing must be read so that we "see reflected in the particularity of each corpus the lineaments of some particular woman's life experience as dialectically constructed both by cultural imposition and by her own countering agency."[56] However, later critics, Sidonie Smith most prominently among them, read autobiography not as a linguistic construction, but rather as a performative act, which is also "inescapably intersubjective . . . a practice not only of recollection of a past *by* a subject, but of recollection *for* another subject."[57] In her earliest journals, Lady Charlotte plays the role of both these subjects at different points in time. In these later journals, she makes her husband the textual embodiment of this intersubjectivity. The result is a merciful release from what frankly can only be described as her obsessive rereading and commentary.

In addition to the textual construct of John Guest replacing Lady Charlotte's rereading herself in these later journals, the collections of biographical excerpts and "Oriental Notes" in her early journals are also replaced by new textual constructs—again associated with John Guest. Early in their marriage, he presented Lady Charlotte with a copy of Mrs. Ellis's *Wives of England*, an early Victorian conduct book. As might be expected, much of Mrs. Ellis's advice is frankly dated. Particularly offensive to a twenty-first-century sensibility is her firm reliance on the Victorian ideal of separate spheres, as well as the notion that a woman's satisfaction should derive from self-effacement and generosity to others, rather than achieving her own desires. Even worse is Mrs. Ellis's claim that a wife's happiness lies in her inferiority to her husband; in a passage particularly germane to the unabashedly ambitious Lady Charlotte, Mrs. Ellis goes so far as to argue that "in the case of a highly gifted woman, even where there is an equal or superior degree of talent possessed by her husband, nothing can be more injudicious or more fatal to her happiness than an exhibition even of the least disposition to presume upon such gifts."[58]

Despite such obviously unpalatable sentiments, some of Mrs. Ellis's advice remains surprisingly practical and up to date—in particular, her counsel that, although the goal of marriage is mutual improvement, many marriages founder on a desire to change too many of a spouse's habits. Instead she suggests a husband be "kindly allowed to rest himself, if he chooses, in an awkward pose and to wear an unbecoming coat because it is a favorite,"[59] so that the wife might save her energy to correct him from habits that are genuinely objectionable. Moreover, there are some genuinely funny passages in the book, such as her delicate aside:

> If it were possible to whisper upon paper, I should here avail myself
> of a convenient *aside*, to hint that there is often a great deal of un-

necessary bustle and importance when men have anything to do. But why should we mind that—why should we not allow them the satisfaction of feeling, that as regards the little world in which they rule supremely all space is their's [*sic*] and all time? And if we have not patience to look on, and see the order of our house overturned, our dinner waiting, our servants called away from their work, one to fetch paper, another string, and a third to wait until the mighty affair is complete; we have at least the advantage, when the same thing has to be done again, of taking the opportunity to do it ourselves.[60]

Yet, these graceful accommodations are quickly balanced on the following page by the stern injunction, "Never deceive!" Perhaps sensing that the line she has drawn between accommodating one's husband (often referred to with the telling synonym "managing") and deceiving him, Mrs. Ellis provides a road map of the slippery slope down which the unwary wife can tumble. First comes concealment. Next come "false pretenses, assumed appearances and secret schemes," which lead inexorably to falsehood itself.[61] Mrs. Ellis concludes her grim syllogism with the ominous warning that there is "no fellowship in falsehood."[62]

It would be overly facile to point out the seeming contradiction in her logic. It would also be facile to point out the paradox of such advice appearing in a conduct book, which is itself a set of rules. Instead, it is perhaps more useful to see the paradox she creates in literary terms. Mrs. Ellis's easy notion of the interchangeability of verisimilitude and veracity depends upon the romantic commonplace that content gives rise inevitably to the poetic form that will best express it. Indeed, Mrs. Ellis is repeatedly at pains to emphasize that a wife's good behavior must be organic, stemming from her own desires to nurture others, not a series of strictures. Yet, she also suggests that, at least in educating young women, the process can work in both directions: Observing the outward forms is in fact the best way to condition a young woman's heart.

In addition to Mrs. Ellis, the newlywed Lady Charlotte read Hannah More's *Coelebs in Search of a Wife*. While Mrs. Ellis at least offers the occasional humorous aside, the earnest More offers no such respite. Receiving ambivalent reviews even upon its original publication in 1805, her book has little to recommend it, apart from its arguably being an early source for *Mansfield Park*. In general, the book rehearses the argument of More's earlier and more famous *Strictures on the Modern System of Female Education*, in which More argues for serious education for girls instead of the curriculum of useless and decorative "accomplishments" common at the time; and also for the encouragement of a robust Christianity, which, she insists, will conquer by example without undue female assertiveness. This is all connected with her overarching concern with social stability and the effectiveness of women in their proper domestic spheres.[63]

It would seem there could hardly be a less congenial educational approach to the intellectual autodidact Lady Charlotte—even without the following exchange between the priggish Charles (the eponymous Coelebs, which simply means "unmarried") and Mr. Stanley, the father of the woman Charles will actually grace with a marriage proposal:

> I often called to mind that my father, in order to prevent my being deceived and run away with by the persons who appeared lively at first sight, had early accustomed me to discriminate carefully, whether it was not the *animal* only that was lively and the man dull. I have found this caution of no small use in my observation on the other sex. I had frequently remarked that the musician and the dancing ladies, and those who were most admired for modish attainments, had little *intellectual* gaiety. In numerous instances I found that her mind was the only part which was not kept in action; and no wonder, for it was the only part which had received no previous forming, no preparatory moulding.
>
> When I mentioned this to Mr. Stanley, "The education," replied he, "which now prevails, is a Mahometan education. It consists entirely in making a woman an object of attraction. There are, however, a few reasonable people left, who, while they retain the object, improve upon the plan. They, too, would make a woman attractive; but it is by sedulously labouring to make the understanding, the temper, the mind, and the manners of their daughters, as engaging as these Circassion parents endeavor to make the person.[64]

The adjective "Mahometan" is a particularly telling one in light of Lady Charlotte's "Oriental Notes." It would seem that More could give the newly married Lady Charlotte no more direct order to put aside the intensely romantic textual models of her youth and replace them instead with the model of a decorous Victorian wife. That Lady Charlotte felt considerable ambivalence at the models Mrs. Ellis and More offered is reflected in both her life and her journal, in particular the following passage recorded in response to a contretemps with her husband, in which "[s]he had asked his opinion about an idea she had and he had replied, half in jest and half seriously, that he would never seek his wife's view on such a subject. Characteristically, she agreed and laughed 'yet the words he had spoken sank deeply into my heart and clouded all that evening.'"[65]

In the privacy of her journal, she expanded on her reaction, writing:

> How deeply I have felt this inferiority of sex and how humiliated I am when it is recalled to my mind in allusion to myself! Knowing that most wives are but looked upon as nurses and housekeepers (very justly too) I have striven hard to place myself on a higher level—and dear Merthyr, who knows how sensitive I am on this point and who really does think that some women are rational beings—has always aided and encouraged me—I have given myself almost a man's education from the age of twelve when I first began to follow my own devices—and since I married I have taken up such pursuits as in this country of business and ironmaking would render me conversant with what occupied the male part of the population—Sometimes I think I have succeeded pretty well—but every now and then I am painfully reminded that toil as I may, I can never succeed beyond a certain point and by a very large portion of the community my acquirements and judgements must always be looked upon as those of a mere woman.[66]

Both formally and emotionally, this example illustrates a new textual strategy that Lady Charlotte adopts in this portion of her diaries. She may rehearse the rhetoric of submission, but it scarcely takes a Derridean reading to see the stubbornness with which her actual writing attempts to counter it. Guest and John have already pointed out that what is most striking about the passage is its dependence on caveats and parentheses, which in turn inscribe a constant tension between self-assertion and self-effacement. Yet, even as she counters the model, she internalizes it. Mrs. Ellis's ideal wife is no straw (wo)man to attack, but literally part of the diction with which Lady Charlotte attempts to rebel. The two voices inhabit each other —nowhere more so than in the fact that this very ambivalence between form and content, or verisimilitude and veracity, is precisely the conduct that Mrs. Ellis recommends in a wise wife.

Elsewhere, the ambivalence evinced in this passage is much closer to outright dividedness. Even allowing for Bessborough's interfering editorial hand, Lady Charlotte's diaries during her marriage to Sir John Guest have an annoyingly schizophrenic quality, jumping from Dowlais to London to Canford and back again; from the birth of her fifth child, to her race to publish her version of *Peredur* before Villemarque published his French one; then to the Resignation of the Whigs, caused by the Chartist riots, in the space of two pages.[67] The peculiar diversity of Lady Charlotte's interests leads Guest and John to compartmentalize their biography, treating each of seven perceived personas in turn instead of trying to create a chronological narrative.[68] Such a division, especially in terms of discussing a woman's life, is quite theoretically permissible. Indeed, if one follows the lead of Anderson and Zinsser, who argue in *A History of their Own* that women's experience is better described in categories of experience, rather than in a masculinist, chronological narrative dominated by political demarcations, women's biographies might be best constructed this way. However, it is useful to at least begin with a chronologically organized resume of her life during her first marriage.

Lady Charlotte married John Guest on July 29, 1833, when she was twenty-one years old. The marriage lasted just short of twenty years, ending with Sir John's death on November 26, 1852, which left her a relatively young widow of forty. John Guest was an ironmonger, who had inherited the Dowlais Iron Company from his father and grandfather before him. It was John, however, who transformed it into the largest ironworks in the world. He died a wealthy man, leaving a fortune of a half a million pounds and a working country estate at Canford, in addition to the works and house at Dowlais. In addition, he left behind a baronetcy, which was bestowed upon him in Queen Victoria's Coronation Honors in 1838. Lady Charlotte was Guest's second wife; his first, Maria Ranken, had died in childbirth.

In contrast with Guest's first marriage, the union with Lady Charlotte produced ten children over the course of thirteen years. Although the impression may be partly due to Lady Charlotte's reticence in writing about such matters, she seemed, with the exception of her last child, to handle pregnancy and birth easily, her confinements causing her barely to pause in her routine of writing, managing, and socializing. For example, when her daughter Constance was born, Lady Charlotte:

> walked to the furnaces with her husband, learned some German poetry and read in the library. She was about to dress for dinner and

rang for the maid "But my dressing was never accomplished for I was suddenly taken ill and had to send the maid for the nurse. The works bell rang six o'clock just as I got into bed which I did forthwith. In less than twenty minutes later another dear baby was added to our family." Her husband had no idea that anything was the matter.[69]

At least according to the recollections of her daughter Enid, Lady Charlotte was a distant mother. Their governess, Miss Kemble, was "more of a mother to us all than ever our own mother who was far oftener away from us."[70] Yet, whatever Lady Charlotte's mothering skills, all ten of her children survived to adulthood, quite an accomplishment in and of itself. In addition, several of her children went on to make highly successful marriages—an ambition for her children which Lady Charlotte was never shy of admitting. Her eldest son, Ivor, married Lady Cornelia Spencer-Churchill, the daughter of the Duke of Marlborough; the Guests' eldest son was created Baron Wimborne in his own right. Lady Charlotte's daughter Enid married the discoverer of Nineveh, Austen Henry Layard. Interestingly, Layard, who was a contemporary of Lady Charlotte, was rumored to be in love with Lady Charlotte herself. Indeed, the relationship between Lady Charlotte and Layard led Sir John to create a scene when

> One Sunday in late March 1848 the family went to church and Lady Charlotte stayed behind writing. Afterwards Sir John confronted her with his suspicions—"it was as though a thunderbolt had fallen at my feet." For two extremely painful hours he talked seriously to her . . . "it was too extravagant, for the moment it really seemed a sort of frenzy."[71]

Despite Sir John's not infrequent,[72] and perhaps not unprovoked, attacks of jealousy, Lady Charlotte's diary portrays their marriage as an idyllic one, beginning when Guest took her to Dowlais to live near the ironworks. Her first reaction could certainly be no more gratifying to a newlywed industrialist:

> The country *did* smile as we started on our Journey and I could not have entered my new abode under more favorable circumstances . . . By the time we reached the house it was quite dark and the prevailing gloom gave full effect to the light of the blazing furnaces, which was quite unlike all I had ever before seen or even imagined . . . Merthyr took me through the furnaces and the forges after coffee,

and after dinner I saw them cast the iron. In the broad glare of the fires, from a little distance, the workmen formed groups which might yield fine studies for the painter, especially in respect to the lights and shades cast upon their figures.[73]

She never lost this early enthusiasm for the industry. Her journal is rife with detailed discussions of the iron trade, such as that of March 3, 1838, when the Guests took

an expedition to Millwall to see a Manufactory which Mr. Fairbairn has there for making Iron Steam Boats. They were constructed much in the same way as boilers except that the plates do not overlap, but, having their edges placed evenly together, they are connected by a flat piece of iron placed on the inside and to which they are strongly rivetted. The holes for the rivets are all countersunk so that their heads do not project at all, and the exterior surface of the vessel is perfectly smooth.[74]

On August 16 of the same year, on a trip to Zurich, she wrote of her visit to the machine shop of a Mr. Essher:

The man who went round with us did not know where the Bar Iron came from, but in poking about in the forge I found two or three bars upon which was the mark *"G.L. best"* [Guest, Lewis & Co., clarification Bessborough's], which settled the question very satisfactorily. It gave me for a moment as much pleasure to find my own Iron in this remote spot as anything has done during the whole journey.[75]

There is no question that Lady Charlotte was genuinely fascinated with technology. Two of her most charming artifacts are tucked into a set of ladylike sketches of architectural details saved in one of her journals. They are a pair of wonderfully detailed sketches for an "Ironing implement using Charcoal in the interior" and a "Hand Mangle for Female Things." The latter sketch also includes precise measurements.[76] Nonetheless, another explanation for this unexpected enthusiasm for industry is that it provided Lady Charlotte with an immediate vehicle to identify herself as extraordinary. For example, when she was invited to fulfill the traditional wife's role during the laying of the Taff Vale Railway:

I went through the form of laying mortar with a pretty little trowel, but when the stone was lowered to its place, and the Engineer brought an equally interesting Liliputian [*sic*] hammer from his pocket for me to strike with, the idea appeared to me so absurd that I rebelled outright and insisted upon using the wooden mallet, to the no small amusement of the workmen. I then said a few words of the pleasure I had in performing the ceremony.[77]

Once again, Lady Charlotte's behavior highlights the paradox that Nancy K. Miller describes. In this episode, as well as many others where Lady Charlotte leapt on boats, descended into abandoned ceramics kilns, and negotiated perilous viaducts, she proves herself memorable as a woman specifically by violating the conventional roles assigned to women. Now, however, it is Lady Charlotte who defines herself in this way—at least in her actions. Her words, however, immediately intervene to negate the effect of her actions, for, as soon as she rejects her feminine identity by demanding the mallet, she hastily recoups it, saying the conventional few words on the pleasure she had taken in the ceremony. (This is by no means to accuse Lady Charlotte of hypocrisy. It is certainly quite possible that she took a genuine pleasure in discomfiting the engineer.)

Still a third reason for Lady Charlotte's fascination with the iron industry was its location in Wales. As might be suspected, Lady Charlotte quickly romanticized Wales, and with it Welsh nationalism, especially when it was embodied by such outlaw figures as the Rebecca Rioters, who disguised themselves as women to attack the toll gates of West Wales.[78] Lady Charlotte met their leader, John Hughes, on the eve of his transportation to Tasmania, describing him as "my poor Welsh rebel with all his faults and all his grievances and all his romance."[79] She also had political dealings with Dr. William Price of Porth y Glo, described by many as "a fit subject for the lunatic asylum," who

> drove around in a carriage drawn by goats and wore full Bardic costume "of red and green and his lambskin on his head with the four lambs [*sic*] tails hanging about his eyes" . . . It was Price who, years later, was responsible for the legalization of cremation after his court case over the burning of his illegitimate child, whom he had called Jesus Christ.[80]

With this immediate embracing of Wales and Welsh nationalism also came an embracing of Welsh culture. Scarcely a week after Lady Charlotte had arrived in Wales, she began Welsh lessons with the local rector, Evan Jenkins.[81] At first, the gesture was nothing more than that of a devoted linguaphile wife—a substitution of the Welsh language for her Persian vocabulary and Arabic sonnets. Furthermore, a smattering of Welsh would appeal to the many amateur antiquarians in whose social circles Lady Charlotte now moved. For example, Benjamin and Lady Augusta Hall, a couple whose social, financial, and political situations closely paralleled the Guests, "promoted Welshness like Renaissance patrons," Lady Hall going so far as to offer prizes for collections of designs for traditional tweeds.[82] Nonetheless, the immediacy and enthusiasm with which Lady Charlotte took up the cause of Welsh manuscripts was certainly extraordinary.

During the first year of their marriage, the Guests became founding members of The Society of Welsh Scholars of Abergavenny.[83] Soon after that, in 1835, Lady Charlotte proposed an independent project to Elijah Waring: creating a collection of legends and superstitions of Wales.[84] Nothing came of this project, but in 1836 she was involved in a new venture, the Welsh Manuscripts Society, which had just obtained access to Mr. Justice Bosanquet's copy of the tales from the *Red Book of Hergest*.[85] In keeping with Lady Charlotte's ambitious temperament, the idea of translating these manuscripts arose at the same time as she was working on her (never to be completed) history of the iron trade. Her entry for November 29, 1837, records, "[Dr. Aukin] has written a good deal upon the Manufacture of Iron, and I feared had forestalled much that I intended my history to comprize [*sic*], but I found his Lectures chiefly related to antiquarian researches among Hebrew, Greek, etc."[86] The entry for the very next day includes the historic notation:

> Mr. Justice Bosanquet, has, through Tegid, kindly lent me his copy of the Llyfr Goch y Hugest, the Mabinogion, which I hope to publish with an English Translation, notes, pictorial illustrations. Price of Crickhowel and Tegid have promised their assistance, and by God's blessing I hope I may accomplish the undertaking.[87]

At the outset, there was some resistance to her taking on the work. Her entry of December 8 records

> The M.S.S. Society wants to take the Mabinogion into their own hands, believing that I have given it up. We have to arrange to prevent this, and also to go into some plan for translating Justice Bosanquet's Copy, as I do not feel inclined to give up my scheme of publishing it myself . . . Mr. Jones . . . has taken Justice Bosanquet's M.S.

and is to copy from it one story at a time in a fit manner to go to the Press, vis: in Modern Orthography which would be more generally useful, and send them to me to translate.[88]

The translation, which occupied her from 1838 to 1849, appeared in eight installments, culminating in the three-volume complete edition, lavishly bound and illustrated, that appeared in 1849. It was a project that she began seventeen days before the birth of her fourth child. (She was back at work five days later.[89]) The project concluded a year after the birth of her tenth and last child, Blanche.

As massive an undertaking as a four-hundred page edition of a medieval Welsh manuscript was, it was by no means Lady Charlotte's sole contribution to the Welsh and Wales. In Dowlais, she is remembered to this day for her work as an educator, a fact that is somewhat ambivalently attested to by a pub being named for her.[90] Lady Charlotte's interest in education was an extension of that of her husband, who had, very early on, established schools modeled on the Rev. Andrew Bell's National Society, funded in part by his company. His efforts were praised in an 1847 parliamentary inquiry, and the boys' senior school at Dowlais was described as "by far the best provided in Wales."[91]

As with much liberal reform in the nineteenth-century, John Guest's concern with education can hardly be described as devoid of self-interest. His primary motivation was developing a more technically competent workforce; a secondary motivation was appeasing the Chartist agitation that constantly threatened the status quo at the Guest ironworks. Lady Charlotte herself did not get seriously involved in the cause of education until 1848. When she did, however, she threw herself into the project with her customary energy. By all accounts, she was an admirable educator, dedicated to the point of annoying her husband,[92] actively teaching, substituting whenever required, and experimenting with innovative classroom methods such as visual aids. The culmination of Lady Charlotte's educational drive was the opening of the Dowlais Central Schools on September 11, 1855:

> a showpiece containing seven schoolrooms and a large central hall lit by four perpendicular traceries windows. They accommodated 650 boys and girls and 680 infants. The total cost of the land, design, buildings and fitting reached £20,000—the same amount as that set aside for the schoolroom building of England and Wales in the first government grant of 1833.[93]

Interestingly, despite her involvement with translating the *Mabinogion*, Lady Charlotte did not emphasize Welsh culture in her schools.[94] Instead, "Her own background and standards made her initially somewhat unrealistic. After one examination she wrote that '*some* young ladies of ten years old could not spell Thessalonica.'"[95] In these attitudes, Lady Charlotte was reinforcing the cultural discourse established by her husband's educational programs. Not surprisingly, this discourse privileged "desirable" capitalist values such as hard work and technical skill. The humanities, along with the more conventionally "feminine" spheres of infant education and continuing education for young girls to which Lady Charlotte devoted herself, were largely ancillary to the schools' practical purpose, for, as Walter Benjamin argues,

> that the same knowledge which secured the domination of the proletariat by the bourgeoisie would enable the proletariat to free itself from this domination. But in reality, a form of knowledge without access to practice, and which could teach the proletariat nothing about its situation, was of no danger to its oppressors. This was particularly the case with the humanities. The humanities represented a kind of knowledge far removed from economics, and consequently untouched by the transformation of economics. The humanities were satisfied "to stimulate," "to offer diversion" or "to be interesting."[96]

The symbiosis between education and ideology posited by Benjamin in turn gives rise to the issue of class consciousness and its relationship to morality. Benjamin believes that the conscious elements in the formation of ideology are overestimated, which leads to the fundamental misunderstanding that "exploitation conditions false consciousness, at least on the part of the exploiter, because true consciousness would prove to be a moral burden."[97] Instead, Benjamin suggests that the emergence of a class morality is an unconscious process; indeed that "the bourgeoisie did not need consciousness to establish this class morality as much as the proletariat needs consciousness in order to overthrow that morality."[98]

Certainly, Lady Charlotte demonstrates a morality suitable to her class in passages such as the following, which she wrote in response to the second wave of Chartist riots in 1848:

> We talked about the poor and the feeling of the lower classes to the rich, and what he said quite confirmed my views of the unsound state of society and the necessity of educating, or humanising, the lower

grade. But I know one cannot make people good and religious by an act of Parliament. The first step is to make them comfortable and happy, and for this purpose all the sanitary and social reforms are most important. [99]

Yet, applying Benjamin's analysis to Lady Charlotte's situation is complicated by the fact that, as a woman, she is simultaneously oppressed by the ideology that she is attempting to impose on her workers. The education that Sir John offered his male workers might, in fact, allow them to make the transition to the bourgeoisie, as did the man Lady Charlotte encountered on a channel crossing in 1873, who

> introduced himself to me as a former Dowlais schoolboy, and told me he was now a partner in a rolling mill near Stockton-on-Tees. He said, having been a poor boy, he owed all his success in life to his teaching in the Dowlais schools, and remembered on one occasion, my having patted him on the head and told him to be a good boy . . . He seems to have well obeyed my instructions. [100]

It is a commonplace of Marxist thinking that allowing certain, highly talented members of the proletariat into the bourgeoisie, is in fact simply another strategy to reinforce the overall oppression of the proletariat. However, there is an important difference between Lady Charlotte and her literally exemplary pupil. Education remained largely a decorative diversion to Lady Charlotte. Instead of having practical value in increasing her wealth, as it did for her ex-student, all education could accomplish in Lady Charlotte's case was to transform her into Disraeli's creature of "languages and learned books; Arabic and Hebrew, and old manuscripts." [101]

Paradoxically, Susan Miller's argument in *Assuming the Positions* suggests that this very exclusion from the prevailing cultural discourse allows Lady Charlotte a freedom from its influence that was unavailable to the laborer who had risen from the proletariat. In contrast to Benjamin, who argues that teaching the humanities is largely a diversionary tactic, Miller argues that the hierarchies of texts taught in public educational systems serve to reinforce the hierarchies of values in the prevailing cultural discourse. Of course, Lady Charlotte, like most well-bred girls of her time, was taught at home. This very exclusion, however, arguably allowed her to regard all cultural capital as private cultural capital—something that she had collected, like the excerpts in her commonplace book. As such, she could share with that intellectual capital the kind of relationship that a collector shares with objects in his collection—a relationship that Benjamin argues allows the collector to enter into a relationship with the past that is at least fleetingly freed from the prevailing cultural discourse.[102]

Despite this intimate association between Lady Charlotte and the Welsh, there was a period, beginning in 1843 and lasting until the death of Lord Bute in 1848, when the Guests' continuing association with Dowlais and Wales seemed very much in question. Lord Bute, whose ancestor had leased the land to John Guest's business partner's father in 1759, was disinclined to renew the ninety-year lease. Sir John, who was in increasingly bad health at that time, was unwilling to pursue the lease aggressively. The significance that Lady Charlotte attached to Dowlais can best be judged by her diary entry at a point where she thought she would be forced to leave it. On December 22, 1847, she wrote,

> I asked Merthyr to go into the Works with me. I wanted once more, while they were in full operation, to go through the dear old works, leaning as of old on my dear husband's arm . . . I nerved myself to bear it, for it was very painful to think of thus taking leave of the dear old home.[103]

Yet, barely a month earlier, she could address the issue of the lease with her usual practical acumen:

> Mr. Divett's opinion entirely coincided with Merthyr's, that is, if the Lease could be had on really advantageous terms, it would be well to take it . . . Say the profits have been £50,000; of this the Royalties demanded by Lord Bute would absorb £25,000 leaving the other £25,000 for the Leases. But the capital &c., in the works if withdrawn would yield £15,000, so that the £25,000 to be expected on renewal would only give a gain of £10,000.[104]

At the same time the Guests were involved in negotiating with Lord Bute over Dowlais, they were also involved in a protracted negotiation to purchase a Dorset property, Canford, from Lord De Mauley. That negotiation was as least as fraught as the one over Dowlais, involving as it did three heirs, one of whom was a minor whose interests were represented in chancery. The symbolic value of the purchase, however, may have been as fraught as the negotiations themselves, for Canford was a working estate that produced its own incomes from tenants, rather than a leased site for industry. The move to Canford thus represented the final step in the Guests' move from being "in trade" to being members of the landed gentry. That Lady Charlotte attached such significance to the move might well be extrapolated from the fact she hired Sir Charles Barry, the architect of the Houses of Parliament, to remodel the place, a decision that led to some marital tension over the costs of the renovation.[105]

Shortly after the Guests had begun the transition to life at Canford, word came that Lord Bute had died suddenly "within six weeks of the expiration of the great Lease, which has remained unrenewed only owing to his grasping obstinacy. For years . . . Lord Bute has been *the* person to thwart and annoy us, perhaps I should say was the only enemy I felt conscious of possessing."[106] The lease was renewed, leading Lady Charlotte to reflect, "In days of witchcraft I might have been disposed to feel superstitious about it . . . for although I wished him no ill, I certainly loved him not, and as I said before, it is an awful thing when one's only enemy dies suddenly."[107]

The new lease, however, was not to Sir John, but rather to his nephew and business partner, Edward Hutchins. Nonetheless, Lady Charlotte still regarded Dowlais as her home—a situation that led to frustration on both sides. One feels a certain sympathy for the nephew, trying to set up a household and a career under the conditions set forth by his aunt-in-law:

> I gave him my views, as unauthorized, of what Merthyr might probably agree to, viz: that each should take his own Department; Merthyr, the London House with the general supervision of all the branches, Edward the Manufacture, residing 9 months in the year at Dowlais, on a fixed salary. Then I told him we should pay occasional visits to the Works, and I thought that, all circumstances considered, and being the senior partner and by far the largest proprietor, Merthyr should be at liberty to go and reside at Dowlais if ever he wishes it for two or three months, on giving the Hutchinses reasonable notice. All this I thought he seemed pretty well to concur in, though he still made some allusion to his desire "to manage the London House whenever Merthyr should be out of town."[108]

The caveat "as unauthorized" hints at how well the increasingly acrimonious encounters between Lady Charlotte and Hutchins illustrate the peculiar textual struggles between the assertive Lady Charlotte and the ideal of modest female behavior suggested by such model texts as *Wives of England*. Her demands are insensitive, if not downright audacious, and in fact were destined to cause a rift between Hutchins and Sir John. Yet, there is no apparent duplicity in her belief that these are in fact her husband's desires. Indeed, she is scrupulous about identifying their lack of finality, first by identifying them as "unauthorized," and secondly by carefully phrasing them in a conditional, "what Merthyr might probably agree to."

Whether out of respect for Lady Charlotte's gender or the sheer force of her personality, Edward Hutchins was apparently hiding his real feelings. The next day, Lady Charlotte wrote,

> Edward Hutchins called again and . . . Merthyr sent for me to join the conference. When I came down I found Edward in a very different mood from that which he was in the previous day. He was insisting that, if we were to come to Dowlais at all, it should be at a stated period of the year, to be fixed now at this present time for all the years to come.[109]

Lady Charlotte eventually won this territorial war, in an episode that will be discussed later. What is more significant at this point is the reciprocal relationship between Dowlais and the Guests' other residence, a leased house in Spring Gardens, London. The two homes both provided loci for audiences that observed Lady Charlotte. However, where Dowlais provided an adoring audience that saw Lady Charlotte primarily in terms of a female ideal, accepting "generously offered cheers" from the populace and bestowing largesse as well as knowledge in return, Lady Charlotte had to struggle simply to be visible in London society.

It was a struggle that seemed largely uncongenial to her; nevertheless, it was an extremely important one, for Sir John was an MP for Merthyr. Although officially an Independent, John Guest was most closely associated with the Whigs and sometimes even with the Radical party. He was, if not a self-made man, the son of self-made men, a member of the rising bourgeoisie, and one of the founding members of the Reform Club, "established in 1836 'for the purpose of bringing together the Reformers of the United Kingdom,'"[110] with Joseph Hume as its first chair. Guest was, as pointed out above, a dedicated educator of his own workforce, creating schools that were acknowledged to be among the best in Wales. An early identification as "The Poor Man's Friend" during the Reform Crisis cost him his seat in Parliament, albeit temporarily.[111] He stood against the

Corn Laws, as well as government expenditures, to the point that Gwyn A. Williams observed, "whenever Guest spoke at length in the House, someone lost money."[112]

Yet, for all his liberal identification, John Guest was a member of Parliament, an institution that only represented men of property. Liberal or conservative, Whig or Tory, all the members of parliament were men with a vested interest in preserving the order from which they had arisen. Furthermore, like any good industrialist, Guest was dead set against trade unionists.[113] In addition, he presumably married into the aristocracy quite deliberately and apparently was more than happy to receive elevation to the baronetcy as a reward for his diligence.

Sir John's political career, thus, provided yet another textual model for Lady Charlotte's autobiography, for, as Leonore Davidoff argues in *The Best Circles*, the rules of Victorian society were very much an unwritten text—made the more absolute and authoritative because it was unwritten.[114] It was also the one text that remained stubbornly resistant to Lady Charlotte's efforts to incorporate and manipulate it—perhaps because she attempted to approach it with her customary intellectual rigor, writing,

> I had intended to study Society and attempt success in it—The object would have amused me the aim was not great enough to give me the least disappointment had I failed [*sic*]—This idea was hastily adopted and more because I wanted the excitement of aiming at something other than from ambition (which relating to Society I cannot feel) but I have quite given it up and I am glad I have—it is useless to catch an ugly butterfly not worth having—it would be worse than useless—criminal—to waste time on the pursuit of it; but that I would never have done.[115]

In writing thus, she is adopting an almost Balzacian stance as a detached observer of society. However, because of her status as a political wife, it was not a stance she could sustain, either textually or actually, for her husband's career was vitally linked to her social success. Indeed, it would have taken a detachment close to schizophrenia to see the comic side of an episode such as the party Lady Charlotte gave, where Mrs. Wyndham Lewis told a "shocking story" and "All the Mammas looked grave and the young ladies shocked, and I was red with anger that such a thing should have happened in my house."[116]

At other times, Lady Charlotte's social disappointments were far crueler, including at least one outright slap in the face, when Lady Stuart called and

> was remarkably civil, staid [*sic*] half an hour and talked about nothing . . . she says she is delicate about introductions which is to say she will make none. She says it is extremely difficult to get to any of the good parties, and does not offer to assist me to any of them. Even introducing me to the foreign Ambassadors, which at first she said she could accomplish, she now cannot promise, and I think her offer of giving some of my cards to young men was the only result of the half hour's conversation. I spoke to her coming to dine with me and she talked of Lord Stuart's coming alone and she said she seldom went out except to Balls with her daughter . . . I believe I must depend on myself for getting on.[117]

It would be romanticizing Lady Charlotte's situation, however, to see her as an external observer of London society who was forced against her will to participate in it. Passages such as the following demonstrate that Lady Charlotte was capable of demonstrating significant social snobbery of her own:

> Conceive the horror of seeing a fat woman sit opposite to one in a *yellow* gown, and an *amber* cap with *red* flowers, and the still greater horror of that fat lady claiming to be an acquaintance. She proved to be Mrs. Hudson, and the only other people in the room that I knew were Major Gore Brown and his wife, with his sister, Miss Buryon. The Browns and the Hudsons were almost the only two families in London that I have taken pains to avoid having any communication with, so that I was supremely unlucky to have met them there.[118]

The ambivalence in Lady Charlotte's positions as simultaneous observer of and participant in London society is reciprocated by an ambivalence concerning her roles as observer of and participant in her husband's actual political views. As should be evident by now, Lady Charlotte was incapable of behaving as a simple, passive observer in any situation. Instead, despite the fact she could not vote or otherwise engage in politics, she was an active political wife, well beyond her efforts as a hostess in London. She canvassed for her husband, and her diary shows a fine understanding of political issues, although it was often undercut by an insecurity that it was unbecoming for a woman to have political views. Her situation is well-illustrated by her account of the bitterly contested election of 1840. It opens with an admirably precise resume of the position:

> I must give a little review of what has been going forward in the political world . . . Opposed and harassed by their never tiring opponents, the Whigs have been bound to take a course worthy of them. In bringing forward the budget they proposed a measure for reducing the tax upon corn and bringing it to a fixed duty, 8/- per qr. They have met with the most determined resistance from the shortsighted landowners of all parties, and the people have been slow to second them with their approbation.[119]

Despite her clear understanding of the issues, during the election itself, she went to wait at the Castle for fresh orders, at her husband's request.[120] Nonetheless, later in the day, she eventually ventured into the chaos that was taking place at the hustings. What is most interesting about the episode is the position in which she at last finds herself:

> I walked into the field and got a good place close to the hustings, but sufficiently in the background for Merthyr not to see me. I feared my presence might make him nervous, if he were aware of my being there. I heard pretty well. Merthyr's speech was a good one. He dwelt on the Corn Laws, and shewed the price of labour not regulated by the price of corn, but by demand and the price of iron . . . Morgan Williams made a very long and prosy speech, part Welsh, part English. I could not follow him, but he chiefly gave statistics, whether correct or not I cannot tell, which however I am sure no-one understood.[121]

The passage is almost a set piece, illustrating the feminist struggle between self-assertion and the conventional silent role assigned to nineteenth-century women. Nowhere is that more evident than in the last lines of the passage, where Lady Charlotte cleverly couches an acute criticism of the speaker in a conventional profession of female ignorance. However, the passage also foregrounds the extreme intersubjectivity of Lady Charlotte's narration. Sidonie Smith has suggested that autobiography, in addition to being an intersubjective act between the narrator and a posited reader, is also an intersubjective encounter among four different "I's": the "real" or historical "I"; the narrating "I"; the narrated "I"; and the ideological "I."[122] The distinction between the narrated and narrating "I's" is that "the narrated "I" is the subject of history, whereas the narrating "I" is the agent of discourse."[123] These are both distinct from the ideological "I," which "is the concept of personhood culturally available to the narrator when he tells his story."[124] All of these "I's" are at play in the above passage, as Lady Charlotte narrates the acute inner commentary of her "narrated" self, even as her "ideological" self remains properly silent on the edge of the hustings in obedience to her husband's command. However, this ideologically correct retreat actually reverses the relationship between Lady Charlotte and Sir John as her ideal reader, for her hiding from her husband's gaze places her in the position of being able to observe him instead. That Lady Charlotte is aware of the power she accrues from this reversal is evident in her concern about how it will affect her husband if he sees her.

Another episode, this one at a dinner party at Canford in 1850, casts such light on the ambiguity of Lady Charlotte's role as a political wife that it is worth quoting in its entirety:

> I had set my heart on saying a few words. It was the moment to do it. I trembled, and almost hesitated, but there was no time for more consideration and in a moment we should have been scattered. I summoned courage and rose. I saw Merthyr was astonished and his visitors too, but I could not now have retreated, even had I wished it. I proposed that another toast should be drunk, the labouring classes; and I said a few words upon the subject, and in praise of the peasantry of England, above the same class in every other part of the world. Once launched all my diffidence vanished. Of course I had never spoken in publick before, except to my own people at home, in my school in Wales, but I felt when I had once begun that I could have gone on with my subject, which is one I have much at heart, for any length of time. But the emotion with which I spoke gave me I think the appearance of being timid. I know my voice trembled, but I know also that every word was distinct and even measured and could have been heard all over the Hall. I apologized of course for the unusual step &c., or rather I made a little preface, and my toast was received with all due acclamations. This was the last scene of the dinner, where all the nine children at home had added to the picturesque effect.[125]

At least to the reader, if not to the writer, the episode is a slyly humorous version of a woman learning to speak for herself. The urgency with which Lady Charlotte understands that her opportunity to speak must be seized at once, before it vanishes forever, is balanced nicely by the imagined astonishment of John Guest, who might have well been wondering whether his headstrong wife was suddenly in her cups, even if, presumably by this point in their marriage, he was well aware of his wife's penchant for dramatic effects, whether they involved overacting in family theatricals[126] or leaping onto a steamer that bore her name.[127] Yet, the very fact that Lady Charlotte's voice trembled speaks more eloquently than any words could about how inappropriate this need to express herself publicly was, at least in her own mind. Still, what is perhaps most interesting is the peculiar *aporia* that results from this trembling, for it is an *aporia* of reception, not of meaning. Lady Charlotte has no doubt of the meaning of what she is attempting to say, nor presumably of the ultimate truth value of the claims that she is making on behalf of the laboring classes. Nor has she doubts about the rightness of what she is saying, or, presumably, of people correctly determining it. What she doubts instead is the correctness of her audience's reception of her as the deliverer of the message: her fear is not for the truth of what she is saying or that people will correctly interpret that truth, but instead for how people might believe she feels about delivering that truth.

What allows her to seize the moment and deliver the truth is an acute consciousness of her effect on her reader—or, put more broadly, how she functions as the object of the gaze of others. Lady Charlotte may perceive her timidity about speaking as undermining the forcefulness of her self-assertion, but such timidity is also a conventionally desirable feminine quality, making the overall assertiveness of her gesture more attractive. Certainly, there is little more femininely attractive than the last effect she presents, that of her being surrounded by her nine (Muse-like) children—even if the sharp-eyed critic might note that the fact they remain unnamed suggests they were valued more for their picturesqueness than any inherent personal qualities.

What is perhaps most significant in this passage is Lady Charlotte's consciousness of where she would be permitted to speak freely: in her schools and in Wales. This perception on Lady Charlotte's part supports Judith Johnston's claim that colonial women, while on the one hand often identifying very strongly with the indigenous people they are colonizing, on the other hand find themselves in a position of relative power that they would be unable to

taste in their homeland.[128] Johnston's argument, however, emphasizes the importance of power in this position, rather than the importance of relativity. Arguably, what is most important about Lady
Charlotte's relationship with Wales and the Welsh is that they provide a dialogic alternative to her existence in London, just as her existence in London allows her to exist in dialogic relationship with
Wales. It is a relationship that is perhaps best illustrated by Lady
Charlotte's wearing Welsh flannel to the Cambrian Ball in London,[129] while wearing a dress that was "exactly similar to what the
peasants wear about Merthyr except that the material instead of
woollen was satin wove to the proper pattern on purpose, the hat
was black velvet instead of beaver and that the whole had a sprin-
kling of gold over it to give candlelight effect" to a fancy dress ball in
Wales in 1837.[130]

Instead of creating a double-bind, these opposing presentations
of self allow Lady Charlotte to open up a crucial space for self-definition. In both cases, she is at pains to portray herself as memorable,
and, in both cases, that memorability stems from difference. This
difference, in turn, defines her as extraordinary. Her extraordinari-
ness, however, is not solely dependent on gender. Moving the question of difference to nationality—unlike the Welsh in Wales, unlike
the English in London—allows Lady Charlotte to distinguish herself
not just as an extraordinary woman, but as extraordinary, regardless of gender. This perception suggests a refinement to Johnston's
claims: the most critical part of an imperialist woman's encounter
with a foreign, colonial culture is this heightening of difference,
which, in turn, allows the woman to distinguish herself as extraordinary.

Wales and the Welsh, thus, provided a means for Lady Charlotte
to define herself as an extraordinary woman without violating the
norms of conventional female behavior. Such a compromise was
crucial, for, despite her ambitious nature, Lady Charlotte seemed
remarkably comfortable with patriarchy. Indeed, the overall impression one garners from her writing is that, not only was she more
comfortable in the company of men, but she was susceptible to half-
acknowledged "sentimental friendships" that might be termed
"crushes" in a crueler environment. Certainly, her journals are difficult to reconcile with Bella Brodzki's claim that "the autobiographical project symbolizes the search for origins, for women a search for
maternal origins and that elusive part of the self that is coextensive

with the birth of language . . . To be exiled from the maternal continent is to be forever subjected to rules of a foreign economy for
which one also serves as the medium of exchange."[131] Instead, Lady
Charlotte turns to the masculine in her search for language. It is,
therefore, perhaps significant that Lady Charlotte's prowess was always with *foreign* languages. For certainly it is arguable that the phal-
locentric order of language was a foreign discourse for Lady Charlotte. Yet, the relationship between Lady Charlotte and her mother
made any attempt to search for maternal origins of language impossible. Indeed, Lady Charlotte's relationship with her mother could
be characterized as nothing so much as a series of frosty silences.

Many incidents separated mother and daughter, but the most
dramatic took place when Lady Charlotte's rejected suitor, Mr. Martin, the tutor, asked Lady Charlotte's stepfather, the Reverend Pegus,
to influence the Bishop of Norwich to ordain him, and the Reverend
Pegus refused. The Rector of Uffington then incurred Pegus's eternal enmity by supporting Martin, and, when the Guests dined with
the Rector of Uffington, Pegus was so furious he offered to call out
John Guest over the incident.[132] The incident escalated and culminated in Pegus telling "Poor Lindsey," the heir to the earldom, that
Charlotte and her husband wanted to take out a Statute of Lunacy
against him.[133] With Pegus's encouragement, the accusation con-
vinced Lindsey first to cut off the entail to his estate, then to write a
will that specifically excluded all of Lady Charlotte's children from
ever succeeding to the Uffington estate.[134] The friction culminated
in a genuinely painful scene between mother and daughter:

> [I] was surprised by a note from Mamma saying . . . that she wished
> to see me . . . I doubted at first what I ought to do under all the cir-
> cumstances of their conduct to Merthyr. But he himself thought I
> ought not to refuse to go to my own mother . . . It was a great effort,
> but I was determined to be calm and I succeeded. I think however it
> was very cruel in my present state of health to drag me to so needless
> an interview. We were on both sides very cold and civil. Two common
> acquaintances could not have been more so, and what object there
> could be in thus trifling with my feelings I cannot imagine. No allu-
> sion whatever was made to any differences between the families, but
> when I went away Mamma asked to see the children. I said that from
> all that had taken place I could not feel there would be any real af-
> fection for them, and that I could not therefore consent to her doing
> so. This may seem harsh. But when it is considered that by the direc-

tion of her husband, and I doubt not by her connivance, those children are sought to be excluded *by name* in a legal document . . . I
think the refusal is sufficiently justified.[135]

It is tempting to read Lady Charlotte's narrative in psychological
terms, seeing the absence of both parents in her life, one literally
and one figuratively, as driving her to turn to an idealized patriar-
chal order. Yet such an argument is complicated by the fact that her
highly unsatisfactory stepfather was a clergyman, a profession that is
normally accorded authority in the matter of any idealizing move.
Furthermore, at least in matters of religion, Lady Charlotte stead-
fastly resisted the transcendental move to the realm of the symbolic,
for she was a dedicated foe of the Puseyite clergy—the high Angli-
cans who insisted on the importance of symbol and ritual in wor-
ship—often to the point of comedy. The nadir of this war took place
in 1851, when Edward Hutchins had the misfortune to invite a
Roman Catholic bishop as a houseguest at Dowlais. The arrangements for the visit were made on the assumption that the bishop
would arrive the day after the Guests left; however, when it was discovered that the bishop was scheduled to arrive a day earlier, Lady
Charlotte insisted that the bishop must delay his visit by a day. Edward Hutchins' wife, however "chose to assert her authority, and
one would have thought to hear the tone and clamour of them both,
that we were the junior partners newly admitted to the concern . . .
and that they were the old respected owners."[136]

When the bishop arrived, Lady Charlotte refused to leave her
room to join the company at dinner; furthermore, she was more
than a little disappointed that her husband did choose to dine with
her perceived enemy, writing,

> I was struggling for a great principle of what I deemed the right, and
> I little dreamt that he would have left me to combat alone and have
> thus abandoned me, after all he had felt and expressed, and almost
> seemed to reproach me and take part with my enemies. But he
> thought he was doing right and acting on a principle of Christian
> Charity, what could I say?[137]

The episode degenerated into low farce when Lady Charlotte was
told that Dr. Brown, the bishop, had gone out to breakfast, and she

> went into the dining room to breakfast accordingly. I was scarcely
> seated and a cup placed before me, when someone went by the win-

dow. I knew it was the priest returned . . . I hardly know how I got away, but having declined to meet him I could do no other in consistency . . . and I since found Dr. Brown had been told it was illness that had caused my absence from table on the two preceding days.[138]

Dr. Brown was apparently more perspicacious than Lady Charlotte or less stubborn, for the episode concluded when he

left suddenly by the midday train. A letter was supposed to have recalled him, but I could not help surmising that he at length suspected how uncongenial his presence was to my husband and myself, and that he had acted with gentlemanly feeling and withdrawn himself.[139]

Even Lady Charlotte's most fervent apologist could scarcely claim that the episode reflects well on her. What is most off-putting about the episode, however, is that its—presumably unintentional—irony all derives from the problems of language it presents. Lady Charlotte's defense is that of sincerity and consistency: as a member of a church that prizes truth over symbol, she feels she cannot so much as dine with a proponent of the other view. She insists on adhering to the right and supporting it with consistency, even if that goes against the actions of her husband, who dined with the bishop for propriety's sake. Yet, when her stance is in danger of being smoothed over by a social lie, she escalates, so that the bishop cannot help but be aware of her objection. In direct opposition to her own insistence on truth and clarity, she next shows herself an adept reader of the bishop's own social lie, and furthermore commends his using it as "gentlemanly feeling." She then ends the entire episode on a final evasion: that it was not only her feelings, but also those of her husband, that the bishop was attempting to spare.

The comic linguistic anecdote does have an epilogue, however, that demonstrates that something very material was at stake in all these language games. Not unexpectedly, Edward Hutchins was "greatly aggrieved about [Lady Charlotte's] conduct about the Romish Bishop at Dowlais,"[140] and these feelings were certainly a contributory factor in his decision four days later to sell his shares in the Dowlais Works back to Sir John Guest. Lady Charlotte's written reaction is expectedly ambivalent:

I had hoped and earnestly wished for this arrangement to be concluded, I had scarce dared to expect that it would be brought to pass

... I sat down and wept bitterly, and yet I know that it was right and best. He gives no help but much anxiety to my dear husband, by his unintentional counteractions in business. The Roman Catholick [*sic*] influence ... is most pernicious. He had not depth, no real business-like views, and really his removal will be a relief to Merthyr. But to look further: if it pleased God to remove my dear husband, his influence and interference, in such a position as this, would have been objectionable [*sic*]beyond anything I can imagine now or detail; I shudder to think what might have been the consequences.[141]

It did please God to remove Sir John scarcely a year later, a development that could not have come as a surprise to Lady Charlotte, for her husband was in poor health for many years. Sir John had long ago demonstrated his faith in his wife by making her the sole executrix for her children; the removal of Hutchins meant that Lady Charlotte was left to manage the works with only the assistance of John Evans, whom she found congenial. And, for all its bitter weeping and deference to God's pleasure, the passage demonstrates a very clear-eyed consciousness of this consequence of the situation.

Did Lady Charlotte exacerbate the incident with the bishop in order to drive Edward Hutchins out of the Dowlais Iron Works? Her intentions are quite frankly lost to us; all we can discuss is her narrative of these events. There is a certain delicious pleasure in reading them as a Machiavellian discourse of a woman who is doing what she must do in order to protect her children's inheritance—a mission that, given her belief that her own inheritance had been snatched from her, seems quite justifiable. Yet, the text itself refuses measurement against any "objective" standard outside itself, precisely because that standard is continually incorporated into her version of events. In the end, it is simply impossible to judge sentences such as "I sat down and wept bitterly, and yet I know that it was right and best."

Perhaps the only unequivocal conclusion one can reach is that Lady Charlotte claiming to know anything at all during this fraught period is testimony to her extraordinary strength of both intellect and character. For Sir John, who was twenty-seven years older than his wife, was in largely poor health due to bladder stones for the last several years of his life. In addition, during at least the last two years of his life, he was subject to bouts of dementia, including the rather horrifying incident in 1851, in which he "had taken a fancy our poor dear innocent Ivor had made an imprudent marriage, had been raising many thousand pounds—had come home from Harrow. I assured him it was entirely without foundation and reminded him that I never deceived him about anything."[142]

The last sentence points to the peculiar difficulty Sir John's condition created for Lady Charlotte's autobiography: even before his death, she had lost her ideal reader, for Sir John's mistrust of her veracity implicitly violates the compact she had established between herself and him at the beginning of their married life. It should thus come as no surprise that during this period, she began rereading and commenting on her journals again, citing, for example, the above passage in an entry a year later, with the single sentence "See this day last year."[143]

Furthermore, while Lady Charlotte was thus groping to reestablish an ideal reader for her autobiography, she also seems to have been groping for new exemplary texts to replace Mrs. Ellis's *Wives of England*. The presence of a clipping in one of Lady Charlotte's diaries is no guarantee of its chronology; the clipping describing Ivor's coming of age, for example, is found in volume 9, before he was born. However, volume 15 contains a clipping of a genuinely execrable example of high Victorian verse—a startling anomaly in a woman whose usual tastes ran to Virgil. The poem, by one M. F. Tupper, is a ballad on the motto, "Aspire!" It begins

> Higher, higher, ever higher,—
> Let thy watchword be "Aspire!"
> Noble Christian youth;
> Whatso'er be God's behest,
> Try to do that duty best
> In the strength of youth.

After four more verses in this muscular vein, it concludes, even more awfully,

> Higher then, and always higher,—
> Let Man's motto be "Aspire!"
> Whoso'er he be!
> Holy liver! Happy dier
> Earth's poor best, and Heaven's quire,
> Are reserved for *thee!*[144]

Granted, the context of the poem, as well as Lady Charlotte's reason for clipping it are unknown. Indeed, she may not have been the one to clip it at all. Nonetheless, one would think that the "holy liver" would smack enough of vivisection to cause Lady Charlotte to consign the poem to a merciful oblivion were she not distracted by her husband's imminent death.

That unhappy event was recorded in a set piece with which Bessborough concludes the first volume of her memoirs:

> When we stopped at [Canford's] door, I got out silently, and leaving them all went straight to the Library, where luckily there was a light. A slight veil had been thrown over [the deceased John Guest's] bust, which at once I removed and then I flung my arms around it, and remained clasping it for some minutes, kissing the cold lips—not colder than his own when I kissed them last—and shedding torrents of passionate tears. And this cold marble is now all that is left me![145]

Sir John Guest died in 1852, leaving Lady Charlotte a relatively young widow of forty years old, with ten children, none of whom had reached their majority. Conventionally, her husband's death would dictate that Lady Charlotte retire to private life, spending at least a year mourning her dead husband before she ventured back into the peculiar half-world of the dowager, participating in society primarily as a mediator of her husband's memory and her children's needs. And so Bessborough's choice of conclusion implies. Yet, in fact, she was thrust immediately back into the very real world of business when the couple's solicitor arrived on January 18,

> in the morning, bringing with him the Bute lease for my signature. It is granted to me as being the sole acting trustee for my life. When this paper was shown to me I was completely unnerved, so many associations of sorrow and anxiety seemed revived; I covered my face with my hands and for a moment wept bitterly, it was no use trying to repress it. A minute after, I had signed the important document.[146]

It is testament to Sir John's good sense, Lady Charlotte's acumen, and the strength of their relationship that Sir John appointed Lady Charlotte sole executrix of her children's estate. Her reaction to this news exemplifies the tension between conventional and extraordinary woman that we have come to expect from her. On the one hand, she bursts into the tears one might expect of a recently bereaved widow. On the other hand, she retains the presence of mind, not only to recognize the document's importance, but to sign it.

Within a year, Lady Charlotte was called upon to demonstrate a similar intelligence and presence of mind in her reaction to the colliers' strike. Her handling of the situation amply justified Sir John's faith in her. In her role as executrix of the children's estate, Lady Charlotte took over control of the iron works in the name of her son, Ivor, with the advice of John Evans. Within a year, she was faced with a situation that called into question any assumptions she might have had about the natural relationship between the beneficent upper classes and deferential lower classes: a strike in the ironmongeries. The other ironmasters met with Lady Charlotte, suggesting collusive wage practices in order to break the strike. In her journal, Lady Charlotte wrote:

> It seems to me monstrous to tell our steady good men that unless (as it were) they *compelled* their refractory neighbours to go to work we would revenge it upon them and throw them out of bread—But they were all against me—even *Evans*—they said it would never come to *that*—that with the month's notice—if not within the week —all would be at work—that only strong measures could be of any use.[147]

She acceded to the ironmasters' plan, only to immediately send Evans to revoke her decision. She then began to worry that her credibility was at issue and took a hard line with her own miners. The result was a hybrid that was known later as "The Respectful Strike," during which one labor leader called attention to the fact that the strike was taking place in a factory "principally ruled by a lady, whose excellent qualities all willingly acknowledge, and whose claims to their good wishes could scarcely be overstated (Applause). No lady in the kingdom had such cares to bear as Lady Charlotte Guest."[148]

The strike was eventually resolved, but the episode crystallizes the shaky triangulation among idealism, gender, and materialism that characterized the twenty years of Lady Charlotte's marriage to John Guest. The relationship between Lady Charlotte and her miners is a reciprocally idealizing one: she perceives her men as "good" and "steady," in opposition to their "refractory" neighbors; similarly, they perceive her as possessing the ideal, "excellent qualities" of a lady. These parallel ideal structures allow Lady Charlotte and the workman to communicate in a way that is impossible between her and her fellow ironmasters. That relationship is governed by a continuing, unsuccessful dialectic that remains stalled in the tension of negation, without moving forward to any meaningful resolution. Interestingly, however, in maintaining her idealized relationship with her workmen, Lady Charlotte succeeds in displacing her own self-assertion as an industry owner onto the other ironmongery owners, who, in the tradition of good cops and bad cops everywhere, are effectively set up as the "heavies" in the strike. Nonetheless, Lady Charlotte was capable of considerable self-assertion, as demonstrated when she faced down the strikers at Dowlais:

> one man in the party loudly dissented; he said the colliers expected their money to be given back at once and he thought, if it were not, they would all strike again tomorrow. To this appeal I remained quite unmoved. I said: Very well, I had stood that once, I could do so again, but they might be sure that when I said a thing I meant it, and that nothing could make me change my mind. If they were not satisfied, so be it. His tone changed upon this, and the others interposed and said they were very grateful, and knew they had sacrificed all claim to [the money] at all, whereupon I desired such as were satisfied to hold up their hands, which they did forthwith unhesitatingly.[149]

Interestingly, Lady Charlotte's self-assertion in this episode is primarily rhetorical: the basis of her claim is that the strikers might be sure that when she said a thing, she meant it. She underscores such rhetorical firmness quite literally by signing her diary entries C. E. Guest or C. E. G., a recurrent habit during stressful portions of her life. It is tempting to read both gestures as demonstrating her resolve to take control of her autobiography—both literally and figuratively—at a moment when she has lost the ideal reader that lent stability to the "text" of her life. Yet, other passages, dating from the same year, demonstrate how fragile Lady Charlotte's control of rhetoric was following the loss of Sir John. A particularly poignant entry shows how her husband's death left her literally and figuratively groping for forms:

> *March 24 [Canford].* . . . My equanimity overset by Mr. Ponsonby sending word that he intended stripping the church of the mourning put up in respect for my dear husband . . .
> *March 25.* . . . I had a very kind note from Mr. Ponsonby saying that if I had any feeling on the subject the mourning should not be removed from the church. I replied that I only wished what was

usual, and that hoping to hear by the morning's post what the rule was (from precedents) I begged to wait till then before anything was done . . .

March 26. . . . I find that although in public, i.e., Royal funerals, it remains up but six weeks, yet that it is the custom in private ones to keep it up much longer. In this county Lord Eldon's remained a twelve-month, Lord Shaftesbury's fourteen months, from which may be argued that at all events the rule is such in this part of the country. I wrote all this to Mr. Ponsonby, and in reply he sent me a note to say he had already decided to make no change, which I answered by a letter of thanks; and thus it has ended, but the affair has worried me a good deal . . .[150]

To the modern reader, Lady Charlotte's concern with the niceties of hanging bunting is a Victorian oddity as silly as Lady Dunraven's claim to the Guest carriage horses as a heriot, "a feudal duty due to a lord upon the death of a tenant, consisting originally of the horses and arms lent by the lord to his man."[151] Yet, her concern also vividly demonstrates the destabilizing effect of the loss of Sir John, not only as a husband, but as an external standard of judgment. Literally at an *aporia*, Lady Charlotte turns to convention and precedent as a method of asserting what she feels is due her husband's memory.

Given Lady Charlotte's struggle to maintain rhetorical control during this period, it is ironic that chance has dictated that this period also affords us the most complete view of the texts that make up Lady Charlotte's autobiography. For, although her collected personal journals fill nine cardboard boxes at the National Library of Wales, these were not the only journals that she kept. In addition, in her informal capacity as Sir John's secretary, she kept extensive business journals as well. If these journals still exist, they remain in family hands. However, eight photocopied pages of one of these journals, which was in the possession of John Guest in 1976, are enclosed in volume 15 of her journal. The pages cover the events of July 18 to July 22, 1853—some of the most dramatic episodes in the colliers' strike. Juxtaposing the two sets of entries provides new insights into what constitutes the "complete" text of Lady Charlotte's autobiography.

The differences between the two sets of entries are not unexpected. The works diary is shorter and discusses only matters pertaining to business. Its overall tone is less personal, with fewer "I's," no personal details, and less evocative language. The similarities between the two sets of entries, however, are striking and suggestive. Perhaps the most significant is the fact that Lady Charlotte records the same incidents she describes in her works diary a second time in her personal diary, often providing even more detail in the personal diary. For example, in an episode that epitomizes both her good will to her workers and her blindness to the inequity of the underlying social conditions, she notes on July 18, "Found in this level an air door boy under 9 years old—who is to be moved and put to some other occupation—not discharged—for the boy told the truth about his age, which many of them will not do."[152]

Even this brusque entry provides autobiographical detail about Lady Charlotte's ethos: She will not discharge a child for telling the truth. However, the incident only obtains its true narrative value in her personal journal:

> A pretty little boy was "keeping a door" here. I asked him his age and he answered me with great simplicity that he was "going his nine." His being there at all was consequently illegal; often they are put to this work while under the prescribed age, but they are taught to say they are over ten and thus it is difficult to do anything, until you can disprove it. I was delighted by this boy's simplicity and candour. He must of course be removed from where he is, but he must not lose by it. I shall find him an easy berth above ground, poor infant, and make him know that he has it because he told the truth.[153]

The immediacy of Lady Charlotte's emotional involvement, as well as her sharp ear for the child's language, makes this one of the most appealing self-portraits in her journals—as does the fact that she cares enough about the little boy's fate, not only to find him a new, safer position, but to tell his story in her personal, as well as her business, diaries. Nonetheless, one cannot help but feel a certain frustration at her obliviousness—even in the throes of a strike—to the larger social ills that forced the child to work in the first place. In particular, her blaming the boy's parents for breaking the law, rather than her being appalled at a law that allows children to work at ten, lends weight to the striking miner's grievances.

This duplication of effort in keeping two sets of journals is not only testament to the sort of Victorian textual industry that seems so unbelievable in an age of photocopiers and text messaging. It also illustrates how completely Lady Charlotte saw her life as the head of the ironworks as interwoven with her life as a whole—as with the entry for July 18, which begins with "Euclid till breakfast. Then saw

Evans before his going down to Board of Health."[154] It closes with a similar blend of business and personal life:

> I believe the plot is thickening. I shall be very glad when it takes a definite form . . . for I really want to join the children. Our colliers just sent out 1655 Tons of Coal on Saturday, which does not look like discontent. My evening was spent with Beethoven & I went to bed at 11 calmer and less tired than usual.[155]

Indeed, there is at least one work-related entry that appears in the personal journals, not the business journals:

> Wales told me the air was worse here than in any other part of the colliery. The men told us there had been fire on going in the first thing this morning. Wales tried to show me that his candle lengthened a little as he held it up toward the roof with his hand in front of it. It was not, however, very striking to my unpracticed eye.[156]

Lady Charlotte's self-deprecating "unpracticed eye" would never have appeared in her business journal. Nonetheless, it should not blind anyone to her clear-eyed evaluation of the demonstration. Wales has, in her mind, failed to prove his point.[157]

On the whole, the differences between the two sets of journals are not unexpected. Yet, Lady Charlotte can never completely suppress her flair for language even in her business journal entries. Her entry describing the furnaces being turned off to shut down production not only personifies the machines as condemned, but endows them with a Byronic defiance that would not seem out of place in the striking colliers themselves: "The glare of the condemned furnaces, that seemed to flame with surpassing brilliancy tonight . . . was the most magnificent sight I ever saw."[158]

The prose of her personal entry recording the event is equally beautiful; nonetheless what is most striking about the passage is Lady Charlotte's firm determination to pursue her course of action:

> I sat watching the magnificent glare of the condemned furnaces— which flamed wildly—more beautifully than ever—but it was fitful & uncertain. I never saw anything like the effects they had made on the surrounding scenery—How melancholy it was!—but quite right and as much as it grieved me, I felt perfectly satisfied.[159]

Perhaps the most telling detail among all these entries, however, has nothing to do with the strike. Instead, it is Lady Charlotte's sudden interest in Euclid. Indeed, by this point, Euclid had become a bit of a passion for Lady Charlotte. In addition to turning to Euclid to escape from the rigors of the strike, she also takes refuge in him after a particularly unpleasant fight with Mr. Pegus.[160] Euclid also figures in a study plan that is ample testimony that Lady Charlotte had lost none of her intellectual energy:

Algebra—up to quadratic equations	done (Go further.)
Euclid—Bks I II	do (write out) esp. defn
Virgil Aeniad Bk 1	do
Cicero De Senetude	do
Homer Iliad Bk I	to write out in MS Book
Gospel of St. Luke	to go over
Cicero de Amicite	
Xenophon Mem Bk I[161]	

This passion for Euclid is an early indication of the arrival of a new figure destined to play a significant role in Lady Charlotte's life: Charles Schreiber, fourteen years younger than she, and Ivor's new tutor, engaged by the family at Mr. Pegus's recommendation. This is not, however, his first appearance in Lady Charlotte's diaries. On that occasion, Lady Charlotte records that she paused between church services to have "a short walk round the garden in front with Mr. Schreiber to whom I had a good deal to say about Ivor."[162] No mention is made of what, if anything, Charles Schreiber had to say.

The full scale of the role Schreiber was destined to play in both her journals and her life becomes evident in June of that year, when Schreiber fell gravely ill and asked to see Lady Charlotte. It was, to say the least, an unconventional request, and her first concern in recording this event was to establish the propriety of the situation:

> . . . finding Mr. Schreiber had expressed a wish to see me I went to him, and very glad I am that I did so. I felt a little prudery about it at first—for it is difficult for me who was comparatively a young woman last year, to feel and believe myself, as I am, an old woman now.[163]

For all its concern with propriety, the passage represents a radical shift in Lady Charlotte's construction of both meaning and self, for with Lady Charlotte's appearance at Charles Schreiber's sickbed, the figure of the ideal reader represented by Sir John is eradicated from her journals for good. In this passage, Lady Charlotte irrevocably appropriates the right to observe—to read the text of another's life, and with it, her own. The underlying justification of her seizing this right is the fact that Lady Charlotte is now an "old woman," invisible to the male gaze. No longer the object of male desire, she can enter a man's bedroom, an action that would have been unthinkable in a woman who was still perceived as a sexually desirable object. Needless to say, it is clear from her hasty claim that a year ago, she would have been young enough to make the situation a delicate one, that Lady Charlotte has her regrets about relinquishing her status as a sexually desirable woman. Yet, she chooses to avail herself of the new freedom of being an independent, judging observer, rather than clinging to her status as object of the gaze and leaving the room in girlish modesty.

Schreiber immediately reinforces Lady Charlotte's seizing of the gaze in this episode by offering her an opportunity to stand in judgment of him. As he was in delirium, "all his youthful unrepented sins came thronging before him, exaggerated doubtless by his condition . . . There had been no-one to whom to pour out his heart and his fears, and now I heard it all, only, it is true, the usual generalities, anguish at ever having sinned, ever forgotten God, and neglected so many opportunities."[164] Lady Charlotte's discomfort with her new ability to stand in judgment of Charles Schreiber is clear in the excuses "exaggerated doubtless by his condition" and "the usual generalities," both of which defer judgment to an imagined standard of conventionality. Yet when offered a new opportunity to change her role so radically, she again accepts it, even if she reacts to the breach in convention represented by his confessions in the most conventional way. She "ventured on a short extempore prayer beside his bed . . . [suggesting] that if he should be raised and devote his energies to God's glory, his present illness might prove to him to have been a signal blessing."[165]

More praying ensued after Schreiber's recovery, when he left on a journey to recuperate. Lady Charlotte:

> . . . felt I ought not to let him go without fulfilling a promise that I had made him when he was so very ill; it was to the effect that, if he would but tranquillize [sic] himself, I would undertake to remind him on his recovery of all he had suffered with the fear of impending death before his eyes. He seemed quite to remember all that had passed then, and he took all I now ventured to say in very good part . . . Another mind is added to the very few I value and am interested in. I pray God I may be instrumental for its good . . . it seems to me as

if that young life had been granted me, given me back, as it were from the very grave; and shall I not strive earnestly for its welfare? Is it not my duty so to do? By God's help I will do it . . .[166]

The extended episode is an appropriate introduction to the role Charles Schreiber was destined to play in Lady Charlotte's later journals, for just as her entry into his bedroom threatens to violate Victorian convention, the figure of Charles Schreiber violates the textual conventions of Lady Charlotte's earlier diaries. It is she who stands in the position of clear-eyed reader, while Schreiber is in delirium, a state of mental incapacity, helpless on his sickbed. However, it is important also to note that although Lady Charlotte's power in the episode is a mental and intellectual one, and although it arises directly from the newly discovered sexual invisibility that allows her to attend his bedside, the culmination of the episode is decidedly passionate, swelling from the final two rhetorical questions to the pure desire of her last vow—which, even this early in their relationship, seems to involve more than honing his intellect. This balance between passionately desiring subject and clear-eyed observer is the hallmark of the next fifteen years of her diaries.

That the balance was often uneasy is clear from a new coyness in her prose. According to Bessborough, as the romance gained momentum, "the daily references in the diary to Charles Schreiber take two separate forms. As tutor and companion to her son he is referred to as 'Mr. Schreiber.' But there are constant references to her feelings towards an unnamed person, and her desire to become his wife, and there are also very frequent allusions to her correspondence with him under the heading of 'letter to Cambridge' or 'letter from Cambridge.'"[167] Lady Charlotte was apparently equally circumspect in actual conversation. For example, "when she discussed with Maria the minds of those possessing practical wisdom, she confessed that in addition to the four they singled out, 'I could I believe have added a fifth—but I forebore.'"[168]

This coy allusiveness culminates in a passage of September 1853, which reads, "I am gradually regaining my usual tone and the stereotyped manner continues unmoved. I feel now that there must have been some great misapprehension and must hope to put all straight."[169] It is no exaggeration to say the passage is impossible to parse—mainly because of its inherent contradictions. The first sentence makes a virtue of the forms, not the meaning, of speech. On the other hand, the second sentence asserts the conventional value of truth as meaning what one says and virtue being contained in the seamless relationship between signified and signifier. That initial contradiction is intensified by the fact that the signifier is ultimately absent in this entire passage. Indeed, in an almost Derridean gesture, the signified is, in fact, a misapprehension. The only meaning that can be unambiguously determined from the passage is the author's desire to "put all straight." Any other deductions, as to with whom the misunderstanding arose, over what, what the truth is, or indeed whether Lady Charlotte understands that truth, are nothing but a projection on the part of the reader.

Perhaps because of this newly discovered reticence—equally describable as "becoming" or "annoying"—it is very difficult to track the course of Lady Charlotte's romance with the "fresh, young, pure, enthusiastic, beautiful" Schreiber.[170] Indeed, even after their marriage, Charles Schreiber remains largely an absent figure. An ex-tutor, he had neither title nor wealth. Nor was he particularly ambitious: he served two brief stints as an MP, one for Cheltenham and one for Poole, but he was content with the role of leisured intellectual and collector financed by the remains of his wife's wealth.

This impression, however, may be attributable in part to the fact that all of Lady Charlotte's biographers and editors were Guests, not Schreibers.[171] Revel Guest and the Earl of Bessborough certainly give short shrift to Lady Charlotte's second marriage, even though it lasted nearly ten years longer than her marriage to Guest. Revel Guest dismisses Schreiber as "a shadowy figure."[172] And Bessborough's second set of journal extracts, which cover the last forty years of her life, comprise only 202 pages, as opposed to 302 pages for the twenty years of her marriage to John Guest.[173]

Even shadows, however, leave traces, and the traces that Schreiber leaves are two of the most charming in Lady Charlotte's journals. A single, white flower was pressed between pages 310 and 311 of Journal 15. Unlike loose sheets of paper, a flower stains the pages when pressed, so it is clear this was where it was pressed originally. It is impossible, of course, to know to which of the four entries on those pages the flower pertains, or even if it is related to any entry at all. However, the entry of April 14 is highly suggestive:

> When I walked home after Mr. Schreiber followed me & we were out til near 8 o'clock in different parts of the works. First I went to the iron works where John Evans met us. Found several new works I had planned in progress & nearly completed. Left Evans at his house . . . .

Things are slack and must be looked up. Labour scarce . . . Returned
by garden . . . gate.[174]

Almost as pleasing as the hint of romance in this passage is the way
Lady Charlotte unselfconsciously embeds it in the clear-eyed practi-
cality of her tour of the works. Equally pleasingly, a second leaf can
be found in Journal 16. Although it is currently tucked in the back
cover, it is clear from the staining on the pages that it was originally
pressed between pages 184 and 185, by the entries for May 13–14,
1854. In this case there can be no question that the leaf is associated
with the entry describing Lady Charlotte's visit to Ivor and Charles
Schreiber at Oxford. In the garden of Trinity College "Lilies of the
Valley [were] growing luxuriantly, of which Mr. S gathered some for
me."[175] And, in fact, the dried leaf is clearly a lily of the valley leaf.

Nonetheless, despite these lovely traces, Schreiber's silence seems
infectious, for the next fifteen years of journals are the spottiest of
Lady Charlotte's life. There are no journal entries from Christmas
1854 until the day of her wedding, over three months later. Furthermore, the wedding itself is recorded as an absence or suspension.
On April 10, the day of her wedding, her entry records, "now I have
reached the 10th of April, and, after much trial and inexpressible
opposition, expect in a few hours to be the wife of Charles Schreiber."[176] Her next entry, on May 9, records somewhat prosaically:

After writing here on April 10 I had much to do . . . We had not far to
go from Usher's Hotel, where we were staying, to St. Martin's Church,
where the ceremony was to take place by special license, at 12 o'clock
. . . Dear Charles met me and we shook hands; as soon as all was
ready we proceeded to the Altar, and I became his happy wife.[177]

Arguably, silence before Lady Charlotte's marriages seems to be
a trend: there were also no journal entries for the period that immediately preceded her marriage to Sir John. However, there is a
significant difference between the silence that preceded her first
marriage and the one that preceded her second. Lady Charlotte
wrote in her journal during the period immediately preceding her
marriage to Sir John; however, she burned the entries. In the case
of her wedding to Schreiber, in contrast, she seems simply to have
ceased writing—perhaps because she feared discovery by her family, who were adamantly opposed to the marriage, even after it took
place.

The newly-wed Schreibers' honeymoon is equally absent. Lady Charlotte describes it once more retrospectively as "three most blessed weeks . . . that it would be vain to attempt to describe." And, although she does concede that "They are engraved on the memory of my dear husband" as well as her own, the textual Charles Schreiber has already been reduced to an abstraction, "a fresh, young, pure, enthusiastic, beautiful being."[178] Significantly, without any other identifying context, it is a description one would be more likely to assume applied to a young wife.

Very few specifics of the honeymoon are given, beyond "Much talk with dear Charles about my former life, and about much that I suffered with and for my poor late husband . . . "[179] One has to fight down a certain sympathy for Charles Schreiber, when one considers that this was the highlight of his new wife's honeymoon. Yet, textually, this passage marks an important turning point: Schreiber is finally openly presented as an object of affection by the use of his first name. Concurrent with this new foregrounding of Schreiber as an open object of desire is Lady Charlotte's equally open acknowledgment of her first husband as a cause of suffering. Since Sir John functioned as Lady Charlotte's ideal reader, the implications of this transformation are significant, for the textual construct of a reader, whether her husband or herself, always seems to have been a source of anxiety for Lady Charlotte—perhaps because her intellectual nature made any act of reading also an act of judgment. Her anxiety over this posited judgment makes her adolescent diaries, in particular, very fraught, unpleasant reading. Granted, maturity, as well as success as a works manager, a translator, and an educator, were probably as influential in the transformation in the diaries as any freedom from an ideal reader. Regardless of the reasons for the change, however, Lady Charlotte's voice grows increasingly more engaging in her later diaries—funnier, sharper, and far more direct.

She needed all those qualities particularly during the next several years, for her second marriage was, if not scandalous, certainly an unconventional one. Although Schreiber was well-educated, he had neither Lady Charlotte's wealth nor her social position. He was also fourteen years younger than she. In addition, the marriage itself took place within three years of her first husband's death—leading to the inference that she had become romantically involved within a year of her first husband's death. Both her friends and relatives found such behavior indecorous—so much so that, if the first half of Lady Charlotte's journals are instructive, the second half are, well, juicy.

It would be overstating the case to say Lady Charlotte was ostracized socially over her second marriage, despite the reaction of such old friends as Lady Augusta Hall, whose response was

> . . . very mischievous and her manner vexed me when I saw her in town last year. I befriended her years ago when she was in trouble and when her husband's conduct made her grateful for sympathy, though I always assumed to *know* nothing that could hurt her or reflect upon him, and this has been my return—she is the only person in the course of all the differences of opinion about my marriage that has shown me personal coolness amounting almost to incivility.[180]

In fact, for the first several years of her marriage, Lady Charlotte attempted to maintain her position in London society. Her efforts, however, resulted in many uncomfortable moments. As a newlywed, Lady Charlotte had to be presented to the queen a second time; somewhat awkwardly, this occurred at the same time as her daughter Katherine was presented at court. Lady Charlotte's reaction is understandable: "I was rather put out, and I am afraid I was not so self-possessed as I should have been."[181]

However, there were auspicious moments as well. For example, "I gave my first party in London under my new name . . . I had a great many old friends and some new ones, and this my new *debut* might be considered perfectly successful."[182] Yet, only a week later, Lady Charlotte was to be disappointed when "My first ball took place. Now this ball was a great event. I had taken great pains about it . . . after the success of the concert it was expected to be very brilliant. However it did not succeed so well as I anticipated."[183]

Her summary of the season, yet another week later, is hopeful, but with a perceptible undercurrent of self-justification:

> A great deal had been said to make the children uncomfortable as to doubts of how I should be received on account of my second marriage. All this has been set at rest by the result. They must now be content to believe that my position is as good if not better than ever; and Charles himself appears so popular that on that head also they must feel satisfied.[184]

Like Jane Austen's modals, that final "must" brings with it a host of meaning; its mood is at once predictive, exhortative, and imperative.

The same words could be used to describe Lady Charlotte's relationship with her family during this period, for the marriage remained an ongoing source of tension long after it took place. The Peguses and Lady Charlotte's half-sister Mary "all but disowned Charlotte when she remarried."[185] Among her children, her sons eventually accepted the transformation of their tutor into their stepfather. Her daughters, in contrast, violently objected to the relationship. At least in retrospect, Lady Charlotte's daughters Blanche and Katherine were upset with how quickly their father's memory was forgotten. Fights erupted over the trivial, but charged issue of Lady Charlotte coloring her white hair, a change to which her daughters objected, but which Schreiber endorsed.[186] Furthermore, Lady Charlotte suspected that Katherine had feelings for Schreiber herself—a charge that Katherine later dismissed as "absurd."[187] A third daughter, Maria, was, according to Lady Charlotte,

> unable to accommodate herself to the present state of affairs. She has been touchy and dictatorial, in fact her manner has been our one great trial . . . For a very long time she found it impossible to provoke [Schreiber], but at last continual contradiction and the assumption of authority over us all produced some effect, and his replies became, on one or two occasions only, a little more decided.[188]

It thus comes as little surprise that Enid wrote, upon her marriage to Henry Layard in 1869, "None of us had a happy home and we were all glad to get away."[189]

Not only did this conflict with her children undoubtedly create significant personal pain, it also represents the rejection of her children as potential new "ideal readers" for her journals. However, this rejection was neither immediate nor absolute. In at least one instance, Lady Charlotte did use her daughter Maria to regulate judgment in the journals, dragooning her into acting as a go-between as Lady Charlotte attempted to reconcile with her half-sister, Lady Huntly. The episode bears quoting at length:

> *April 20* . . . My sister . . . sent for my children to see her, and on Sunday they went. She gave Maria a message of reconciliation for me, and Maria managed to deliver it in such a manner as to make it appear to be an insult. I had been led to expect that my sister was sorry for her interference with my affairs and for her very harsh conduct towards me, and I thought she meant to call on me on coming

to town, but the message that reached me was to the effect that I might if I pleased go to her, and she would be glad to see me. Now this seemed unbearable; to be ignored for a whole year, and then graciously permitted to go and make peace. I chafed at this idea very much, more for the sake of my position with those around me than for any pride of my own in the matter. Ill feeling I have none, nor ever had . . . Having consulted Mr. Bruce what to do, I put on paper my reasons for being unable to accept such terms, and told Maria to communicate them to her aunt. Lady Huntly upon this disclaimed the message and said she had meant to call upon me, and only wanted to know if I should be glad to receive her. Explanations have been sent on both sides, but she is now, of course, annoyed at my note, and Maria, with her unconquerable reserve and mystification is the very worst envoy that could be employed. So hitherto we have not met and it seems to me very probable that we are further than ever from doing so.

April 26 . . . Before going to my party I wrote a short conciliatory note to my sister. I knew now her message had been most incorrectly delivered, and was sure she had never received any of mine, and I felt I should be as glad to see her as she expressed that she would be to see me. I put this on paper and sent it to her.

April 27 . . . We had just sat down to luncheon when my sister, Lady Huntly, was announced. I went down to her in my room and we had a very affectionate meeting, though no explanation passed or anything that had previously occurred was alluded to . . . The whole interview went off quite satisfactorily. She thought me looking wonderfully well. I did not think the same of her, she varied in colour, and seemed altered since we last met, but she was probably agitated, and her being *enceinte* of her ninth child may make a difference.[190]

There is a peculiar fittingness in the fact that, in the middle of all these machinations, Lady Charlotte attended a reading of *Hamlet* by Kemble, with which she was highly dissatisfied. The doubts and misinterpretations governing Lady Charlotte's family dynamics are worthy of those at Elsinore—nowhere more so than in the fact that throughout the passage, interpretation precedes utterance. Lady Charlotte begins the story with an understanding of her sister's willingness for a reconciliation—an understanding that is contradicted by the actual message she receives from her sister. Lady Huntly is in turn angered, not by her sister's response to her actual message, but by Lady Charlotte's response to her—possibly erroneously—perceived intentions.

What makes this failure ironic is the exquisite devotion to precision in language that both parties display. Lady Charlotte in particular displays a lawyer-like nicety in committing her grievances to paper. Indeed, it is striking that she feels she needs to consult with Mr. Bruce before she so much as takes the step of writing. Yet, even writing fails to guarantee perfect communication, for Lady Huntly applies her own, hostile, interpretation to Lady Charlotte's message. The failure in communication is only at last regulated by creating a scapegoat to replace the *aporia*. The unhappy victim is Maria, who is already in her mother's bad graces over her attitude toward her new stepfather. Only when Maria is duly excoriated can the reconciliation take place.

Yet, when it does take place, even though it is pronounced "very affectionate," the reconciliation offers no interpretive satisfaction. The sisters do not resolve or even discuss their earlier differences. Furthermore, Lady Charlotte's final comment on the scene betrays a fatal lack of self-awareness as she accepts her sister's evaluation of her looking wonderfully well at face value, even as she cattily points out that her sister's pregnancy is taking its toll.

In contrast to such scenes, the most balanced reaction to the marriage came from a surprising source, Schreiber's mother. As Lady Charlotte describes it:

> Charles Schreiber came and joined me, and we went to his rooms and concocted a letter to his mother, which, I trust, for a time may put matters at rest. She writes to make enquiries, and there is one sentence in her letter that I should wish to record. She says: " There is nothing to be ashamed of, though there may be much to be said, for and against, on both sides."[191]

The elder Mrs. Schreiber was clearly a sane and sensitive woman. She was also a closet postmodernist, content to leave her final judgment in a state of suspension. Lady Charlotte was fortunate to have such a mother-in-law, for at the same time that she was struggling to have her own family acknowledge her second marriage, her relationship with them was under attack from another quarter as well. Within a year of Sir John's death, Mr. Pegus, her stepfather, at last put into motion a plan Lady Charlotte had been able to stave off while she was married to Sir John:

> [Pegus told Lady Charlotte] that my poor brother Lindsey had had a fit . . . My first impulse was to go and see him, but I found on enquiry

that he was staying at the house of a woman Mr. Pegus pays to live with him! . . . But my consternation was greater still when I found my other brother Bertie was staying with her, too, and was actually being nursed by her for inflammation of the eyes![192]

Later events more than confirmed Lady Charlotte's seemingly comic suspicions. After the death of Lady Lindsey in 1858, Pegus, "very angry to see he was neither asked to live at this house, nor even made executor,"[193] began to put in motion his plans to marry off Lindsey to Mrs. Maitland, the woman he had paid to live with Lindsey. Bertie, by this time, was married to a wife of his own, Felicia, and was determined to take Lindsey into his own custody. Pegus countered by telling "Lindsey that his brother and Felicia had an interest in poisoning him" and Lady Charlotte would "contrive to put him in a lunatic asylum."[194] The quarrel dragged on for four years, but terminated with the happy event of Lindsey expressing "himself with a clearness and propriety of words and of thought that quite surprised [Lady Charlotte]. He declared his desire to get rid of Mr. Pegus entirely . . . A paper was drawn up as a memorandum of his wishes, which he signed, and which seemed a great relief to his mind."[195] Even given the rather obvious opportunity for projection on Lady Charlotte's part, the episode is a happy reversal of the misunderstanding with her sister, in which a previously occluded meaning is not only clearly ascertained, but also committed to writing by a person previously deemed unable to communicate clearly.

Perhaps not surprisingly, Lady Charlotte reacted to these tensions by increasingly valorizing private life. On October 25, 1853, she wrote of a "Long talk at breakfast . . . about all the children, and my duties . . . May God support me to execute these duties, but may he grant me a release some day! May I hope at length to be allowed to retire 'into private life,' and to enjoy the comforts of repose?"[196] It was to be the first of many entries on the theme.

This desired withdrawal, however, did not happen immediately. Lady Charlotte still spent much of her time preparing Ivor to take over the manor at Canford; presenting her daughters and marrying them off ruthlessly; fending off a fortune hunter who wanted to marry Merthyr; and establishing Montague in an army career. Her activity continued until Ivor's coming of age party in Canford in 1856, which was the last great party that she gave. It was entertainment on a grand scale, including a daytime party for eight hundred children, with a Punch and Judy show and games, followed by night-time illuminations, fireworks and a ball for eight hundred. Interestingly, Ivor was asleep by two o'clock, and, at least in the opinion of his indefatigable mother, his absence was not noticed. Lady Charlotte herself stayed up until "God Save the Queen" was played at six in the morning.[197]

Nonetheless, she increasingly separated such public efforts on behalf of her children from her private life as Charles Schreiber's wife. No better example of this separation can be found than the manner in which she received the news that Montague's regiment was under orders for India. Lady Charlotte "went upstairs to Charley and had a hearty cry upon his shoulder . . . to the boy himself I wrote that I doubted not he was glad to go and have an opportunity of seeing active service."[198]

The Schreibers' retreat to private life was also marked by intermittent but significant attempts at regaining a public life in the shape of a political career for Charles.[199] It is difficult to determine whether he had any particular affinity for such an endeavor, although he did serve twice, once as an MP for Cheltenham in 1865, and later as an MP for Poole in 1880. It is inarguable, however, that Schreiber's entry into politics was destined to create marital tension, for he was a Tory, while Lady Charlotte retained her liberal tendencies. In fact, she and Schreiber were of such divergent views that "we determined never to speak on politicks [*sic*] to each other at all, a rule which we have always strictly adhered to."[200]

Nowhere was this divergence more unpleasantly evident than when Schreiber chose to blame Lady Charlotte's "radical politicks"[201] for his first electoral defeat. His scapegoating his wife led to a significant marital rupture:

> I felt as if a crisis in my life had come. Charles said no word to me. At Swindon where we had to change carriages, he went and got into a carriage by himself, taking no notice of me, so that in searching to find where he was, I was nearly left behind. But I did find him, and we had happily a compartment to ourselves. Before we reached London I insisted on having it "out," spite of [*sic*] of his assertions that he meant to go to a lodging in town, and leave me, and not come near me for some weeks. I fought him very hard; I never had such a fight in my life. I made every allowance for his natural vexation at the issue of the election contest, but I told him the truth, and did not spare where I knew him to be in the wrong, and, praise be to God, I conquered. He came home with me. It was late in the evening; I read him prayers when we went to bed, and by degrees all was well once

more. Doubtless everything in this world is ordered for the best, and I shall ever believe that when the election was lost my husband was saved to me.[202]

The passage is far from an ideal portrait of a marriage. Given the absence of any underlying, unstated motive for the couple's quarrel—and one is led to suspect from the violence of his reaction that such a motive indeed existed—Schreiber's reaction is simply childish. Yet, Lady Charlotte's customary rationality and determination seem almost Gradgrindian. One does not envy the husband whose wife's idea of a reconciliation in the bedroom is reading prayers. Granted, the couple was groping to respond to what appeared to be both a catastrophic public and personal failure. Nevertheless, it would perhaps have been best if the scene had been confined to the privacy of their shared carriage.

Indeed, it is quite possible that such was Lady Charlotte's initial impulse. For it was during this period that she began abandoning her journals and then returning to them. For example, volume 17 of her journals begins—uncharacteristically—on the first of January with the following entry:

New Years Day—A New Year has begun for me & I am going once again to attempt to renew my old habit of writing a journal—however short. The old journal has been discontinued now for many months—I doubt if any of it can be recovered—certainly nothing more than a mere sketch—and where I shall find time for even that I cannot tell—

My new record must commence by acknowledging with the deepest gratitude my present happiness—blessed as I am by my darling husband—and surrounded by my children.[203]

Journal 17 is relatively complete; however, the next journal, which contains the description of Schreiber's electoral defeat, is marked by significant gaps. The most significant of these occurs after February 16, 1859, when Lady Charlotte stops writing for six months. She begins again with this entry:

Six months have elapsed since the above was written and many things have befallen—but, after such an interval how can I record them? I feel that all I can attempt now to do is to put down a few dates that I have carefully preserved & that will give me in future time some indication of the whereabouts of the family during this important portion of my life. Three great facts have taken place within these six months—Mr. Pegus has been deposed and banished from Uffington—My husband has contested, with great distinction though without ultimately success, a seat in Parliament—and I have the blessing of seeing a daughter happily married.[204]

Over the next several pages, she does valiantly attempt to fill in all the events of the missing six months—including the story of the contested parliament seat. Her narration of the ugly scene is, thus, a retrospective one. It would be simplistic to assume that this gap in the journals simply reflects Lady Charlotte's inability to write immediately about what was obviously a painful rupture in her marriage. Nevertheless, the manuscript does offer two strong indications of editorial distancing. The first is the underscoring of the words "I fought him." Usually, Lady Charlotte only underscored upon rereading, but in this case it seems to have been done at the time of the entry, suggesting that she already saw herself as a reader of the episode, rather than a participant in it. The second indication is the quotes around the word "out." It is hard to imagine a woman immediately in the throes of a marital crisis providing such a careful indication of a word's slanginess.

Whatever the reasons underlying this six-month gap, this return to her journals lasted only a few months. Then there is another gap until New Year's Day, 1863. That entry reads,

How long it is since I have written here—months—nay Years! And now I am going to force myself to try to write again, though indeed with sad heart & broken spirit. Alas, how much of sorrow I have gone through since last I wrote here in Sept. 1859.[205]

This "sorrow" can be ascribed to the death of her son Augustus, probably due to complications from scarlet fever. Nonetheless, the entry is very difficult to parse, since no mention of his death is made in the entry itself. Instead, the events it actually records are joyous ones, such as weddings and births. Given that these weddings and births are of Lady Charlotte's daughters and grandchildren, it is impossible not to see at least part of Lady Charlotte's sorrow as stemming from her daughters' taking over her roles as wife and mother.

The impression that this last gap is more significant than the others is exacerbated by a matter of chance, for the journal volumes for the years 1863 to 1869 are missing. Furthermore, the journals after 1869 are significantly different from those before 1869. The first difference is a physical one: Lady Charlotte switched from conventional journals to smaller, soft-covered notebooks that more closely resembled a ledger. More importantly, however, Lady Charlotte's regular journal entries now also include detailed notes on acquisitions for her ceramics collection—notes that would eventually be published by her son Montague in 1911 as *Confidences of a Collector*. These notes dramatically change the character of Lady Charlotte's journals, making them much closer to a catalogue than a diary. Indeed, the first fifty pages of the 1869 journal are simply titled "Particulars of some Specimens in CS's collection," and consist of nothing but a very precise ledger, categorized by manufacturer, and providing details for each piece including cost, description, and purchase date. The journals themselves begin on page 51 and are entitled "Notes Sept 1869—Ceramic."

Despite such an anodyne title, however, Lady Charlotte's flare for narrativity is evident from the first entry:

> Determined to beat up Holland, in detail, and find if any English China was to be met with there, we set off on Tuesday the 28 Sept by the 7.40 AM train from Charing Cross—took the Steamer from Dover to Ostend (having a lovely, calm, hot passage—the sea as smooth as glass) and reached Antwerp by $^1/_2$ past 5. Put up at the Hotel de L'Europe place Verte—very good.[206]

Nonetheless, these collectors' journals are far from a conventional diary. It is nearly impossible to convey their effect without quoting from them directly. The following is a comparison of Bessborough's and Montague Guest's presentation of the events surrounding the Schreibers' visit to Spain in 1870:

February 22 . . . Stopped a long time at a sale of the Demidoff[207] pictures, brought from San Donato, near Florence, where we had seen them all last spring. The sale was going on at 26 Boulevard des Italiens. Only modern pictures were sold today. I did not care for any of them, but it was a curious scene. We saw the Ary Scheffer of Francesca da Rimini[208] sold for £4,000. Delaroche's Lady Jane Grey went even higher. Yesterday Lord Hertford bought the Bon-	22nd. I walked with Lane to the Rue Jacob about some marcasites for Merthyr, which, however, I did not purchase. About 2, we went out for our daily walk. Stopped a long time at a sale of the Demidoff pictures, brought from San Donato, near Florence, where we had seen them all last spring. The sale was going on at 26 Boulevard des Italiens. Only modern pictures were sold to-day; I did not care for any of them, but it was a curious scene. We saw the Ary Schef-

ington "Henry IV Playing with his Children."[209]

Before starting on their journey south the Schreibers sent letters to Spain to know if it was safe to go there as there were rumours in Paris of Carlist risings. On arriving at Montpellier on March 3rd they found a telegram from the British Consul at Barcelona: "Advise delay, will write." On the 8th, however, they received a further message from the Consul reassuring them, and the same day they left Montpellier, and reached Barcelona three days later. A few days after their arrival they found everyone in a state of excitement at the news of the Duke of Montpensier's duel. The Infante Prince Henry of Bourbon, brother of the ex-King Consort of

fer of Francesca da Rimini sold for £4,000. Koches' Lady Jane Grey went even higher. Yesterday Lord Hertford bought the Bonington, "Henry IV. playing with his children." [Now in the Wallace Collection.] From the sale we went again to the Fourniers to deposit our purchase of the George III tea-jar in their case, and we engaged to take one of their Sevres cups and saucers, gros bleu, with gold decoration, and a painting of musical instruments as a trophy. We are to pay £10. It is an experiment for us to touch Sevres, but this seemed tempting at the price, and the Fourniers are such pleasant folk and so civil to us that we wished to do some little business with them. On our return we looked into one or two shops, and visited the Salles des Ventes which was a still more curious scene than that we had been at in the Boulevards. Such noise! such bustle! Amidst such rubbish it might occasionally happen that something good might be found here.[210]

3rd. Visited the three (so called) antiquaries and at the shop of one of them found an intelligent youth who volunteered to accompany us and to show us over the town. He sometimes picks up things himself, and promised, on our giving him notice, to look out for specimens for us should we come to Nismes again. His name and address—"M. Suel Alfred, Rue St. Paul 41." First we went to the Maison Caree where we found a wretched collection of modern pictures desecrating the old Roman Temple. Then to the gardens, with the Baths and Temple of Diana, and

Spain, had recently declared that the Duke was concerned in an Orleanist conspiracy against Napoleon III, and "that this braggart of a French pastrycook" had no support in Spain. On March 12 the Infante and the Duke fought a duel in Madrid. At eight yards the Infante fired first and missed. The Duke then took deadly aim and killed his opponent. A court martial condemned him to a month's exile and to pay the Infante's family 6,000 dollars, but refused to censure him.

up to the Tour, which is a most inscrutable building. It commands a fine view; the concierge was away so we could not mount it, but its site gives a magnificent prospect. Lastly to the Amphitheatre which is very perfect, but is not nearly so large as that at Verona, and did not impress me nearly so much. We looked into the old Cathedral, the interior of which is wretchedly spoilt, but which has some beautiful remains in the facade. Our last act in leaving the town was to buy a coffee pot of the tortoise-shell Avignon ware at a broker's shop at the corner of the Rue Guizot in the Boulevard Grand Cours, by name, Banquiere, price 16/-. We left Nismes by a train at $1/2$ past 2 and in about an hour found ourselves at Montpellier in pouring rain. Hotel Nevet. Here a telegram met us from the English Counsul at Barcelona— "Advise delay, will write." This upsets all our plans, which had been to the effect that we should go on to Perpignan to-morrow, and reach Barcelona on Saturday. Went to two antiquaries at the house of one Daumas, Rue St. Foy, close to the Hotel, we bought for 16/- a good Wedgwood Coffee Pot, transfer printed in red with subject, Minerva and emblems, and legend "Let wisdom unite us," birds, stags, and other ornaments. Also two Chelsea stags of goodly size in bocages, pretty perfect. These are the only thing we saw at Montpellier. Excellent table d'hote. Washed up our china and faience in the evening . . . .[211]

March 13 (Barcelona) . . . We had planned to come take a drive in the afternoon, and Balçon the guide to

13th. Barcelona full of excitement at the news of the fatal Montpensier duel. We went to the principal Club

come to us with a carriage. To our consternation, he appeared in time with a regular Court conveyance—a splendid open barouche decorated with blue and silver, with gorgeous lamps, and with two servants in State liveries to correspond! Too absurd. It was a great relief when we found this stupendous vehicle could not ascend to the Fort; and after some delay a more modest equipage was procured.[212]

(called, I think, the Equestrian) for C.S. to see the papers, and then looked into the Church of Santa Maria del Mar. Took lunch at the Consul's where were the officers of an English Ship of War, stationed off the coast. We had planned to come take a drive in the afternoon, and Balcon the guide to come to us with a carriage. To our consternation, he appeared in time with a regular Court conveyance—a splendid open barouche decorated with blue and silver, with gorgeous lamps, and with two servants in State liveries to correspond! Too absurd. It was a great relief when we found this stupendous vehicle could not ascend to the Fort; and after some delay a more modest equipage was procured. While this was being arranged we went and saw a private collection belonging to a dentist just opposite to our Hotel, which was for sale. I never saw so much hopeless rubbish in my whole life. At length we ascended the Castle, and a more delightful view is nowhere to be found. Walked about there some time, returning only in time for table d'hote. We had been told that this excursion would occupy a whole afternoon, whereas we might easily have made a pleasant walk of it. We feel an additional interest in Barcelona by reason of the curious old prints we have of the siege of the palace by Lord Peterborough in 1705, which we had so much difficulty in verifying, as the margins had been destroyed and there was no text to inform us what town was represented. Letters till late after going to see the commencement of a play on the life of Christ.[213]

Bessborough's interfering editorial hand is immediately evident, as he goes out of his way to minimize the effect of Lady Charlotte's obsessive notes on collecting, in order to highlight the actual narrative of her life. Indeed, in the case of the Montpelier duel, Bessborough goes so far as to substitute his own narrative of the lurid events surrounding the duel; Lady Charlotte's actual entry is much more concerned with the coffee pot of tortoise-shell Avignon ware. In making such decisions, at least from an editorial point of view, Bessborough is quite correct: there is a peculiarly anesthetizing quality to Lady Charlotte's meticulous notations. Events as the fatal duel get swept up into the tide of buying and selling, of examining and evaluating—entire lives reduced to insignificant hitches in the greater, more mesmerizing rhythm of the marketplace. Indeed, Lady Charlotte barely seems to notice the human drama surrounding her in Barcelona, even when it threatens her directly in the form of imminent civil war. Instead, she is far more interested in an earlier uprising, the siege of the palace by Lord Peterborough in 1705, but only because she had difficulty in authenticating a set of prints that depicted the event.

This preoccupation with the act of collecting is equaled only by her interest in food. Indeed, Lady Charlotte's obsession with the table d'hote is worthy of no lesser a literary figure than Pooh. From Brussels to Berlin, her journals offer meticulous details on the values —and timing—of tourist meals, such as the intriguing, but ultimately inscrutable, "Joined a *table d'hote dejeuner a la fourchette* soon after 10, which amused me from its novelty and was a very good repast."[214]

It might be argued that such a preoccupation with food echoes the Schreibers' equally obsessive consumption of objects,[215] which is enumerated in a detail that can only be described as obsessive itself. At conservative estimate, 70 percent of the nearly one thousand pages of the two volumes describe the couple's buying decisions, including those items they did not buy. For example, on April 20, 1872:

> C.S. and I went with Giovanni to look at an "Urna" (cabinet) in the Alcala, which did not suit. Then to Lorenzo's, where we concluded for a very good Urna and Mesa (table) (1500 reals) and bought some other trifles. We also got a miniature and some D.V. tea-jars in the Calle del Prado.[216]

Lady Charlotte's obsessive energy in recording her every transaction is matched by the obsessive energy with which she pursued her quarry. The Schreibers often rose at five or six in the morning in order to shop all day, and, after a brief respite at the table d'hote, went back out to conclude purchases in the evening. An anecdote Joseph Joel Duveen, the art collector, related about Lady Charlotte has become the defining legend of her energy and tenacity. Montague Guest tells the story:[217]

> He happened to be over in Holland searching for "objets d'art" when he heard of some wonderful pieces of china in a little village a long way from any town or railway; to get to this out-of-the-way place entailed a long and tedious journey by carriage. He started off on his expedition, but as he was nearing his destination he observed a fly driving out of the village towards him; he looked into it as it passed, and he saw the face of my mother; he felt at once that he had been forestalled, and he continued his journey, only to find that she had snatched the prize, which she was carrying off with her.[218]

Duveen's portrait of Lady Charlotte is unfeminine, undignified, and absolutely delightful. She has beaten the boys at their own game and is clearly thrilled to have done so. In the words of the psychological theorist of collecting, Werner Muensterberger, "This lonely, defensively rigid girl had turned into an impressively astute woman, energetic, single-minded, and often better informed than her suppliers."[219]

Muensterberger's further commentary on the scene, however, is decidedly more disturbing. He writes,

> There is no question that this is a modified version of the successful hunt or the chase and capturing the trophy; in Lady Charlotte's case, I see her mode of action as an attempt to prove her dominance vis a vis her stepfather, and also to enhance her self-esteem. At its simplest, it can be a fleeting impulse, like bringing home a souvenir. At its most committed, it assumes the proportions of a kind of aggression with masculine potential, if not dominance or an all-consuming, sensuous activity surpassing rational ends.[220]

Muensterberger is a Freudian and therefore sees all collecting as a neurotic attempt to compensate for Oedipal lack. Nonetheless, his predisposition to see collecting in terms of a disease or symptom does nothing to excuse the blatant sexism of his defining Lady Charlotte's aggression as potentially "masculine," as if that were a neurotic symptom in and of itself. Furthermore, his reading of collecting as a symbolic experiment in self-healing that reveals the "need of the phallic-narcissistic personality . . . while they use their objects for inner security and outer applause, their deep inner function is to screen off self-doubt and unassimilated memories" quickly begins to feel doctrinaire.[221]

Jean Baudrillard offers a more measured assessment of the psychological roots of collecting in lack. Beginning with the definition of an object as "anything which is the cause or subject of a passion," he characterizes collecting as the "process of passionate abstraction we call possession," in which an object is "divested of its function and made relative to a subject . . . thereby [constituting] themselves as a *system*, on the basis of which the subject seeks to piece together his world, his personal microcosm."[222] Baudrillard's analysis makes the feminist nature of Lady Charlotte's triumph clear. If she is the object of a man's passion, it is Duveen's passionate envy—for she has appropriated the subject position for herself, using her china collection as a system to order her own personal microcosm.

Yet, the system created by Lady Charlotte's china collection is far from a completely internal one. Indeed, what is most peculiar about Lady Charlotte's collecting is that she went to Europe in order to find examples of English pottery. Her justification for this was completely pecuniary: she felt that she obtained better prices in Europe, because the dealers there were not well acquainted with English china. The very statement, however, suggests a process that neatly echoes Lady Charlotte's self-definition in Wales: The foreign context offers her a kinder epistemological standard—or at least a better rate of exchange—by which to judge her relationship to England and the English.

The analogy between epistemological standards and rates of exchange is not a frivolous one. Indeed, Lady Charlotte's collector's diaries are a paean to the interpretative value of money.[223] She never describes a piece as beautiful, or, for that matter, even as useful. Instead, she discusses the pieces entirely in terms of what she paid for them or what was asked for them, in comparison to what they were worth.

There is, of course, a certain reassurance in the absoluteness of this external scale of value. Monetary valuation not only has the advantage of being mathematically inarguable. It is also resituable, providing a standard by which, for example, a Meissan teapot can be reliably measured against a silver snuff box—although the reliability of such a measurement seems suspect indeed, when Lady Charlotte can, in the same day, reject a 7 shilling figurine as being beyond what she can afford, and then pay 100 pounds for a screen without batting an eye. And, in fact, the "objectivity" of such external standards as monetary valuation has long been problematized—most famously by Jacques Derrida in "White Mythology." Derrida begins with Karl Marx's interrogation of the peculiar relationship between currency and interpretation, "Whence did the illusions of the monetary system arise? The mercantilists . . . regarded gold and silver, not simply as substances which, when functioning as money, represented a social relation of production, but as substances which were endowed by nature with peculiar social properties."[224] Derrida responds to Marx's question by expanding on Anatole France's discussion of metaphor in *The Garden of Epicurus*, demonstrating the essential similarity between linguistic constructs and currency by showing that neither have any value unless they are put into circulation.

Derrida's argument leads inevitably to the conclusion that even such apparently "objective" standards as money are in fact intersubjective. Mieke Bal has responded that regardless of which term one chooses to employ, "objectivity" and "intersubjectivity" are still similar in that they both refer to something outside the subject, whether that is a cultural code or an empirically observable object. Interestingly, Bal goes on to argue that both collecting and narrative are loci where the individual subject negotiates inserting the system of his "personal microcosm" (Baudrillard's term) into such larger external contexts.[225]

It is thus a happy coincidence—or arguably no coincidence at all —that embedded in all the monetary valuation of Lady Charlotte's collector's journals, one can find the one unrepentantly fictional construct of her entire *oeuvre*, the sketch, "The Adventures of a Bottle." Written by Lady Charlotte, the story concerns the acquisition, loss, and reacquisition of a peculiar, gourd-shaped piece of German Delft ware. From its very first line, the story assumes the form of an exemplary tale, beginning thus:

> In the very cold February of 1873 it happened that C.S. went alone on an exploring expedition to Holland. He came home pretty well laden with objets d'art, and having but two hands of his own, and being without those of his wife to help him, he was fain to leave behind him two specimens . . .[226]

The narrative's jokey, self-conscious tone is not as unusual as a comparison to the rest of Lady Charlotte's journals suggests. Such literary productions as family gazettes were a favorite pastime of the Guests. Indeed, there was a private printing press at Canford, and the family often amused itself with publishing private magazines and journals. However, this narration is unlike anything else in her actual journals.

What is even more unusual is the fact that the protagonist of the tale is not the journals' protagonist, Lady Charlotte, but rather Charles Schreiber, whose initial situation is that of any fairy tale hero, setting out on a quest, alone, to a foreign land, without the aid of his family. The fact that Schreiber was the one who initially set out alone most likely dictated Lady Charlotte's making him the hero of her tale; however, his role in this tale also underscores a significant difference between his and Sir John's function in the diaries. Instead of functioning as a locus of judgment, an ideal reader, Schreiber plays the role of the desiring subject who sets out to determine his place in the universe.

Moreover, Schreiber is also a surrogate for Lady Charlotte—a fact that becomes more clear when later in the tale they become allies in the pursuit of the piece. The surrogacy become even more evident when the two main characters change from the protagonist "C.S." and "his wife," who remains at home, into two near-interchangeable sets of initials, C. S. (Charles Schreiber) and C. E. S. (Charlotte Elizabeth Schreiber), who voyage together to Rotterdam to retrieve the purchased bottle, along with a bowl that Schreiber had also purchased.

The pair immediately meet their first obstacle: the dealer was still offering the pieces for sale. Given the fact that Schreiber had already paid for them, the dealer's act is a theft, which is, in turn, an act not only of capitalist, but also of mythic, transgression. The story of Prometheus is the touchstone narrative of theft violating the boundaries of self and other, mine and yours, gods and men. It is also one of the primal stories of self-assertion through the pursuit of an object. That self-assertion takes on an additional significance in a capitalist system, where property becomes a system of value. Theft then threatens not only the system of values but the very symbolic underpinnings of society itself. It is thus textually satisfying that, although the attempted theft of the Schreibers' bowl and bottle is quickly resolved, it leaves behind a situation of epistemological instability:

... now the question was, what it could be. Was it Delft? Was it some other manufacture? Was it not, at all events something good and rare? So thought C.S., so thought C.E.S. But Bisschop, the great Hague painter, well versed in these Delft products, declared it was only German, and not at all to be prized. So what was to be done? Was it worth carrying all the way to England?[227]

Next, the pair meet a helper in the form of an anonymous dealer at Utrecht, who believed he could sell the bottle to an equally anonymous amateur. In a fit of pique, Schreiber abandons the quest, snapping, "Then for goodness' sake let him have it." Thus, according to Lady Charlotte, ended "the Second Act of the Drama."[228]

The quest was, of course, not abandoned so easily. On the appropriately ominous 13th of October of the same year,[229] the Schreibers received the unwelcome news that, although the amateur had been happy to pay 100 florins for the bottle, his friends had told him it was valueless and he had returned it to the dealer. Schreiber was, naturally, "very sorry to have to carry about so despised a piece of goods" and sold it in Antwerp for eighteen shillings. The entire drama seems to end once more, this time with Charles Schreiber content that he had "disembarrassed himself of [the troublesome bottle] at very little loss."[230]

However, fate had a final twist in store for the questing pair. On yet another thirteenth of the month, August 13, 1874, the stability of value and judgment that they seemed to have achieved by admitting they had made a mistake in purchasing the piece was abruptly reversed. While traveling in Normandy, the Schreibers visited the museum, where,

> Oh horror! Oh despair! what should meet their eyes, set on the most conspicuous shelf, in the very place of honor, but bottles exactly similar in style, shape and decoration to that which they had once possessed and in an evil hour had sacrificed.[231]

What is perhaps most striking about this reversal is that, despite the absolute nature of the museum's placing the reviled bottle in the "very place of honor," it depends on an epistemological impossibility, "exact similarity." Something is similar or it is identical; it cannot be both. Yet such a simply stated impossibility is a fundamental component of both the theory of metaphor and the theory of monetary exchange. For, in fact, nothing is identical unless it is in fact itself. Both metaphor and money address this problem by providing systems of exchange that allow one to measure the relative values between similar things. However, any such system is by its very nature imperfect.

This central impossibility of "exact similarity" is the story's lesson, one that is learned with appropriately mythological "wailing and gnashing of teeth! To have been unconsciously possessed of such a treasure, and to have been at such pains to have deprived oneself of it was almost more than amateur nature could endure!"[232] Yet, such outsized despair belongs to the mythic realm, not the actual, and the purpose of any fairy tale is the successful education of the hero. Consequently, C. S. and C. E. S., having learned their object lesson in the instability of judgment, are allowed a final resolution. After having "returned to England, sadder and wiser, they remained there a week, and then their restless dispositions prompted them to set out on their travels again."[233] In a nondescript shop in Brussels,

> having well ransacked it without any result, they were on the point of leaving it and had reached the door when C.E.S. happened to cast her eyes to a topmost shelf, on which a bright familiar object met her astonished and delighted gaze: "What is that I see above?" said she. "Oh, it is only an old bottle of German ware," said the dealer, and he reached it down. There was no mistaking it now. It was the long-lost, much-lamented bottle, which their better educated sense now showed them to be of the priceless Rouen fabric. C.S. was overjoyed at the recovery of the beloved object, and he instantly paid whatever he was asked without any demur.[234]

The Schreibers' final financial outcome in the entire transaction has a fairy tale's even-handedness of valuation. The original—too good to be true—purchase price of one sovereign is gone forever, the victim of the protagonists' short-sightedness. However, having gone through the long and painful educational process of the narrative, the Schreibers are still allowed a surplus, purchasing it for forty francs, a price more than the original bargain, but still less than the piece's true worth—a fact confirmed by the tale's ending, which compares the Schreibers' judgment favorably with their fellow amateurs, who, not having undergone such a painful education, overlooked the bottle when they saw it.

The tale's denouement also offers an interesting insight into the couple's relationship as connoisseurs. For, although it is Charles Schreiber (C. S.), who originally notices and attempts to purchase the piece, it is Lady Charlotte (C. E. S.) who notices it the second time. There is certainly a nice post-modernist fable to be read in the surplus that is created by the letter *E* as she attempts to replicate an act of judgment. For an act of judgment can never purely be replicated, since it is always influenced by the surplus created by the history of previous judgments. What is more overtly readable than such speculation, however, is how the episode reflects the relative connoisseurship of the couple. There is no question that the china collecting was a shared passion[235] and that Charles Schreiber went out on many individual, and often uncomfortable, forays to find china, often at five in the morning or nine at night. Yet, it is equally clear that, although Lady Charlotte perceived their collecting as a joint venture and more or less ceased collecting when Schreiber died, she is always credited with the connoisseurship of the pair—as is perhaps inevitable with such a forceful personality.

Bessborough gives the four years from 1873 to 1876 as the height of the china mania, and there is no reason to question this dating. Certainly, by 1879, Lady Charlotte was putting more of her energy into cataloging her china than collecting it—and she had also developed secondary and tertiary interests in collecting playing cards and fans. In 1880, Charles Schreiber once more stood as a member from Poole. Lady Charlotte's description of the election give striking evidence of the change wrought at least in part by her collecting. Schreiber's election was a—skin-of-the-teeth—triumph:

> March 31 . . . The polling began at 8 and closed at 4 . . . I have employed my solitary day by abstracting the Wedgwood entries from the catalogue. It has helped to turn my attention from the momentous issues of this day and my dear husband's prospects . . . I went on steadily working, till interrupted by the shouts of the crowd, and by Mrs. Williams rushing in to tell me it was all over and that my husband had won . . . but presently there came a pause, the noise ceased, it was rumored that all was uncertain.[236]

Eventually, Schreiber won, by only six votes. However, that year, three of Lady Charlotte's sons were also running for office. Of them, Ivor and Arthur lost; only Montague (the editor of *Confidences*) won. The position of Henry Layard, Lady Charlotte's old admirer and her daughter Enid's husband, as ambassador to Constantinople was also significantly jeopardized by the elections. These facts alone might explain why, instead of venturing triumphantly on the hustings, as she did with Sir John, Lady Charlotte spent the next few days "alone; it poured with rain, so I wrote letters, verified the salt glaze stoneware catalogue, and was fully employed."[237] Some of this change might also be attributed to a natural quietism that occurs with maturity, and even more of it might be attributable to the difference between her Liberalism and Schreiber's Toryism. Yet, it also seems quite arguable that cataloging the china, assembling its provenance—and therefore value—provided Lady Charlotte with an arena of pure and absolute valuation that offset the often conflicted as well as conflicting political aspirations of her husbands and sons.

Upon his election, Schreiber took a renewed interest in his political career, so that he and Lady Charlotte saw less of each other than they were accustomed to do. Instead of mourning his absence, Lady Charlotte, never at a loss to occupy herself, was inspired by her firsthand witnessing of the situation in Constantinople, where Henry Layard was ambassador, to engage in relief work selling the embroidery of Turkish refugees in England. It was a task she accomplished with her usual furious efficiency, selling embroidery to everyone from her aristocratic acquaintances to Oscar Wilde.[238] The couple did, however, continue to travel and collect when Parliament was not in session. In 1880, they went to Oberammengau to see the Passion Play, with which Lady Charlotte was very impressed, asking the actor who played Jesus whether he was not very tired, after having spent twenty minutes on the Cross.[239] She was less struck with Wagner's new theater at Bayreuth, dismissing it as "a hideous building, and apparently inconveniently distant from the town. What made him fix upon such a desolate place as Bayreuth to build in, I am at a loss to imagine . . . It seemed a miserable deserted town."[240]

In 1883, Charles Schreiber fell ill with a lung ailment from which he never fully recovered. A sea voyage to South Africa was recommended. The trip was largely an exercise in frustration, relieved only by the evident closeness of the couple, as Schreiber took relief in Lady Charlotte's reading to him.

Little is said in Lady Charlotte's diaries about the state of Schreiber's health. At nine P.M. on the night of March 28, 1884, she wrote, referring to her Turkish embroidery, "I have already sold 3 sets . . . with hopes of doing more . . . could not get the samples shown to the Queen, which I am sorry for—but perhaps some other opportunity may arise."[241] The only sign that she might be anxious about her husband is that she initialed and dated her entry, always a sign of stress in her texts. Certainly, there is no reason to suspect that on the very next day she would write,

> And now it is all over. The eleven months of anxious care and watching are past, and he is gone . . . he died in my arms about 4 o'clock. A little before he passed away he asked: "Where am I?" to which I answered: "With your own dear wife." He replied: "God bless her," and those were almost the last conscious words he spoke.[242]

Even more striking than Lady Charlotte's words is the fact that four lines of this entry are obliterated—apparently at the time of writing. It is arguably the only time in her journals that she ever excised her original text.

Two days later, Lady Charlotte concluded, "And so ends my life on earth. It has been a very happy one, and I have very much to be grateful for. Henceforth I have but to bow the head in patience, working and waiting till it shall please my Merciful Father to call me hence."[243] A valedictory entry indeed, but Lady Charlotte was destined to live eleven more years, to the age of eighty-three. Work and wait she did for those eleven years, but it must be said that working was, of the two, the more congenial to her naturally energetic temperament. Her first endeavor, begun within two months of Schreiber's death, was to present their collection of English porcelain to the South Kensington Museum (later incorporated into the Victoria and Albert Museum) as a gift in memory of her husband. As obvious—even inevitable—as this step may seem, it caused some friction between Lady Charlotte and her son Ivor, who was also a collector. Perhaps justly, he was annoyed that he not been consulted about the gift, and that he could furthermore say nothing when he learned of it, as the gift had already been announced in the newspapers.[244] Yet it is difficult not also to read into his pique a remnant of the tension between Lady Charlotte and her children over their father being supplanted by a much-younger stepfather.

In giving their china collection to a museum, Lady Charlotte was arguably following the wishes of her late husband, who had reflected "what a pleasure it would be to collect national objects for the benefit of the country."[245] Yet, the gift was also a final reification, inscribing the couple not only in a collection of objects and a pair of portraits of the couple commissioned to accompany the collection, but also with a catalogue, Lady Charlotte's final piece of writing. Lady Charlotte began working on this and other catalogues of her collections in 1884; she continued working on them even after blindness caused her to give up her journal in 1891.[246]

A second, more idiosyncratic memorial to her late husband was her concern with the refurbishing of a statue of Achilles that stood in Hyde Park—another cause that Schreiber had espoused. In January 1885, she was happy to report:

> My dear Monty has most kindly taken up the subject of the Hyde Park Achilles. There is a letter from him on the matter in this morning's *Times.* Very few people know that the statue is from a Greek model, the Castor and Pollux at Rome, and that it was cast at the expense of the ladies of England, of cannon which we took from the French in the war terminating with the battle of Waterloo.[247]

The passage is the epitome of a favorite dotty old aunt, keeping her old age interesting with a succession of eccentric causes. Indeed, there is a certain music-hall comedy to Lady Charlotte's passionate espousal of a variety of missions that ranged from finding a pug dog to send to a friend in Lisbon[248] through a brief flirtation with photography lessons[249] to getting her maid Moody's sister a respectable place as an actress.[250] Lady Charlotte also underwrote the cost of a shelter for hansom cab drivers, being careful to supply a copy of *The Times* daily for the cabmen's edification. Eventually, she was dismayed to discover that the cabmen would actually prefer more copies of a cheaper paper, and finally compromised by deciding "that *The Times* delivery should be continued, because of the usefulness and variety of its information, but that a copy of the *Daily Chronicle* should be added, so that the cabmen might be given both sides of politics."[251] Her concern with the cabmen also led her to take up knitting once more, eventually producing a red woolen muffler each day for their relief. That habit produced a memorable picture of her in old age. In her seventy-ninth year,

> Lady Charlotte now started the habit of taking exercise every morning by walking up and down her long drawing-room for some hours, knitting the while; one day she would recite aloud "Chaucer's dear old prologue" which she calculated took thirty-five minutes to repeat; another day it would be *Childe Harold.*[252]

The comedy of all this frantic activity is offset by how obvious it is that Lady Charlotte was desperately trying to stave off the twin losses of her husband and her eyesight. Her late diaries are imbued with the same sense of nostalgia and loss that characterize her early diaries. This time, however, her sense of loss is focused on Schreiber—sometimes in ways that are completely unexpected, such as her entry for February 7, 1885:

> I never write the date of 7 Feby [sic], but I think of my first Latin grammar bought in 1825, if I mistake not, just 60 years ago, with almost the first money I ever had. I was so conscious of inaccuracy then, that I thought studying the learned language would help to correct this grave fault. I have the book now and will take it out and look at it before I go to bed. No, I was wrong, my little Latin grammar bears date [sic] of 1826, which I used to call "that hot and happy summer." On the 10 May of that year my darling [Schreiber] was born.[253]

Even religion provided little refuge, for going to church reminded her painfully of Schreiber. Instead, she read the service to herself, usually in Regent's Park, for:

> Sunday is always such a sad day with me. I cannot bear to go to church with anyone, and when I am alone I find myself brooding over the past, and the happy days when we went together, and he always held my hand in his dear hand during the lessons and the sermon.[254]

Equally devastatingly, Lady Charlotte began to lose her sight, most probably from glaucoma. She mentioned the problem first in 1884, the year of Schreiber's death.[255] For the next six years, she chronicled the decline of her vision, along with the various treatments she sought. In January 1887, she underwent an operation that was performed in her bedroom under conditions of strict secrecy. Rather typically, she threw herself into activity the day before, not knowing how long it would be before she would see again.[256] The operation was a qualified success; however, two years later, she was attempting the more appalling treatment of having electricity applied to her eyes. Despite her doctor's assertion to the contrary, she believed the treatment harmed, rather than helped her.[257]

Despite her best efforts, her blindness continued to increase, forcing her to become dependent on others. In 1888, she ceased reading, relying on her maid, Moody, to read to her instead. Moody was eventually joined by her sister, whose stage tour of America had failed, reading Shakespeare, and a Mr. Upton, who, Bessborough claims "moistened his throat for reading aloud by a visit to a publican in the neighborhood."[258] The aplomb with which Lady Charlotte apparently handled his drunken stumbling is offset by her genuinely sad entry of January 6, 1889:

> I can only record a painful increase of depression. All are very kind to me, and I do my best to be or to seem cheerful. But I am getting less and less able to sustain the mask . . . What I most like here is to sit in Ivor's room with my eternal knitting . . . There I sit, revolving many things.[259]

The passage's despair is offset by the fact it is a mythic image, a Norn, a Fate, an old woman sitting by herself, shut off from the world, eternally knitting as she revolves things only to herself. And that mythic solitude is a fitting solution to the recurring questions of judgment and value throughout her journals. The circle of eternity has replaced the dialectic of judgment. The judging Other—whether herself or Sir John as ideal reader, the textual models represented by Mrs. Ellis or the rules of society, or the objects in her collections —has vanished, leaving Lady Charlotte in almost complete internal dialogue with herself. However, her solitude has paradoxically provided her with an almost Cartesian belief in herself: she at last accepts the validity of her own thinking, and reference to any external standard is perceived as inherently false, a mask.

It is difficult to think of the eternally restless, acquisitive Lady Charlotte as ever at peace, but it is at least pleasant to think that this final retreat into the self that she had pursued for so many years underlies the graceful calm of the entry with which she closes ten thousand pages and sixty years of journals:

> *1891, February 24 [17 Cavendish Square].* And here I close a journal which I have kept for very many years. I can no longer see to write, or to read what I have written. I am, thank God, perfectly well in health though growing feebler every day, and I feel confident the end cannot be far off. I am most kindly cared for by all that are dear and I bless them for it . . . and now, adieu to all.[260]

2

Rhonabwy's
Virtue-bearing Stones

LADY CHARLOTTE'S DIARY ENTRY FOR NOVEMBER 30, 1837, MARKS
the beginning of the project that not only ensured her lasting scholarly fame, but also established one of the most significant cultural
icons of the Victorian era. On that date, Lady Charlotte recorded
that Mr. Justice Bosanquet agreed to lend his copy of the tales from
the *Red Book of Hergest* to the recently founded Welsh Manuscripts Society, which was dedicated to "promoting and publishing" old manuscripts.[1] It was Lady Charlotte who, on behalf of the Society, took on
the task of translating and publishing the tales from Bosanquet's
manuscript, beginning with her 1838 translation of "The Lady of the
Fountain." The remaining tales were published in seven parts and
were then republished in 1849 as a sumptuously illustrated and
bound three-volume edition.[2]

There had been previous attempts to translate these tales. The
most notable was that of William Owen Pughe, serialized in the
Cambrian Register from 1796 on. Although Pughe announced that he
planned to translate something he called *The Mabinogion*, the scale
of the project he envisioned is unclear, for he only managed to publish three tales, "Pwyll," "Math," and "Taliesin," before he was side-
tracked by the demands of, among other things, his newfound ad-
herence to the prophecies of Joanna Southcott, "who proclaimed
herself as Revelations' 'Woman clothed with the sun' sent to deliver
mankind."[3] Other scholars who had made translations of the tales included Bosanquet himself.[4] However, it was Lady Charlotte who was
responsible, not only for providing the first complete translation,
but also for transforming this loosely connected, arguably even un-
connected, set of tales into the literary text known as the *Mabinogion.*

Indeed, what first needs to be said about the *Mabinogion* is that no such thing exists. In fact, the word *mabinogion* does not exist in Welsh, though it appears once by mistake in "Pwyll."[5] The translation that Lady Charlotte published in 1849 is, more precisely, eleven tales from the *Red Book of Hergest* (ca. 1400), a manuscript in the possession of Jesus College Oxford, along with the tale of Taliesin from a later manuscript.[6] There are other versions of these tales, most notably the earlier and incomplete *White Book of Rhydderch* (ca. 1325) and a few other fragments, the oldest of which is Peniarth 6 (ca. 1225).[7] In addition to being the latest version, the *Red Book* is the most complete version; however, whether it is a copy or redaction of one or more of the earlier books, or whether they derive from a common source that no longer exists, is still a matter for scholarly debate.[8]

Of the eleven tales that Lady Charlotte translated from the *Red Book*, only four, "Pwyll Prince of Dyved," "Branwen the Daughter of Llyr," "Manawyddan the Son of Llyr," and "Math the Son of Mathonwy," can properly be termed Mabinogi. However, even these four are identified as such only because each one ends with a variation on the phrase, "So ends this branch of the Mabinogi." If one eliminates the unifying function of this phrase, it becomes difficult to decide whether even the Four Branches constitute a unified work or whether they might better be described as "an imbroglio of anecdotes, allusions, motifs and characters which under close scrutiny reveal the outlines of a number of familiar mythological paradigms within a British setting."[9] Admittedly, it would be folly to look for a nineteenth-century architectonic narrative structure in a medieval piece derived from the oral tradition. However, the internal inconsistencies of several of the tales are glaring, with characters such as Dylan in "Math" appearing and disappearing for no apparent reason. Furthermore, with the exception of "Manawyddan," which begins "When the seven men of whom we spoke above had buried the head of Bendigeid Vran [Bran], in the White Mount in London; with its face towards France," none of the tales refer to one another.[10]

Nor do the Four Branches derive from a single mythological source. "Pwyll" has its roots in both the *Odyssey* and the Irish tales of Cu Chulainn,[11] while "Branwen" derives from Geoffrey of Monmouth and an early Welsh poem "The Booty of Annwvyn."[12] "Manawyddan" seems to have its roots in Irish myth, for Manawddan "is the Welsh counterpart of the Irish god Manandan son of Lir [however] no Irish adventures parallel those of the Third Branch."[13] Finally, Math can be seen equally to derive from the story of Amnon and Phaedra, or that of Ailill in the Irish "Wooing of Etain."[14]

The Four Branches cannot even be claimed to be united by geography or style. "Branwen" and "Math" are set in the north of Wales; "Pwyll" and "Manawyddan" are set in the south. Perhaps because of this difference in location, the southern tales seem to demonstrate a French influence, whereas the northern tales do not. Indeed, beyond some crossing over of characters between the tales, it is quite arguable that what unites the Four Branches is in fact nothing beyond the four markers that conclude the four tales. Viewed that baldly, the Four Branches seem to be an extreme example of Jacques Derrida's claim that every work that belongs to a genre contains a "supplementary and distinctive trait, a mark of belonging or inclusion, [which] does not properly pertain to any genre or class. The re-mark of belonging does not belong. It belongs without belonging."[15] Derrida's mark that "appears only in the timeless time of the blink of an eye"[16] appears grotesquely swollen in the case of the Four Branches into the sole indicator of the works' identity as a set.

Examining the role of these "marker" phrases is further complicated by no one knowing what a *mabinogi* really is. Definitions of the term range wildly, beginning with the Rev. R. Williams' charming speculation in his 1906 introduction to the Everyman edition of Lady Charlotte's work:

> The aspirant to bardic rank was called a *Mabinog*. The traditional lore which he had to acquire was roughly represented by the *Mabinogi*, which seems to have been at once a course of study and a source of income, for the *Mabinog* was probably allowed by custom to recite the tales he knew for pay. Using *Mabinogion* as the plural of *Mabinogi* Lady Charlotte Guest gives it as the general title of all the twelve tales contained in her book, although, strictly speaking, the title is applicable only to the four-branch tale of *Pwyll, Branwen, Manawyddan* and *Math*.[17]

Current thinking depends on Ifor Williams' suggestion that, because *mabinogi* usually refers to the story of someone's youth, the Four Branches might have originally told the story of Pryderi.[18] That suggestion is supported by R. L. Thomson, who points out that the

Welsh *mabinogi* is used to translate the medieval Latin *infantia*.[19] In "Folklore and Myth in the Mabinogion," W. J. Gruffydd provides the most elaborate articulation of this point of view, postulating that the Four Branches are the remains of a Saga of Pryderi, who is the child of a union of the King of Dyfed with Rhiannon, a visitant from the Other World. Part 1 would have been the Conception of Pryderi; part 2 Pryderi's Raid on the Other World; part 3 a Capture and Return of Pryderi, not unlike the Demeter/Kore myth; and part 4 the Death of Pryderi. However, Gruffydd's reconstruction is considerably undermined by the two facts: First, Gruffydd's order and division of episodes is nowhere near the order and division of the stories as they currently exist. Second, Pryderi is a relatively minor character in the current version of the tales. Rachel Bromwich has offered an alternative suggestion, that "*mabinogi* came to signify 'a tale of descendants,' and that the Four Branches actually deal with the children of the early Celtic deities: the families of Llyr and Don, and Pryderi son of Pwyll."[20] However, none of these explanations is universally accepted as definitive.

Despite such significant ambiguities as to what it represented in the Middle Ages, the vexed title *The Mabinogion* crystallizes two highly significant issues in terms of the nineteenth-century study of such texts. The first of these issues is the reification of loosely connected traditions into titled collections. The most prominent example of such an eponymous collection is, of course, the work commonly known as *Grimm's Fairy Tales*—as if Jakob and Wilhelm Grimm were legendary storytellers like Mother Goose rather than philologists attempting to explore the development of the German language by comparative analysis of folk tales.[21] However, British antiquarians such as Richard Hurd, Thomas Percy, and George Ellis also created similar collections of medieval ballads.[22] Thomas Crofton Croker published his collected *Fairy Legends and Traditions of the South of Ireland* in 1825, a collection that was translated into German by the Grimms. The tradition extended well into the twentieth century with Andrew Lang's *Fairy Books*, which are still in print.

One of the most influential of these British collections, *Minstrelsy of the Scottish Border,* was published in 1802 by Lang's fellow Scotsman, Sir Walter Scott. Scott was even more influential, however, in establishing the second great issue crystallized by the title *The Mabinogion*: the close connection between these collections and children's literature. In 1810, in his notes to *The Lady of the Lake,*

Scott suggested that "the mythology of one period would . . . appear to pass into the romance of the next century, and that into the nursery tale of the subsequent ages."[23] Although Scott went no further in studying or supporting his theory, this idea of the devolution of myth into children's literature was eagerly taken up by other antiquarians such as Sir Francis Palgrave and Thomas Keightley.[24]

This belief in the relationship between myth and children's literature, as well as the close relation of the word *mabinogi* to "*mab*," the Welsh word for boy, led to the common perception that Lady Charlotte believed *mabinogi* meant a story for children and intended her collection to be one of fairy tales for children.[25] This point of view is supported by her loftily Victorian dedication of her first published translation to her two oldest sons, who were three years old and newborn, respectively, at the time:

> To Ivor and Merthyr
> My dear Children,
>   Infants as you yet are, I feel that I cannot dedicate more fitly than to you these venerable relics of ancient lore, and I do so in the hope of inciting you to cultivate the literature of "Gwyllt Walia," in whose beautiful language you are being initiated, and amongst whose free mountains you were born. May you become early imbued with the chivalric and exalted sense of honour, and the fervent patriotism for which its sons have ever been celebrated. May you learn to emulate the noble qualities of Ivor Hael, and the firm attachment to your Native Country, which distinguished that Ivor Bach, after whom the elder of you was named.
>
> I am,
Your affectionate Mother,
C. E. Guest.
Dowlais, August 29th, 1838[26]

The idea that Lady Charlotte was writing for children is reinforced by her Bowdlerization of what she considered immodest sexual references. For example, she routinely softened rapes into forced marriages. More notoriously, she excised a passage from "Pwyll" that she considered indelicate: the fate of Arawn's wife when he and Pwyll exchanged kingdoms, disguised as one another, for a year. Gentleman that he was, Pwyll, whenever he went to bed with Arawn's wife, "turned his face to the edge [of the bed] and his back to her, nor did he speak another word before morning."[27] When

Arawn returned to bed with his wife, he reproached her for not speaking with him. She in turn replied that they had not spoken in bed for a year. Arawn then:

> told her what had happened, and she said, "I confess to God, you made a strong pact for your friend to have fought off the temptations of the flesh and kept faith with you." "Lady, that was my thought when I was silent." "No wonder," she said.[28]

If Lady Charlotte did in fact translate the *Mabinogion* for children, she would certainly be in good company—in particular that of the Brothers Grimm, whose scholarly three-volume exploration of the roots and development of language through nursery tales quickly evolved into a one-volume children's classic. Nonetheless, there are those who believe that the notion that Lady Charlotte was writing for children has contributed to the unfair marginalization of her scholarship. Donna R. White, in particular, has attacked this long held commonplace about Lady Charlotte's intended audience, arguing,

> Specialists in children's literature would be amazed at this charge and would also object to the underlying and all-too-common assumption that children's literature is a lesser breed of writing. The charge is ludicrous. Nobody has ever published for children a massive, bilingual, multi-volume collection of tales accompanied by voluminous scholarly notes and appendices. Nor is there any evidence that the books were marketed for children or reviewed as children's books. In fact, in the preface to the second edition, Guest refers to her "learned" reader. Nowhere does she indicate that her intended audience was children.[29]

White is particularly dismissive of the "evidence" of Lady Charlotte's first dedication, arguing persuasively, "it is a mistake to conflate dedicatees with audience. Some authors dedicated their book to their cats or to deceased relatives, but no one assumes an intended feline readership or an audience of ghosts." [30] She goes on to conclude her essay with what is inarguably the most spirited defense of Lady Charlotte among modern critics:

> Lady Charlotte Guest's situation amongst her Welsh academic peers bears a striking similarity to an episode in "Manawydan fab Llyr," when Manawydan had taken up the crafts of saddle-making, shield-making, and shoe-making, and had become so proficient at the work

that the other craftsmen sought to slay him. Perhaps, in a similar way, Lady Charlotte's own proficiency may have led to this groundless character assassination.[31]

White's defense may be little more than an exquisitely turned analogy; however, it is a fact that Bowdlerization is the least of the charges that have been leveled against Lady Charlotte. At best, she has been seen as an inspired amateur, who, despite her many erroneous understandings, managed to create the first popular translation of the *Mabinogion*. At worst, she has been accused of blatantly taking credit for translations that were in fact done by two Welshmen, the Reverends John Jones and Thomas Price, who were known by their bardic names of Tegid and Carnhuanawc, respectively.[32] These tensions and accusations go back to the work's very inception and the Welsh Manuscripts Society itself, which seemed to have believed at one point that she was uninterested in the project.[33]

Indeed, Lady Charlotte's first major battle over the *Mabinogion* occurred within a year of her beginning the translation, when, nine months pregnant, she was caught up in an undignified race to publish a translation of "Peredur" in English before a Frenchman named Theodore Hersart de la Villemarque did in French. Sadly, the imbroglio began as a civilized academic exchange. Villemarque provided Lady Charlotte with a transcription of the "*Chevalier au Lion*" from the French, which she published as an appendix to her own work.[34] Next, however, Villemarque grew "wild in his notions and presumes on my good nature, because he corrected the press of the last part of the Chevalier au Lion (which was necessary he should as no one could correctly read his transcript so vilely was it written) he writes insisting on Rees' signing his name to the printed copy and saying it is published by him. Poor Rees is annoyed. Of course I can consent to nothing of the sort."[35]

A year later, Villemarque entered an essay on the influence of Welsh tradition on European literature in the Abergavenny Eisteddfod, which not only used Lady Charlotte's work without attribution, but also "delicately insinuated that I did not write the book myself (a degree of moral turpitude which he dare not openly accuse me of.) The secret of all this is his anger at being unable to forestall me in the publication of Peredur."[36]

A comparison of their current reputations makes it clear Lady Charlotte survived Villemarque. However, she remains the victim of the condescending ongoing perception that she "didn't really" translate the *Mabinogion,* a charge that is inextricably linked with her "amateurism." What is cruelest about this charge is that, 150 years after the fact, it is completely unprovable. It is also completely conjectural, being based largely on the logic that Lady Charlotte would have been unable to master enough Middle Welsh in a scant five years to complete a scholarly translation. Lady Charlotte's current defenders range from White's staunch claim that "A woman with such a strong drive for perfection and fluency in half a dozen languages would have had no difficulty learning to read Medieval Welsh,"[37] to Rachel Bromwich's more measured, "Whatever may have been the extent of the help which Lady Charlotte received from others . . . it cannot detract from the magnitude of her achievement and her deep interest and involvement in her work."[38] Yet their voices are consistently drowned out by the voices of detractors such as W. J. Gruffydd, "who believed that the main credit should go to the two scholars who 'devilled' for her, Tegid [John Jones] and Price."[39]

Accusations such as Gruffydd's are based on the completely unanswerable question of how much assistance Lady Charlotte received in making her translation. Specifically, what is open to debate is whether Tegid simply provided assistance by copying the manuscript and Price by reading it over, or whether they did the majority of translation work. Unfortunately, at this late date, there is little definitive evidence that can be brought to bear on the question. Lady Charlotte's defenders can point to her description of Price's reading of the first tale: "after dinner we polished off my translation slightly for the Press. But being willing to keep very rigidly to the original, very little alteration could be made in my version, which will, I fear, appear rather clumsy English."[40] However, an autograph letter from Price is more ambiguous. It opens:

> My dear Lady Charlotte,
> The 8 parcels have arrived and I will attend to them as soon as possible and also to your enquiries.—I send you the translation. You will see that I differ from my predecessors in the 8th line. But I am convinced that *cyn cafat* is one word *cynghaffad. Mutual seizure or grappling together.*

Lady Charlotte's detractors will happily latch onto the words "I send you the translation" as proof positive that Price did the work. Nevertheless, it is equally possible to read the letter as Price responding to Lady Charlotte's request for clarification about a specific passage—presumably the most urgent of her enquiries. Indeed, it is impossible to imagine what the eight parcels are, unless they are a draft of a translation she sent to Price to comment on. And certainly the brisk collegiality of the following paragraph, in which Price writes "I am quite disappointed in your treatment of the *Tair Gormes* . . . by your way of telling it you deprive it of much of the interest which it would possess if given as a literal translation," suggests that he regarded Lady Charlotte as an intellectual equal—as does his concluding statement that he will "leave it entirely to your own discretion having stated so much."[41]

On the other hand, there is no denying that Jones's assistance was at best tepidly acknowledged in Lady Charlotte's preface to her 1849 edition, and that Price's assistance was not acknowledged at all. However, these omissions are much more ethically questionable to a twentieth-century professional scholar than they would have been at the time. Without careers to protect, Lady Charlotte and her colleagues were much less concerned with garnering credit for their publications. Acknowledgments were a matter of courtesy rather than appropriate assignment of credit. The omission of an acknowledgment for Price, for example, is normally justified by the fact he was dead by 1849, when the three-volume edition came out.

Admittedly, this defense in terms of disinterested amateurism is somewhat at odds with Lady Charlotte's firm determination to publish ahead of Villemarque. Indeed, it may be simpler to accept that she believed she had done the work and therefore deserved the credit for it. It is certainly this point of view that is taken by her most gallant defender, an appealing clergyman named D. Rhys Phillips, who presented a spirited defense of Lady Charlotte in a pamphlet published by the equally appealing Swansea Mabinogion Society. His methodology is in itself a portrait of a bygone age:

> We asked the late Countess of Bessborough if her mother's *earlier* Journals contained any detailed references to the Translation of the *Mabinogion*: a work handsomely printed by W. Ress of Llandovery, in seven numbers, during 1838-1846, and afterwards bound in three sumptuous volumes.
>
> Though at that time busily engaged as Hon. Secretary of Princess Victoria's Auxiliary Committee for the inspection of the Y.M.C.A. Recreation Huts for Soldiers at the Base Camps in France (which work she did not long survive, for she died in 1919), the Countess kindly replied on September 26, and in the course of her letter said:

> "I delayed answering your letter till I was able to look out ex-
> tracts from my mother, Lady Charlotte Guest's Journal. I now
> enclose you samples of the kind of details I could send you. I
> have typed copies of her unpublished Journals from 1822 to
> 1853, and I find that I have noted in the margin where she al-
> ludes to working at her translation of the Mabinogion; so that I
> could very easily find you a great choice of extracts for publica-
> tion."[42]

The pamphlet then goes on to cite entries from diaries that show
Lady Charlotte at work on her translation. Rhys' research is meticulous, and the pamphlet contains such delightful anecdotes as the
following:

> [Tennyson] was anxious to make [Lady Charlotte's] acquaintance . . .
> He asked her, amongst other things, what was the proper pronuncia-
> tion of the vowel E in Enid. Should it be short or long? In one of the
> passages of his book he had written "Geraint wedded Enid," which
> would be all right with the long E, but was impossible, he said, with
> the short one. When he was told that it should be short, he at once
> altered the word to "Geraint married Enid." It is the custom for
> ladies, in the present day, who have christened their daughters Enid,
> to pronounce it as with the long E, but in this they are undoubtedly
> wrong.[43]

Despite its considerable narrative appeal, as a piece of scholarly
evidence, Rhys' work proves nothing about Lady Charlotte's level of
command of Welsh. Rather, it simply documents the fact that she
did put a great deal of consistent effort into producing her version
of the *Mabinogion*—a fact that has never been contested by even her
harshest critics. Nowhere is this energy and effort more evident than
in her miscellaneous papers at the National Library of Wales, which
include autograph fair copies of text and translation for "Geraint,"
"Rhonabwy," "Branwen," "Manawyddan," and "Math," as well as par-
tial texts, notes, and translations for other stories, all still carefully
bound in faded pink ribbon.[44] That the notes, at least, are her own
work is indisputably proved by a notebook containing excerpts from
Strutt's Sports and Pastimes of the People of England, destined to become
the footnote on women's riding in "Geraint" discussed later in this
chapter.

Furthermore, the underlying agendas of many of Lady Charlotte's accusers are at least as ambiguous as the evidence on her be-

half. In fact, most of them object to Lady Charlotte simply because she is an English noblewoman and industrialist's wife. Revel Guest summarizes the claim of one of the most overt of these critics as follows:

> Another accusation, levelled in an 1921 letter to the *Western Mail* by an anonymous correspondent who signed himself "Ap Dowlais" claimed that Thomas Stephens, a young scholar who later distinguished himself by publishing *The Literature of the Kymry* and a refutation of the Madoc myth, was the true author, tellingly branding his claims as the "joyful assertion that it was a Welshman who gave to the world these Translations and not the intellect of another race."[45]

The notion that a Welshman should be the first person to translate such an important part of the Welsh literary tradition has created a peculiar double-bind for Lady Charlotte. For, even as one set of scholars condemns her for not having translated the text herself, others, such as Judith Johnston, have condemned her translations as an act of self-aggrandizing cultural appropriation, arguing that

> Language, as Lefevere has shown, is not the main problem in translation, the problem lies in ideology, poetics and "cultural elements that are not immediately clear, or seen as completely 'misplaced' in what would be the target culture version of the text to be translated." The target language, shifted out of its culturally significant context, reappears in another form: in the case of tales and legends, for instance, that form is most often locked into a particular mode: quaint, noble savage, child-like.[46]

According to Johnston, this act of appropriating the "exotic," while simultaneously marginalizing it, is particularly characteristic of nineteenth-century women, especially those in exile in a colony, precisely because they are displaced from both the security of their regular society and the restrictions imposed by it. As Johnston claims,

> Although marginalised socially in Wales by her upper-class rank, and by her husband's powerful position as the ironmaster . . . Guest's mobility of class and geography gave her both intellectual and critical advantage. But throughout the published sections of her diary which I have been able to examine, the reader gains an overwhelming sense that Charlotte Guest's was indeed both an imperialist and a feminist project, although never expressed in either of those terms.

As a feminist project she sought for both identity and position, "in opposition," as Wolff puts it, "to linear narratives of the self and essentialist conceptions of gender and place."[47]

The notion that Lady Charlotte's translation is marked as an Englishwoman's because it is somehow quaint and childlike directly contradicts the notion that her translation was in fact done by a pair of native Welshmen. Yet, Johnston's claims have some validity, for Lady Charlotte's translation of the *Mabinogion* did seem to have stabilized her own sense of identity. It is a happy coincidence that Lady Charlotte's commonplace books of Persian poetry and the biographies of her ancestors are contained in the same box of miscellaneous papers as her notes and translations of the *Mabinogion*, for both arguably are collections that she amassed as a form of private cultural capital that reified the romantic streak in her personality. Indeed, Johnston's argument can only lend force to the idea that Lady Charlotte was replacing the "exotic" romantic ideals of her youth represented by her commonplace books with an "exotic" romanticism closely associated with Wales and the Welsh.

Nonetheless, Johnston's argument ultimately falters because she never succeeds in demonstrating that Lady Charlotte's translation is particularly quaint, childlike, or savage. Indeed, Johnston claims, in a side-by-side comparison of several versions of the first paragraph of "Kilhwch and Olwen" that "It is clear that differences in the English translations . . . are minimal."[48] For example, in "Pwyll," Lady Charlotte writes,

> And the year he spent in hunting, and minstrelsy, and feasting, and diversion, and discourse with his companions until the night that was fixed for the conflict. And when that night came, it was remembered even by those who lived in the furthest part of his dominions, and he went to the meeting, and the nobles of the kingdom with him.[49]

Jones and Jones' 1949 translation, accepted as definitive, differs little in diction or detail:

> The year he spent in hunting and song and carousal, and affection and discourse with his companions, till the night the encounter should be. On that appointed night, the tryst was as well remembered by the man who dwelt furthest in the whole kingdom as by himself. And he came to the tryst, and the gentles of the kingdom with him.[50]

Indeed, the most direct prose in a translation belongs to that of Jeffrey Gantz (1976), although one balks at calling it either childlike or savage:

> Pwyll spent that year hunting and singing and carousing, in fellowship and in pleasant talk with his companions, up to the night of the meeting, which the men in the most distant parts of the kingdom remembered as well as he did himself. He was accompanied by the nobles of the realm . . . [51]

Obviously, a comparison of three sentences does not a comparison of translations make; however, further examination of the texts provides no egregious examples of Lady Charlotte's diction being either quaint or childlike. Indeed, Lady Charlotte's choice of diction, along with that of Jones and Jones, might be better described as stylized and deliberately archaic,[52] at least to a twentieth-century ear. Significantly, in their introduction to the text, Jones and Jones make a compelling argument that archaicizing diction is true to the target text itself, for the unity of the eleven tales is "imposed both by their subject matter and their social and literary milieu. The matter is primarily mythology in decline and folklore, though it is unlikely that the story-tellers were themselves often if ever aware of this."[53] The literary context is that of the redactor attempting to preserve on paper "such relics and fragments of the [oral] Celtic tradition as have survived the steep mortality of the years."[54]

Needless to say, there are significant differences in the prose of the various "relics and fragments." According to Jones and Jones, the redactor of the four branches of the Mabinogi "wrote the finest Welsh prose of his age, a grand master who never for one sentence intrudes the veil of style between the reader and what is read."[55] In contrast, "Not so the author of *Culhwch and Olwen*, who deploys with gusto every resource of language and style to heighten the color and deepen the character of the fantastic and primitive world his creatures inhabit."[56] Yet what unites these writers both with each other and with their translator is their position in relation to their subject matter: they are all attempting to give form to something that is irretrievably lost—even though it never existed, at least in the form in which it is being recreated.

Nothing about Lady Charlotte's translation situates it so clearly in the nineteenth-century intellectual *zeitgeist* as this idea that it was a reconstruction of a lost past from a few remaining fragments. Nineteenth-century literary critics, historians, and philologists shared a conviction, born of Viconian linguistics and bolstered by the poetic theories of Herder and Schiller, that such fragments provided a glimpse of a mythopoeic past, during which "primitive" peoples had more immediate, instinctive contact with the realm of myth and expressed this experience in a language that was equally immediately and instinctively poetic. Collecting the fragments that remained in works such as folk tales and ballads was one of the few ways that the degenerate present could come into contact with this lost, pure past.

That Lady Charlotte perceived herself as such a collector first and as a translator only secondarily is made clear by the fact that the first mention of any Welsh literary project in Lady Charlotte's diaries was a reference to collecting, not translating. In 1835, she recorded a meeting with the editor of the *Cambrian Visitor*, Elijah Waring, in which "our conversation turned much upon the superstitions and legends of Wales—I think it might be desirable to make a collection of them."[57] Furthermore, perceiving Lady Charlotte as a collector and scholar, rather than as a translator, creates a whole new perspective from which to view her work—one that has not been significantly addressed by critics. Indeed, once one considers Lady Charlotte from such a perspective, one can easily argue that the main accomplishment of the attack on her abilities as a translator is to render irrelevant the seven-page introduction and 145 pages of footnotes that also make up her *Mabinogion*.

Admittedly, there are legitimate reasons to dismiss her scholarship as the work of a dotty amateur in and of itself. Her notes are a genuine *Wunderkammer*, a collector's cabinet, jammed with curiosities seized without regard for their sources. It was this magpie-like nature of her work that led Roger S. Loomis to complain that her notes must "be carefully sifted, many of the worthless inventions of Iolo Morganwg and of earlier fabricators being mixed in with the genuine traditions derived from medieval manuscripts."[58]

The tale of Kilhwch and Olwen provides some of the best support for Loomis' critique. In the text, Kilhwch seeks a boon of Arthur and his warriors, specifically, "Kai, and Bedwyr, and . . . Gwynn the son of Nudd . . . and Prince Fflewddur Fflam . . . " and so forth for five straight pages.[59] Lady Charlotte is helpless to resist such a tempting list of names. The following is only the opening paragraph of her three page footnote on Gwyn the Son of Nudd, the first of the five pages of names:

In Gwyn ab Nudd, we become acquainted with one of the most poetical characters of Welsh romance. He is no less a personage than the King of Faerie, a realm, the extent and importance of which is nowhere better appreciated, or held in greater reverence, than in Wales. Very numerous indeed are the subjects of Gwyn ab Nudd, and very various are they in their natures. He is the sovereign of those beneficent and joyous beings, the Tylwyth Teg, or Family of Beauty (sometimes also called Bendith I Mammau, or Blessing of Mothers), who dance in the moonlight on the velvet sward, in their airy and flowing robes of blue or green, or white or scarlet, and who delight in showering benefits on the more favoured of the human race; and equally does his authority extend over the fantastic, though no less picturesque class of Elves, who in Welsh bear the name of Ellyllon, and who, on the other hand, enjoy nothing so much as to mislead and torment the inhabitants of earth. Indeed, if Davidd ap Gwylim may be believed, Gwyn ab Nudd himself is not averse to indulging in a little mischievous amusement of this kind; for one dark night the bard, having ridden into a turf bog on the mountain, calls it the "fishpond of Gwyn ab Nudd, a palace for goblins and their tribe," to whom he evidently gives credit for having decoyed him into its mire. Perhaps he may have been tempted to exclaim like Shakespeare, "Heavens defend me from the Welsh fairy."[60]

One can immediately understand Loomis's scholarly frustration. That the passage exhibits a shameless lack of academic detachment is only the first of its sins. More damningly, Lady Charlotte makes no attempt to differentiate a Welsh source such as Davydd ap Gwylim from an English source such as Shakespeare, nor does she attempt to distinguish literary sources from the oral folkloric tradition. Quantity and picturesqueness, rather than authenticity, seem to be her major criteria for inclusion. Yet, the sheer energy of her acquisitiveness, as well as the clear affinity she has for a purely romantic story, give the passage a literary value all its own. Indeed, rather than sharing Loomis's frustration, one can take pleasure in the unconscious self-portrait of a woman who has a greed for narrative curiosities—a greed that foreshadows her later career as a collector.

More importantly, Loomis's frustration obscures that fact that both Lady Charlotte's scholarly heuristic and its intellectual underpinnings merely reflected the intellectual climate in which she was operating—even in passages that at first glance seem to be as purely eccentric as the following:

There is one argument in favour of the high antiquity in Wales of many of the Mabinogion, which deserves to be mentioned here. The argument is founded on the topography of the country. It is found that Saxon names of places are very frequently definitions of the nature of the locality to which they are attached, as Clifton, Deepden, Bridge-ford, Thorpe, Ham, Wick, and the like; whereas those of Wales are more frequently commemorative of some event, real or supposed, said to have happened on or near the spot, or bearing allusion to some person renowned in the story of the country or district ... But as these names could not have preceded the events to which they refer, the events themselves must be not unfrequently as old as the early settlement in the country. And as some of these events and fictions are the subjects of, and are explained by, existing Welsh legends, it follows that the legends must be, in some shape or other, of very remote antiquity. It will be observed that this argument supports *remote* antiquity only for such legends as are connected with the greater topographical features, as mountains, lakes, rivers, seas, which must have been named at an early period in the inhabitation of the country by man. But there exist, also, legends connected with the lesser features, as pools, hills, detached rocks, caves, fords, and the like, places not necessarily named by the earlier settlers, but the names of which are, nevertheless, probably very old, since the words of which they are composed are in many cases not retained in the colloquial tongue, in which they must once have been included, and are in some instances lost from the language altogether, so much so as to be only partially explicable even by scholars.[61]

Perhaps the most pleasing aspect of this argument, apart from its surface logic, is its sheer circularity. Her argument that Saxon place names are largely descriptive tells the reader much more about her perception of the Saxons as practical literalists than about the etymology of the names, which are more likely reifications of a variety of influences, including mispronunciations of the original Welsh or proper names and corruptions of current or forgotten words in the Saxon, as well as simple description, all superimposed on one another. Symmetrically, it is equally likely that a superficial resemblance between Welsh place names and legends led later storytellers to connect the two, rather than the place names serving as a guarantor of the legend's antiquity. Indeed, that a legend can be attached to a geographical feature long after the first instances of the legend were recorded is witnessed by the number of Arthur's Seats in England.

Lady Charlotte's argument descends into the unwittingly farcical as it culminates in her assertion that we can determine the antiquity of geographic features by their referring to events lost in time—even when in fact we do not know the actual meaning of the words making up the place's name. One could spend hours delightedly bathing in that particular *mise en abime* before one even moved on to consider her corollary proposition, that these place names thus somehow prove the antiquity of the legends for which they are purportedly named.

Nonetheless, such fascination with false etymologies and bad euhemerism is absolutely true to the medieval text Lady Charlotte was translating. As Gantz explains,

> A last amusing example of "history" in *The Mabinogion* is provided by the onomastic episodes . . . over-ingenious and inherently improbable explanations which seem to have arisen out of desperation rather than from genuine knowledge. Thus the storytellers of "Math" explain the numerous occurrences of Mochdrev (Pig Town) in Wales by routing Gwydyon's retreat north—with the pigs—through as many of these as possible. Some names appear to have been misunderstood: in "Branwen," the place name Tal y Bolyon (End of the Ridges) is explained by the episode of the colts which were made over to Mallolwch—the storyteller evidently understood (or chose to understand) the name as Tal Ebolyon (Payment of Colts).[62]

More importantly, however, Lady Charlotte's heuristic in this passage is precisely that of the average nineteenth-century romantic philologist. In *The Myth and Ritual School: J.G. Frazer and the Cambridge Ritualists*, Robert Ackerman describes the birth of the etymological approach to interpretation that underlies Lady Charlotte's arguments. He claims that the eighteenth-century rise of the etymological approach to the interpretation of myths and legends, which, in turn, gave rise to nineteenth-century philology, was a response to the rationalist view that myths were "philosophical allegories formulated by the ancient sages."[63] Thinkers such as Fontenelle, Bayle, and most notably Vico and Herder, turned to euhemerism and etymological analysis in order to locate the genesis and meaning of myth in the concrete experience of the people who first told them. Euhemerism attempted to discover myths' meaning by looking for actual events that inspired them, while philology attempted to strip words down to their common roots in Indo-European in the hopes that words' origins might parallel myths' origins.

If a contemporary reader is acquainted with these ideas, it is most likely through Derrida's "Exergue" to "White Mythology," in which he offers a critique of Anatole France's dialogue in *The Garden of Epicurus*. France's description of the development of philosophical language, as formulated by Derrida, is actually a common nineteenth-century philological one, "Abstract notions always hide a sensory figure."[64] Derrida famously goes on to problematize France's claim, by arguing that

> the history of metaphysical language is said to be confused with the erasure of the efficacity of the sensory figure and the *usure* of its effigy. The word itself is not pronounced, but one may decipher the double import of *usure*: erasure by rubbing, exhaustion, crumbling away, certainly; but also the supplementary product of a capital, the exchange which far from losing the original investment would fructify its initial wealth, would increase its return in the form of revenue, additional interest, linguistic surplus value, the two histories of the meaning of the word remaining indistinguishable.[65]

In sharp contrast to Derrida's insisting on the impossibility of grounding language in a system of referents, the nineteenth century saw this search for the lost origins of language in extremely concrete terms. Perhaps the most representative proponent of the nineteenth-century philological point of view was F. Max Muller, who claimed that

> Aryans, by the peculiarity of their language, were doomed never to be permitted to worship their nature gods directly but instead were forced into the most elaborate periphrases to voice their piety. The reason for this state of affairs was that Aryan was a truly primitive language in that it consisted solely of words that expressed action; its speakers could not therefore use it to express abstractions . . .
>
> Every word, whether noun or verb, had still its full original power during the mythopoeic ages. Words were heavy and unwieldy. They said more than they ought to say, and hence, much of the strangeness of the mythological language, which we can only understand by watching the natural growth of speech . . .[66]

The *Star Trek* aficionado may recognize in this argument the roots of the memorable "Darmok" episode;[67] however to any other post-modernist ear, what is perhaps most foreign about this approach is the actuality which words acquire. Words were, for a philologist, facts, and a translator could then be seen as a collector of these facts, a "scientific" approach to language that was well in keeping with the intellectual inheritance of empiricism. Furthermore, earlier words, being closer to their sensory origins, had more meaning than later words, which were abstracted from their meaning.

Understanding this nineteenth-century privileging of the origins and actuality of language is critical to understanding Lady Charlotte's work. In fact, her interest in Welsh literature may well have stemmed from the fact that philologists privileged the Celtic languages as closer to the original Indo-European than any other language—a notion that still persists, albeit in diluted form. Indeed, when she began to study Welsh, she also began to read the philologist James Cowles Prichard. She paid especial attention to his *The Eastern Origins of the Celtic Nations* (1851).[68] Both Prichard's conclusion and heuristic are neatly set out in his complete title: *The Eastern Origin of the Celtic Nations proved by a comparison of their dialects with the Sanskrit, Greek, Latin, and Teutonic Languages: Forming a supplement to Researches into the Physical History of Mankind.* Any lingering question as to the intellectual affinity between Lady Charlotte and her own preferred influence can be quickly resolved by glancing at their similar touch with a footnote: Prichard provides eighteen pages of ten-pitch notes to the first sixteen pages of twelve-pitch text of his book.

Like most of his contemporaries, Prichard's concern was not, in fact, so much with the origin of languages as the origin of peoples. He opens his first chapter by stating this directly:

Many writers on natural history and geography have maintained the opinion that each particular region of the earth must have been supplied from the beginning, by a separate and distinct creation, with its peculiar stock of indigenous or native inhabitants. Among the ancients this notion prevailed almost universally. There existed, indeed, in the pagan world an obscure tradition of a primitive pair fashioned out of clay by the hand of Prometheus or of Jupiter; but this belonged to mythology; which in its literal sense, at least, was of little authority with the best informed, and the frequent occurrence of such term as *autochthones, indigenae,* or *aboriginal inhabitants,* whenever reference is made to the population of different countries, indicates a general prevalence of the ideas which such expressions are fitted to suggest. The prevailing opinion in modern times has referred all the nations of the earth to a common parentage; and this it has done chiefly, as it would appear, on the authority of our Sacred History, the

testimony of which seems hardly to be reconciled with a different hypothesis. Of late, however, many learned men, chiefly on the continent, have been strongly inclined to adopt an opinion similar to that
of the ancients.[69]

Linguistic study (or, more properly, philology) is nothing but a
method that will "furnish great and indispensable assistance in many
particular inquiries relating to the history of and affinity of nations,"
even if Prichard himself must admit, "It would be too much to expect from this quarter to demonstrate the unity of race, or an original sameness of idiom in the whole human species."[70]

The most problematic assumption of Prichard's argument is the
nineteenth-century teleological one that there is a historical progression from primitive to civilized peoples and that the progression
of language parallels the historical one. This assumption is evident
even in such seemingly innocuous statements as "I must confine my
observations to the original materials of speech, and to expressions
which denote simple and primitive ideas," which in fact implies that
simple and primitive materials can always be equated with original
ones. This teleological view of the relationship between language
and history has a particularly significant influence on Prichard's attitude toward the Celts. On the one hand, he affords Celtic language and culture a paradoxical privilege, for, because of their social isolation, "the Celtic people have been more tenacious of the
peculiarities of their language, as they have been in many respects
of their customs and manners, than the other nations of Europe."[71]
On the other hand, the only way the Celts can maintain this intellectual privilege is by remaining in social isolation—or "primitive."

This philological assumption of the purity of primitivism remained an established approach to reading the *Mabinogion* until
well into the 1950s, when W. J. Gruffydd saw in one stratum of the
sources of the *Mabinogion*, a "folk recollection of an aboriginal people living in inaccessible parts of the countryside, having no contact
with the dominant race, and living in fear and suspicion of them."[72]
It is also exactly the same assumption that inspired the Grimms to
go looking for the roots of the German language in the folktales
that had remained socially isolated among the "backwards" and
"primitive" peasantry of that country. However, the roots of such an
idea actually go back much further than that. The notion of such
early, mythopoeic races, Stuart Piggott explains in *The Ancient Britons
and the Antiquarian Imagination*, derives from the Renaissance desire

to place the learning of the Egyptians and pagan philosophers, as personified by Hermes Trismegistus, on an equal footing with that represented by the Bible.[73] The result was the concept of an early race that was not merely antediluvian, but preadamic.

This preadamite hypothesis was given its most complete explication in Isaac de Lapeyrere's *1655 Systema Theologicum ex Praeadamitarum Hypothesi: Prae-adamitae* (published in English in 1656 as *Man Before Adam*). In it, Lapeyrere

> made use of the two unreconciled versions of the Creation, the E text of Gen 1 and the J text of Gen 2, only the second of which names Adam and Eve, and proposed that the E text should be taken to mean that a separate and large population of Preadamites was created before Adam, who was merely the progenitor of the Jews, not of all mankind. This Gentile, non-Adamic, non-Jewish past was of vast antiquity, as was the fund of wisdom and knowledge acquired over this long period.[74]

Primitive races, particularly those of the newly discovered Americas, were the repositories of that knowledge in the modern world, because "The Flood, as an episode in Jewish ancient history, need only have been limited in extent, and far distant regions such as the Americas could have been populated by Preadamites in a remote antiquity."[75] The ancient Piets, and with them the Celts, were quickly identified with the primitive American peoples, leading to the privileging of Celtic antiquity as a preadamic one.

This casual association of the Other with the dark, primitive, and mystical is by now commonplace of postcolonial theory. Few, however, have explicated that point of view in more appalling detail than Matthew Arnold, whose public acknowledgment of his debt to Lady Charlotte may be a factor in Welsh resentment of her accomplishment as a translator. In *On the Study of Celtic Literature*, Arnold infamously attempted to define the "English genius"—primarily by contrasting it to the Saxon and Celtic geniuses from which it is formed. "Genius" is of course a mystical term, meaning the guiding spirit of a place or people. The twentieth-century reader grows immediately uncomfortable, thus, when Arnold essays a material definition of such an ineffable concept. The German genius, he claims is "steadiness with honesty," which, while it offers at its best "freedom from whim, flightiness, perverseness; patient fidelity to Nature —in a word, *science*," is also responsible for Germany's "eternal beer, sausages, and bad tobacco."[76] Somewhat predictably, he goes on to claim

> sentimental, if the Celtic nature is to be characterized by a single term, is the best term to take. An organisation quick to feel impressions, and feeling them very strongly; a lively personality therefore, keenly sensitive to joy and to sorrow; this is the main point.[77]

This clear demarcation between cultural types is paralleled by associated linguistic principles. The scientific principle, which corresponds to the Saxon character, is that of prosaic, but absolutely truthful, language. The poetic principle, which corresponds to the Celtic character, is the "passionate, turbulent, indomitable reaction against the despotism of fact."[78]

Arnold then spends the remainder of his essay defining the English genius as a combination of these two strains, which he treats as definable and separable: when the Englishman is scientific, that is the German/Saxon side of his nature manifesting itself; when he waxes poetic, that is the Celt prevailing. Soon, like a cook dissatisfied with his recipe, Arnold is forced to add a dash of the Norman genius—which excels at rhetoric and has a "Roman talent for affairs"[79]—to explain any behaviors that fail to conform to the other two extremes. Indeed, it is for rhetoric that Arnold claims the English language is best suited:

> . . . perhaps no nation, after the Greeks and Romans, has so clearly felt in what true rhetoric, rhetoric of the best kind, consists, and reached so high a pitch of excellence in this, as the English. Our sense for rhetoric has in some ways done harm to us in our cultivation of literature, harm to us still more in our cultivation of science; but in the true sphere of rhetoric, in public speaking, this sense has given us orators whom I do think we may, without fear of being contradicted and accused of blind national vanity, assert to have inherited the great Greek and Roman oratorical tradition more than the orators of any other country.[80]

Such a definition of rhetoric as a bridge between the polar opposites of poetry and science begins to sound very much like a Hegelian dialectic, situated across races rather than across time. In fact, a similar dialectic across time underlay the contemporaneous speculative approach to history, associated with the Scottish philosopher Adam Ferguson, who charted human development from folk societies, organized around individual bonds such as blood-brotherhood, to modern capitalist nations.[81] Moreover, very similar assumptions underlie Lady Charlotte's characterization of the textual development of the *Mabinogion* as a series of parallel binary oppositions between ancient and modern, simplicity and ornament, and pure and corrupt:

> The Mabinogion, however, though thus early recorded in the Welsh tongue, are in their existing form by no means wholly Welsh. They are of two tolerably distinct classes. Of these, the older contains few allusions to Norman customs, manners, arts, arms, and luxuries. The other, and less ancient, are full of such allusions, and of ecclesiastical terms. Both classes, no doubt, are equally of Welsh root, but the former are not more overlaid or corrupted, than might have been expected, from the communication that so early took place between the Normans and the Welsh; whereas the latter probably migrated from Wales, and were brought back and re-translated after an absence of centuries, with a load of Norman additions. Kilhwch and Olwen, and the dream of Rhonabwy, may be cited as examples of the older and purer class; the Lady of the Fountain, Peredur, and Geraint ab Erbin, of the later, or decorated.[82]

To the modern historian—of texts or of people—such oppositions seem reductionist at best, reactionary at worst. However, that is precisely why they should not be judged according to such a standard. For history was just beginning to evolve as a discipline during the period that Lady Charlotte was working on the *Mabinogion*.[83] If we are looking for a standard by which to judge any of the theories that shaped Lady Charlotte's approach to her text, we must turn instead to the discipline that gave rise to history, antiquarianism.

Stuart Piggott traces the birth of antiquarianism back to the seventeenth-century Battle of the Ancients and Moderns, claiming that antiquarianism evolved directly from the "Royal Society tradition of the empirical investigation of natural and artificial phenomena."[84] Antiquarians attempted to turn this empirical approach to an examination of the past. Their emphasis on assembling evidence rather than theorizing led to a peculiarly omnivorous intellectual standard, which "rather than confining itself to one specific type of source material . . . attempted to marry the literary and material evidences of past ages to preserve, and to transmit the memory of the past."[85] Descriptive classification was the antiquarian's only heuristic, and "Few antiquaries before the advent of specific archaeological method would have seen any need to treat exhumed burial remains

differently than a town charter or a church font. They were as comfortable editing medieval poetry as they were inspecting Roman remains."[86]

One result of this intellectual promiscuity was that antiquarians
were notorious collectors. The collection of Thomas Layton, for example, included, "11,000 books, 3,000 prints and maps, 3,000 coins,
tokens and medals, 9,000 pottery and glass vessels and tiles and
2,600 [assorted] antiquities."[87] Indeed, collection itself was perceived as the primary intellectual activity of the antiquarian, a stance
that is clearly a holdover from eighteenth-century scientific method.
For empiricism only allows theories to arise naturally from observations, or, as Charles Roach Smith argued in his *Collectanea Antiqua* in
1848, "The notion that a record *of facts,* copiously illustrated, and
but sparingly dilated with theory, would be acceptable to the anti-
quary and to the historical inquirer, is proved to have been well-
founded."[88]

Paradoxically, it was this very emphasis on facts without theory
that gave rise to the peculiarly flowery prose style of the antiquarian.
Unburdened by theory, the most significant facts were left to fend
for themselves, in a prismatic, undifferentiated way. As an anonymous archaeologist described his task, he sought to present the past
"in forms full of quaint and original features, which impart a picturesque and striking character to such fitful glimpses of the romance of life in other ages as are thus revealed."[89] Such an emphasis
on impressionism meant that the antiquarian's language "reveals a
greater emphasis on empathy than on analysis."[90]

As her later career as a china collector suggests, Lady Charlotte's
intellectual heuristic is primarily that of an antiquarian, and her
scholarly notes are best understood as an antiquarian collection,
motivated far more by empathy than by analysis, and intended,
above all, to provide "fitful glimpses of the romance of other ages."
Thus, Old French[91] and Old English[92] make their appearance beside
Welsh and English; the Englyn, the folk tale, the ecclesiastical history, and the romance all interact with equal validity as both reference and literary text—as do, in good antiquarian fashion, found
objects such as coins[93] and natural objects such as hills.[94] Indeed, perceiving Lady Charlotte as a collector rather than a writer may go a
long way to explaining why she took on such a vast translating task,
given her possibly uncertain command of Welsh. Antiquarian societies were closely related to printing societies, which published edi-

tions of manuscripts,[95] often in their original languages with the translation as nothing more than a "trot." As an antiquarian, Lady Charlotte may have considered her translating task as ancillary to her role as a collector and preserver of manuscripts. In fact, her diary entry recording that she "returned at dusk and read part of the tale of Kilhwch and Olwen from the *Mabinogion*. It pleases me much. There is a great field for annotation"[96] might well serve as evidence that she saw the texts' value primarily as vehicles for collection.

Whatever Lady Charlotte's motivations, her footnotes demonstrate an antiquarian's ease with mixing material and literary sources, as well as a collector's penchant for including anything and everything she runs across. Although it is quite arguable that in her mind this approach was nothing but appropriate scientific method, the paradoxical result is to make her footnotes in many ways her most imaginative and personal writing. Scholarship seems to provide a distancing mask that allows her to give free rein to a humor and imagination that she seems impelled to control carefully elsewhere. For example, "Geraint the Son of Erbin," provides a priceless glimpse of Lady Charlotte the passionate horsewoman, who named her own mount Llamerei after Arthur's half faery horse. When Gwenhwyvar asks Arthur if she may attend the hunt of the stag, Lady Charlotte hastens to assure the reader

> It was formerly very customary for ladies to join in the pleasures of the chase; and Strutt informs us that when they did so it was usual to draw the game into a small compass by means of inclosures; and temporary stands were erected for them, from which, when not contented with being merely spectators of the sport, they shot at the game with arrows as it passed by . . . Strutt is of opinion [*sic*] that the ladies had even separate hunting parties of their own.[97]

Yet, a touch of the gentlewoman cannot help but emerge just twenty pages later, when she remarks,

> Strutt accuses the ladies of former times of not having adopted a very feminine mode of riding on horseback, particularly when they joined in hunting expeditions; and he quotes the authority of certain illuminations in ancient MSS [which she cites in a footnote to the footnote] which is, I fear, rather conclusive evidence. But the mention of the Lady's saddle and riding-dress in Geraint ab Erbin, will, I trust, rescue the ladies of the present Tale from the imputation of so unbecoming a practice, and show that they wore a particular and ap-

propriate costume whenever they rode out. Catherine de Medicis is said to have been the first who rode like the ladies of the present age, with a high crutch to her saddle.[98]

To the twenty-first century reader, this magpie-like collecting is likely to seem to be a form of psychosis; indeed, any psychological approach to the phenomenon of collecting reads the phenomenon in terms of objects replacing an Oedipal lack.[99] Even in his own time, the antiquarian was a figure of fun, ridiculed by, among others, Jean Baptiste Chardin in a 1740 painting entitled "Le Singe Antiquaire," "in which an erudite ape sits in his fashionable day-gown, surrounded by his numismatic books and collections, peering at a coin with his lens."[100] Yet, for all its seeming silliness to the contemporary reader, the practice of antiquarianism introduced a fundamental methodological issue that is still a central question in reading folklore: that of the relative claims of empirically assembling facts and abstract theorizing.

Vladimir Propp's seminal *Morphology of the Folk[Wonder]tale* is perhaps the exemplar of the approach that privileges abstract theorizing. In that essay, Propp attempted to extrapolate from simple antiquarian collections of folktales a formalist grammar based on two components: "the functions of its dramatis personae"[101] and the sequence of these functions, which is identical across the tales.[102] Claude Levi-Strauss immediately critiqued Propp's work from a structuralist perspective that problematized Propp's insistence on theory, claiming that in Propp's formalism, form and content

> must be absolutely separate, as form alone is intelligible, and content is only a residual deprived of any significant value. For structuralism, this opposition does not exist; structuralism does not treat one as abstract and the other as concrete. Form and content are of the same nature, amenable to the same type of analysis. Content receives its reality from its structure, and what is called form is a way of organizing the local structures that make up this content.[103]

Without content, Levi-Strauss goes on to argue, form "will remain at so high a level of abstraction that it stops meaning anything and has no heuristic value. *Formalism destroys its object.*"[104]

In his extremely heated response, Propp claimed that Levi-Strauss overlooked the planned second half of his study, *Historical Roots of the Wondertale,* which is a Frazerian analysis of the roots of the folktale in primitive initiation rituals that imitated a visit to a land of death. It is, at this point, impossible to tell how much Soviet political pressures may have influenced Propp's sudden shift from the abstractions of formalism to grounding his analysis in the form's historico-material roots. However, what is interesting is that Propp's examination of origins suffers from the fundamental problem of nineteenth-century philology: the postulated ritual is ultimately empirically unprovable.

In "Edward Fuchs: Collector and Historian," Walter Benjamin addresses exactly the same issues with reference to the study of history. In that essay, Benjamin concludes a Marxist argument about the impossibility of any abstract theorizing about history with the claim that "collections are the answers of the practical man to the irresolvable polarities of theory."[105] Benjamin's argument differs from Levi-Strauss's in that he sees any attempt at diachronic theorizing as rendered impossible by the fact that the theorizer is situated in a historico-economic context from which he cannot extract himself in order to gain the absolute perspective necessary for diachronic analysis. Levi-Strauss, on the other hand, sees limited room for generalization in his belief that "the unconscious activity of the mind consists in imposing forms upon content, and . . . these forms are fundamentally the same for all minds—ancient and modern, primitive and civilized."[106] Benjamin and Levi-Strauss are united, however, in their turning to what is very much the antiquarian's heuristic, collecting facts, "sparingly diluted with theory."

Both Jacques Derrida and Michel Foucault have taken this thinking a step further, and in doing so, effectively demonstrate the dangers of attempting to read history in terms established by folklore, which is exactly what occurred in the nineteenth century as antiquarianism evolved into the academic discipline of history. In "Before the Law," Derrida effectively demolishes any transformation of the antiquarians' "Preadamite civilizations" into the speculative historians' "primitive societies" by examining Freud's Ur-myth of civilization, the Oedipal rupture. Derrida demonstrates how Freud implicitly assigns historicity, or at least the "reality of an event" to what is in fact "a sort of non-event, an event of nothing or a quasi-event which both calls for and annuls a narrative account . . . Everything happens *as if.*"[107] The last sentence, which is all but a definition of the word "speculative," foregrounds two essential difficulties with nineteenth-century speculative history's attempt to recast the antiquarians' mythopoeic understanding of the past into temporal and material terms. The first of these is that stories of lost civilizations are nothing but stories—albeit stories good enough to inspire whole branches of science fiction. If this were the only critique of the speculative historians, they could be justifiably left in peace as dotty, if engaging, mystics. It is the "narrative account" implicit in their heuristic that makes nineteenth-century speculative theories of history a Foucauldian discourse of power. For the idea of narrative imposes a teleological structure on the events of history, which in turn brings with it essential ideals of early and late, primitive and civilized, stasis and progress. As Foucault spent an entire career demonstrating, these underlying intellectual assumptions—or methods of discourse—reinforce social power relationships.

What is particularly instructive about Foucault's approach is that he terms the process of defining "those discourses . . . as practices obeying certain rules" as archaeology.[108] The connection with antiquarianism is immediate, if unexpected. For, at first glance, connecting Foucault's ambition to "define discourses in their specificity"[109] seems completely antithetical to the antiquarian's "fitful glimpses of the romance of life in other ages." Yet the two projects are linked by two important intellectual concepts. The first of these is their mutual emphasis on "specificity." Linked with it is their mutual refusal to interpret or allegorize.[110] Instead, both disciplines simply describe. In this, they are both forms of rewriting "in the preserved form of exteriority, a regulated transformation of what has already been written. [Archaeology] is not a return to the innermost secret of the origin; it is the systematic description of a discourse-object."[111] Such systematic description must be sharply differentiated from scholarly commentary, whose only role remains "to say *finally* what has silently been articulated *deep down.*"[112]

The intellectual effect of such a refusal to allegorize or interpret is particularly evident in Lady Charlotte's treatment of "The Dream of Rhonabwy." Her approach to "Rhonabwy" is genuinely peculiar, for she describes it as an exemplar of the "older and purer" class of narrative, when, as Jeffrey Gantz points out,

> The most literary of the tales in *The Mabinogion*, "Rhonabwy" may also be the last to have taken shape. Madawg son of Maredudd—a genuine historical figure—died in 1159, and his brother Iorwerth a few years later; thus the framework of the story cannot be much older than 1200.[113]

There can be no question that Lady Charlotte was well aware of the historical context described by Gantz. Indeed, she devotes five pages of detailed geographic and historical notes to Madawg and Iorwerth, including the information that Maredudd, Madawg's father, "had been one of the most strenuous and successful opponents of the Normans, celebrated by the national records,"[114] while Madawg "was not distinguished for equal ardour in his country's cause; on the contrary, Madawc [*sic*] combined with Henry II in the attacks he made upon Wales in 1158."[115] Her notes then go on to map the dream that the historical context frames in equal detail, beginning with the improbably precise sentence, "In following Rhonabwy on his visionary journey, it may be allowable to suppose him crossing the Vyrnwy at Rhyd y Vorle (Melverley), and then pursuing his course through the Deuddwr, between that river and the Severn, till we come to the plains of Argygroeg. The district traversed is remarkably fertile."[116] Given such persistent literalism, one can scarcely believe that her identifying "Rhonabwy" as an old tale was a scholarly error. Instead, we can justifiably assume that she was ignoring the framing tale and concentrating on the material in the dream itself, especially the mysterious chess game between Arthur and Owain.

This move can be seen as "collecting" the earlier text—removing it from the framing discourse in order to systematically describe it in and of itself. By thus removing the Arthurian story from the larger framing discourse, Lady Charlotte transforms it from a historically conditioned detail into an object that can pertain to the nineteenth century as well as the twelfth century. But how exactly is one supposed to read such an object? The narrative that Lady Charlotte defines as the "early tale" is, to say the least, cryptic. The story takes place seven years after the battle of Camlan,[117] in which Arthur met his final defeat at the hands of Mordred, yet Arthur is still conducting battles. However, he does so by means of an apparently magical chessboard. The reader never sees the actions on the chessboard or the battle; instead, the exchange between Arthur and his opponent Owain is limited to the repeated phrases "Forbid thy Ravens," on Arthur's part, and "Lord, play the game," on Owain's part.

Given the impenetrability of this story, it is perhaps no coincidence that the central problem of the entire early tale is in fact one of interpretation—a problem that is foregrounded by removing the framing tale's description of the story as dreamed on a yellow calf skin, presumably a mantic space. Without this explanatory context,

Rhonabwy—as well as the reader—can understand nothing of what he sees without the aid of Iddawc Cordd Prydain, an intermediary who introduces him to the men of old and interprets their actions. However, Iddawc's role is significantly complicated by the fact that he is a self-proclaimed liar and trouble-maker, who admits "I kindled strife between them, and stirred up wrath, when I was sent by Arthur the Emperor to reason with Medrawd."[118]

What is even more significant about the tale is that Rhonabwy's having seen the vision of the past does not guarantee that he will remember it. He is only allowed to remember his dream because he also saw the ring on Arthur's hand. Iddawc explains that "It is one of the properties of that stone to enable thee to remember that thou seest here tonight, and hadst thou not seen the stone, thou wouldest never have been able to remember aught thereof."[119] The final, peculiar *envoi* generalizes the function of the stone to all readers of the tale:

> And this tale is called the Dream of Rhonabwy. And this is the reason that no one knows the dream without a book, neither bard nor gifted seer; because of the various colours that were upon the horse, and the many wondrous colours of the arms and of the panoply, and of the precious scarfs [*sic*], and of the virtue-bearing stones.[120]

Interestingly, the *envoi* seems to suggest a way of reading the past that is consonant with Walter Benjamin's arguments in "Edward Fuchs"—as well as with Lady Charlotte's antiquarian heuristic. Instead of being mediated by discourse, history is mediated by a series of objects—scarves, stones, or even texts. What unites all these objects is their ability to be removed from one signifying system and resituated in another one. This resituability, which is itself conditioned by the object's specificity, invests the object with a unique potential to escape the interpretability dictated by social discourse. Unfortunately, according to Benjamin, this escape is by necessity fleeting and transitory.

Nowhere is this fleetingness of the escape from one's historical condition more evident than when the material from Rhonabwy was resituated in Lady Charlotte's own context. Within years, the cryptic, near-uninterpretable material of "Rhonabwy" was reified into what is arguably the seminal historical and moral symbol for nineteenth-century England, King Arthur, and Rhonabwy's gnomic chess player became the "selfless man and stainless gentleman . . . the great pillar of the moral order, and the resplendent top of human excellence."[121]

This ideal of the "stainless gentleman" had already been promulgated as a code of behavior for the English gentleman by Kenelm Henry Digby in *The Broadstone of Honour, or Rules for the Gentlemen of England* in 1822. A genuine eccentric who held vigils and staged tournaments at Cambridge, Digby claimed the destiny of the nation depended on the sons of the aristocracy following the models of behavior offered by the great chivalric heroes,[122] summoning his readers to actions with the lofty words

> You are born a gentleman. This is a high privilege, but are you aware of its obligations? It has pleased God to place you in a post of honour; but are you conscious that it is one which demands high and peculiar qualities? Such, however, is the fact. The rank which you have to support requires not so much an inheritance or the acquisition of wealth and property, as of elevated virtue and spotless fame.[123]

The movement known as Young England gave political actuality to moral and literary musings such as Digby's. Frankly reactionary in its idealism, Young England promoted a return to the virtues of "Merrie England" and a neofeudal system of government, in which the aristocracy would see to the needs of their inferiors in the name of *noblesse oblige*. Young England's lasting claim to fame was launching the political career of Benjamin Disraeli; however, in 1846, the party lost credibility, as well as Disraeli, over their opposition to the repeal of the Corn Laws.[124] The political application of the Englishman as chivalric knight, however, continued as an ideal of service to the young Queen Victoria—just as Spenser's knights had served Queen Elizabeth in the form of their Faerie Queene years earlier. This political ideology was deliberately bolstered by both Queen Victoria and Prince Albert in both their persons and their portraits and was given final form by Tennyson's dedication of *Idylls of the King* to the late Prince Albert, in 1861, and his final epilogue, "To the Queen," written in 1872.[125] The ideology was further fixed in the national consciousness by its being reified into a plethora of cultural capital, including paintings, home furnishings, books, and architecture, all of which were snapped up by Victorians as a means of quite literally acquiring these Arthurian virtues.

Perhaps the most seminal reification of the chivalric ideal into moral instruction was the tremendous number of Arthurian children's books that were published later in the century.[126] This transformation arguably lends credence to Scott's theories of the devolution of mythic material into nursery tales; more importantly, however, it bears striking testimony to the clear interpretability that had been attached to the material by the middle of the century. The Victorian's overt allegorization of the Matter of Britain is made clear by Daniel Maclise's "The Spirit of Chivalry," painted for the Lord's Chamber of the Houses of Parliament in 1848. In this fresco, Chivalry, personified by a woman in classical gown and laurel wreath,[127] is attended by the knights who defend her on her right hand, the beneficiaries of her service on her left hand, and the painters, poets, and historians whose duty it is to praise her at her feet.[128] Even more overtly allegorical is the cycle with which William Dyce decorated the queen's robing room in 1847—a commission that was overseen by Prince Albert. Dyce offered the fine arts commission a choice between an allegorical and a narrative approach; not surprisingly, the commission decided on the one that considered "the Companions of the Round Table as personifications of certain moral qualities . . . which make up the ancient idea of chivalric greatness."[129]

Foucault's talents would be wasted reading the implicit allegory in the Arthurian discourse of the Victorians. However, it is important to realize that, despite her much-reviled association with the great Victorian creators of Arthur as the epitome of the English gentleman, Lady Charlotte's reading of Arthur is much more complex. On the one hand, she is as capable as Digby of gushing:

> In [Arthur] we see the dignified and noble-hearted sovereign, the stately warrior, and the accomplished knight . . . His image adorned our earliest visions of Chivalry and Romance, and though the weightier cares of maturer age must supervene, they serve to deepen, not to efface the impression; and while in the eddying stream of life we pause to look back upon the days when Caerlleon [*sic*] and its Round Table formed to us an ideal world, we feel that, in our hearts at least, "King Arthur is not dead."[130]

On the other hand, the woman who refused to translate Arawn's "indulging in loving pleasure and affection with [his wife]"[131] happily includes as an antiquarian piece of evidence the following wholly undignified and completely tangential tale of the death of Huail, the brother of Kaw:

it appears that Huail was imprudent enough to court a lady of whom Arthur was enamoured. The monarch's suspicions being aroused, and his jealousy excited, he armed himself secretly . . . After a sharp combat, Huail got the better of Arthur, and wounded him severely in the thigh, whereupon the contest ceased, and reconciliation was made upon the condition that Huail, under the penalty of losing his head, should never reproach Arthur with the advantage he had obtained over him . . .

A short time after his recovery, Arthur fell in love with a lady . . . and, in order the more frequently to enjoy the pleasure of her society, he disguised himself in female attire. One day he was dancing with this lady, and her companions, when Huail happened to see him. He recognized [Arthur] on account of his lameness, and said, "This dancing might do very well, but for the thigh."[132]

Similarly, despite her disclaimer that "The real history of this chieftain is so veiled in obscurity, and has led to so much unsatisfactory discussion, that I shall in this place only consider him with reference to the position which he occupies in the regions of Fiction,"[133] her note is immediately followed by an antiquarian attempt to map Caerlleon upon Usk to a station of the Roman Second Legion. Lady Charlotte speculates that such a site would naturally appeal to a native sovereign and that

it was the principal residence of King Arthur; and the amphitheatre is still called Arthur's Round Table. In confirmation of this traditionary evidence, Nennius asserts that one of Arthur's battles was fought at *Cairlion*.[134]

The note concludes with an attempt, based on textual citation and etymology, to map this site to the contemporary city of Chester.

This intellectual tension between empirical antiquarianism and High Victorian allegorist culminates in a footnote that defies all notions of reifying the meaning of either text or discourse. The notes to "The Lady of the Fountain" conclude with two general notes, one on the versions of the tale in other languages, the other on "The Forest of Breceliande and the Fountain of Baranton."[135] The first note is a simple scholarly listing of the other versions of the tale in English, French, German, Swedish, Danish, and Icelandic. The versions are presented in chronological order, with no argument made for the primacy of one over another. The note on Breceliande, in contrast, is an explosion of narrative, speculation, text, and landscape, beginning with the story of Merlin and Viviane, taken from Southey, then providing two Old French lays on the wonders of the Fountain and the marvels of Breceliande before concluding with a contemporary description of the forest by Villemarque, published in the *Revue de Paris* in 1837. Lady Charlotte's final comment is that

> All the old traditions which give an interest to the Forest continue to be current there. The Fairies, who are kind to children, are still reported to be seen in their white apparel upon the banks of the Fountain . . .
>
> The Fountain of Baranton is supplied by a mineral spring, and it bubbles up on a piece of iron or copper being thrown into it.
>
> "Les enfans s'amusent a y jeter des epingles, et disent par commun proverbe: '*Ris donc, fountaine de Beredon, et je te donnerai une epingle.*'"[136]

With its combination of multiple texts and speculative fantasy, the entire footnote enacts the conflict between the allegorical and the antiquarian ideal of facts, sparingly diluted by theory. It is thus fitting that the conclusion of the note is not only a citation, but a citation in a foreign language of a proverb. Such a gesture combines, at least for one tenuous moment, the act of collecting, or citation, with allegorizing or translating. Given Benjamin's argument about the evanescence of such a moment, it is perhaps inevitable that such an accomplishment can only refer to the fairy world.

3

Dangerous but
Domesticated Passions

DESPITE THE FACT THAT HER SECOND MARRIAGE LASTED NEARLY TEN years longer than her first, Lady Charlotte is best remembered as Lady Charlotte Guest. Similarly, Lady Charlotte Guest, the translator, is better remembered than Lady Charlotte Schreiber, the connoisseur. The biography of Lady Charlotte Guest overshadowing that of Lady Charlotte Schreiber can be readily understood when one considers that all of her biographers have been descendants of her first husband; moreover, she and Charles Schreiber had no children. The primacy of Lady Charlotte the translator over Lady Charlotte the connoisseur is more difficult to explain, especially when one considers the fact that her accomplishments as a connoisseur of English porcelain could easily be claimed to outshine her abilities as a translator or antiquarian. Certainly the opinion of later scholars is far more respectful of Lady Charlotte Schreiber than of Lady Charlotte Guest. In 1953, at almost the same time that Roger Loomis was publishing his guarded appreciation of her as a pioneering Arthurian scholar, "Mr. O. Van Oss addressed fellow members of the English Ceramic Circle with a paper [on the subject of Lady Charlotte] which was 'an act of piety—almost an essay in hagiology—devoted to the memory of the lady who has the best claim to be considered our patron saint.[1]'" A later scholar, Frank Herrmann, in *The English as Collectors*, goes even further, claiming,

> In the second half of the nineteenth century there were three works in particular which threw much light on the history of collecting . . . [*Ancient Marbles in Great Britain* by Adolf Michaelis. *Art Sales* by George Redford] . . . The third important work consisted of extracts

from a diary kept between 1869 and 1885 largely relating to purchases of ceramics and antiques—the unique, two-volume *Journals* of Lady Charlotte Schreiber.[2]

What is most peculiar about even these accolades, however, is the fact that they rarely mention, even in passing, Lady Charlotte's previous accomplishments as a translator. Nor do writers about her translation of the *Mabinogion* mention her later career as a collector. This division is particularly regrettable, since considering both activities together foregrounds their similarity as crucial intersections between a personally constructed signifying system and the prevailing cultural discourse.

The act of collecting dramatizes this intersection far more clearly than translating. Yet, despite the attention that current theorists—most prominent among them Baudrillard—have given to this issue, the critical work on collecting remains spotty, if often suggestive. Indeed, before Frank Herrmann's 1972 publication of *The English as Collectors: A Documentary Chrestomathy* (revised and reissued in 1999 as *The English as Collectors: A Documentary Sourcebook*), most publications on collecting were either "How-To" manuals with provenances, styles, and valuations, or memoirs—often titled "Confessions"—of such figures as William Hazlitt and the notorious art dealer, J. H. Duveen.

There were two notable early exceptions to this rule—each establishing an important intellectual thread in considering collecting. The first of these was a spate of early essays, such as Walter Durost's 1932 dissertation, *Children's Collecting Activity Related to Social Factors*, which arose from Piaget's and Klein's theories of object orientation in child development. These essays established a psychological critical discourse about collecting, which has been continued most recently by Werner Muensterberger, who reads collecting as a neurosis that results from "a not immediately discernible sense memory of deprivation or loss or vulnerability and a subsequent longing for substitution."[3]

The second major critical thread was established by Walter Benjamin's seminal essays: "Unpacking my Library," "Edward Fuchs: Historian and Collector," and "The Collector" section in *The Arcades Project*. Admittedly, no one would ever apply the word "systematic" to Benjamin's work. "Unpacking my Library" is impressionistic; "Fuchs" is sprawling; and no one really knows what final form *The Arcades Project* was destined to take. Yet, together they established perhaps the central theoretical tenet in all discussions of collecting as a form of amassing cultural capital: the unique ability of the encounter between the individual and the material object to problematize and even override systems of cultural signification.

Benjamin sees this encounter in near-mystical terms, comparing it to the "*topos hyperouranios*—that place beyond the heavens which, for Plato, shelters the unchangeable archetypes of things."[4] Yet, it would be a mistake to read Benjamin's argument in purely idealistic terms. Indeed, in "Fuchs," Benjamin argues that the act of collecting surmounts the limitations of idealism because "The historical object removed from pure facticity does not need any 'appreciation.' It does not offer vague analogies to actuality but constitutes itself as an object in the precise dialectical problem which actuality itself is obliged to solve."[5] In other words, the object's power derives from the fact it is divorced from a system of abstract significance. Instead, a collection of such objects provides an axis of selection for a fresh system of signification that allows the collector to reinscribe history into the present, for

> the world is present, and indeed ordered, in each of [the collector's] objects. Ordered, however, according to a surprising and, for the profane understanding, incomprehensible connection. The connection stands to the customary ordering and schematization of things something as their arrangement in the dictionary stands to a natural arrangement.[6]

Recent theorists have focused on this reading of collections as signifying systems, while avoiding the more mystical parts of Benjamin's discussion. For example, in *Museums, Objects and Collections,* Susan Pearce begins with the premise that "Objects . . . alone have the power, in some sense to carry the past into the present by virtue of their 'real' relationship to past events . . . This 'reality' is fundamental to the impulses which we know as the collecting process."[7] Using the example of the sword carried by Macdonald of Keppoch at the Battle of Culloden, currently on display in the National Museum of Scotland, she describes the underlying relationship that makes this possible in structuralist terms. The sword's power stems from the fact that it is simultaneously *langue* and *parole*, functioning in metonymic relationship with the past and metaphoric relationship with the present simultaneously. The sword's status as artifact is metonymic; moreover, it is contingent: Any other artifact might have happened to survive, but in fact this artifact survived because, after Keppoch died in battle, "His son, Angus Ban, took his father's sword and dirk and hid them in marshy ground, from which they were afterwards retrieved, and after passing through a number of hands, they finally came into the possession of the National Museums of Scotland."[8] On display in the museum, however, the sword is transformed into a metaphor for the Battle of Culloden—a metaphor whose meaning, Pearce points out, has changed from "a symbol of barbarity rightly defeated by English enlightenment" into a symbol of romantic nobility after the novels of Scott changed public perception of the Jacobite rebellion.[9] Following a loose interpretation of Saussure and Barthes, Pearce argues that Angus Ban's hiding the sword was a *parole*, "the actual action, spoken sentence or performed deed by means of which each society creates itself."[10] Yet as a symbol of Culloden, and with it, the Jacobite rebellion, the sword enters the *langue* of the present. Such a dual existence allows the possibility of infinitely resituated meaning, for, as Pearce argues, "Past *parole* continuously becomes a part of contemporary *langue*, which is continuously restructured to issue as contemporary *parole* in a never-ending spiral."[11]

This crucial interplay between metaphor and metonymy also underlies the act of collecting itself, for any object, once selected by a collector, bears both a metaphoric and metonymic relationship to the class of objects it represents as a whole. As Pearce argues,

> By being chosen away and lifted out of the embedding metonymic matrix, the selected collection now bears a representative or metaphorical relationship to its whole. It becomes an image of what the whole is believed to be, and although it remains an intrinsic part of the whole, it is no longer merely a detached fragment because it has become imbued with meaning of its own.[12]

Accepting the Kleinian premise that object relations are primarily an attempt to define oneself, Pearce goes on to argue that the collector's selection process, or the organizing metaphor by which she structures her collection, is critical to how the collector uses the collection to structure her own sense of self. Pearce distinguishes three kinds of organizing metaphors for collections. The first is collecting souvenirs, which she defines as "objects that take their collection unity only from their association with either a single person and his or her life history, or a group of people . . . who function in this regard as if they were a single person."[13] Organizing a collection in terms of souvenirs has the dual function of preserving one's past as a recallable myth, and, in the case of war mementos, for example, making public events private and therefore emotionally and intellectually manageable.[14] In either case, the purpose of the souvenir is to reinforce the idea of the romantic self as the ultimate arbiter of experience, for "Souvenirs are intensely romantic in every way, and especially in the ways in which that idea is now often applied. The romantic view holds that everything, and especially everybody, has a place in the true organic wholeness which embraces human relationships, in the traditional continuity of past into present."[15] Thus, the final purpose of souvenirs is to construct "a romantically integrated personal self, in which the objects are subordinated into a secondary role."[16]

Fetishistic collecting, which is the second organizing metaphor that Pearce describes, is the opposite of collecting souvenirs. The term "fetishistic" derives from Freud's definition of a sexual orientation in which a single body part, divorced from the whole, becomes the focus of sexual gratification.[17] However, Pearce's use of the term focuses on the aspect of separation of the object from the social whole it derives from, rather than on sexual gratification, in much the same way that Terry Eagleton (1983) and Daniel Miller (1987) use the term. Fetishistic collectors simply collect in order to possess things, and "[fetishistic collections] are detached from any context, they are removed from the sphere of actual social relationships with all the tensions, efforts of understanding and acts of persuasion which these imply. This detachment is, indeed, a very substantial part of the attraction for their collectors."[18]

Thus, although "the whole process [of fetishistic collection] is a deployment of the possessive self, a strategy of desire,"[19] its overall effect is to privilege the objects collected rather than the person of the collector. As such, fetishistic collections and collectors "are at the opposite pole to the souvenirs discussed earlier. Here, the subject is subordinated to the objects, and it is to the objects that the burden of creating a romantic wholeness is transferred."[20]

Systematic collecting, the third category that Pearce describes, is the organizing metaphor that one usually imagines when one thinks of collecting. In a systematic collection, the objects are organized by a governing metaphor or taxonomy. The essential difficulty with any such systematic classification, as long ago argued by Nietzsche, is the natural human tendency to believe that "categories have some kind of objective existence of their own,"[21] rather than to acknowledge that they are constructs either of the observing subject or of society. Instead of seeing this difficulty as an *aporia*, however, Pearce sees this as a strength of systematic collecting that allows it to bridge the gap between the two "frozen and static" poles of fetishistic and souvenir collecting.[22]

Systematic collecting's strength, Pearce argues, derives from the fact it is a form of Hegelian objectification," as it is defined by Daniel Miller in *Material Culture and Mass Consumption.* According to Miller, objectification is "the dual process by means of which a subject externalizes itself in a creative act of differentiation, and in return reappropriates the externalization through an act [of] sublation." As an effect of objectification "the gulf between subject and object is healed and neither is elevated at the other's expense. The essence of the link is relationship; that relationship is always in process."[23]

Jean Baudrillard, by far the most prominent theorist of collecting, expands Miller's claim that collecting erases the distinction between subject and object; however, he calls into question Miller's perception that "neither is elevated at the other's expense." Instead, Baudrillard would argue that collecting transforms the object into an "indefinite chain of signifiers [that] brings about the recapitulation or indefinite substitution of oneself across the moment of death and beyond."[24] This substitution is essentially a violent one that depends on a power relationship between the subject and object, for "the object is *a priori* lacking in cohesion; it is easily destructured by thought." This lack of cohesion means that at any moment an object structure can "lapse indiscriminately into a paradigmatic system with which the subject can rehearse a private repertory of meanings."[25]

In thus problematizing the relationship between subject and object that Miller posits, Baudrillard also interrogates the relationship between public and private systems of signification. It is not a question with definite answers; indeed, Baudrillard can only respond with further questions: "Can objects ever institute themselves as a viable language? Can they ever be fashioned into a discourse oriented otherwise than toward oneself?"[26] His answer, although a provisional one, sharply contradicts Benjamin, for Baudrillard concludes that, although in practice the collector rarely regresses completely inward, objects "are too concrete, too discontinuous . . . to be capable of articulating [themselves] as a real dialectical structure."[27]

Complicating any discussion of these various attempts to charac-terize collecting is the fact that, as Pearce has shown, collectors' mo-tivations vary wildly. Moreover, the nature of collectors have changed over time. Although arguably the Romans were among the most ac-quisitive collectors known on earth, the modern type is most con-ventionally traced back to the *Wunderkammers* of the seventeenth and eighteenth centuries. Perhaps the best introduction to these collec-tors is Patrick Mauries' lavishly illustrated *Cabinets of Curiosities*, in which one can find wax figures, death masks, horrifyingly life-like South Sea natives constructed entirely out of shells, crucifixions carved out of coral, babies' heads pickled entirely along with their lace caps, conjoined twins, mermaids' skeletons, automata, a cherry stone carved with thirty miniature heads, and a bezoar cup that could render poison harmless—all of them fit to turn the stomach of even the most hardened connoisseur of kitsch. Indeed, when con-templating a sculpted figure of Daphne, whose fingers and hair are made of bright red strands of coral in order to represent their meta-morphosis, it is hard to imagine any intellectual impetus behind such grotesqueries.

Yet, the peculiar tension of the Daphne in fact reflects the intel-lectual tension that drove these early collectors to deliberately seek out "liminal objects that lay on the margins of charted territory, brought back from worlds unknown, defying any accepted system of classification."[28] The collector then sought to impose meaning on these liminal objects by inscribing them in a structure of classifica-tions which was created by the physical structure of the *Wunderkam-mers* themselves, which placed the collected objects:

> within a special setting which would instill in them layers of mean-ing. Display panels, cabinets, cases and drawers were a response not only to a desire to preserve, or to conceal from view, but also a paral-lel impulse to slot each item into its place in a vast network of mean-ings and correspondences . . . the cabinet [was] a place in which ob-jects were viewed according to a scale, a perspective or a hierarchy that endowed them with meaning.[29]

This emphasis on analogy or correspondence implied a close re-lationship between collections and magic. According to Mauries,

> Cabinets were perpetually susceptible to the passion for finding analogies, a theme that belongs as much to the realm of magic as to that of aesthetics, and which haunts the history of the cult of curiosi-

ties from its beginnings . . . through the revelation of hidden connections invisible to the uninitiated, and through the discovery of an
essential affinity between objects far removed from each other in geographical origin and in nature, collectors offered their visitors a
glimpse of the secret that lay at the heart of all things: that reality is
all one and that within it everything has its allotted place, answering
to everything else in an unbroken chain.[30]

It is precisely this passion for controlling the hidden correspon-
dences underlying the natural world that explains the collector's fascination with such seemingly execrable objects as the half-coral
Daphne. Hybrid objects, half natural and half artificial, were prized
since cabinets were designed to be places where

> artistic masterpieces and virtuoso examples of technical skill jostled
> with evidence of divine omnipotence (such as marvels of nature,
> relics, and the earthly vestiges of miracles). Together these two
> realms formed one complete world, or microcosm, which was a re-
> flection of the macrocosm and of creation in general . . . The collec-
> tor, meanwhile, played the part of a master-mind bringing these two
> chains of being together.[31]

Mieke Bal sees this desire to organize the relationship between
microcosm and macrocosm, beloved of hermeticists as well as collectors, as the collector's central motivation, arguing that the impulse to collect is inevitable "within a cultural situation that is itself
hybridic: a mixture of capitalism and individualism enmeshed with
alternative modes of historical and psychological existence."[32] Using
Pearce's definition of the fetishistic collector, he interrogates the
intersection between Freud's and Marx's use of the term, coming
to the conclusion that objects mediate both the fetishistic subject's gender identification and his historical identity.[33] In contrast
to Baudrillard's reading the subject as creating and controlling the
collected object, Bal posits that the process of amelioration for the
fetishistic subject "takes place at the intersection of private and public, psychic and historic existence, and the episode contributes to
the shaping of this subject as much as the subject shapes the episode."[34]

This ability of the fetishistically collected object to mediate the
collector's relationship with his historic existence can already be
seen by the end of the seventeenth century, when, according to
Mauries, a collection's "didactic purpose [began to take] prece-

dence over the sense of the marvelous."[35] Hybrids and curiosities were relegated to amazing "the 'most vulnerable' in society: 'women, the very young, the very old, primitive people, and the uneducated masses, a motley group collectively designated as "the vulgar." ' "[36] The hallmark of the vulgar was their incapacity for judgment; conversely, the hallmark of the man of taste was his ability to discriminate, first between "works of art [and] works of science; the next [step] was to draw a distinction within the category of works of art between major and minor works, and between fine and decorative art, the latter being a superior form of craftsmanship."[37] Thus, it was the very ability of the collector to distinguish that in turn distinguished him and defined his place in history.

Parallel with this change was the developing antiquarian perception, discussed in chapter 2 of this study, that collected objects could mediate history itself. Especially with the great nineteenth-century English collectors, this mediation could take the form of outright appropriation, based on the underlying assumption that the inherent taste and nobility of appreciation of the collector gave him an inalienable right to the art treasures of other countries. For example, in "The Remarkable Acquisition of Correggio's Education of Venus," Anna Jameson describes how the Marquess of Londonderry obtained the picture, which, having been owned by a series of collectors with an unfortunate propensity for being deposed, was being offered for sale in Verona by Caroline Buonaparte, the wife of the exiled Murat. Jameson admiringly allows the marquess to narrate how he obtained the pictures by playing the English version of the Ugly Wealthy American:

> as it was not imagined I was an amateur, much less a connoisseur . . . I waited immediately upon Prince Metternich, and I asked him if, in the event of my closing a bargain . . . he would obtain for me, as British plenipotentiary, the same liberty of taking these gems to England that he had accorded to Russia? The prince smiled, and looked *en moqueur*, saying "Mais, oui, mon cher! certainement oui!" [italics *sic*] . . . The moment I obtained the order I went to General M'Donald, and enquired how his negotiation stood. He informed me the Russians stood out against taking the whole for the larger price, and wanted the Correggios alone. I asked him if he would close with me . . . and within twelve hours . . . the pictures . . . were conveyed by him to England almost before the Russians knew they were finally disposed of.[38]

Lady Eastlake's 1854 diary entry records an unsuccessful version
of the same story. Her husband, in his capacity as Keeper of the National Gallery, had gone to Tuscany to offer 1,200 pounds for a
Ghirlandaio in poor condition (his mission being described delightfully by Lady Eastlake as being "in full treaty for some *prizes*").[39]
The Tuscan government however, cited its value as a national treasure and purchased it for a third of the price the English offered,
eventually awarding it to the Uffizi Gallery.[40] Lady Eastlake's outrage
at her husband's defeat unselfconsciously contrasts her husband's
honest, English dealing with Continental perfidy, as she claims "The
laws here, as in Russia, are meant to be evaded; but Englishmen,
and especially ones like my husband, naturally begin by acting according to them, and are punished for their upright dealing by
every kind of annoyance."[41] Rather than acknowledging any right of
the Tuscan government to protect its own treasures, she argues

> The reason for the whole lies in the spite and ignorance of the Di-
> rector of the Academy, a man we hear, without the slightest knowl-
> edge of art, under whose *regime* everything is neglected. He is jealous
> of anyone who knows more than himself. Sir Charles' choice of the
> picture has proved to him that it is one of value; and though, had the
> choice not been made, he would have let it perish with perfect indif-
> ference, yet he now affects a zeal for the preservation of it for the Flo-
> rence gallery, and, as he is a trumpery marquis, all the ministers
> think themselves bound to support him. He has gone the length of
> making all believe, as they are as ignorant as he is himself, that this is
> the only specimen of the master left in Tuscany . . . [although] . . . Sir
> Charles has supplied Lord Normanby with a list of other examples.[42]

Collectors such as Eastlake and the Marquess of Londonderry,
thus, used their collections to reshape history by literally resituating
the artistic accomplishments of Europe within the cultural discourse
of the English gentleman. At the same time, another group of collectors was attempting to rewrite English history itself. These collectors were not aristocrats, but rather members of the rising mercantile class, eager to alter the existing discourse about class in society.
Largely from industrial cities such as Manchester and Birmingham,
these collectors sought art for its utility—in particular its ability to
instill social values in the lower classes.[43] In order that art might accomplish this purpose as effectively as possible, they were great
founders of museums—often with extended visiting hours, so that

the lower classes might spend their free time elevating themselves instead of drinking and carousing. A similar emphasis on self-improvement and social mobility through cultural education motivated Lady Charlotte as well. This motivation is, of course, most obvious in her educating the Welsh workforce. However, her preface to the catalogue of her playing card collection shows she lost none of this motivation when she turned to collecting, for she writes that she has reproduced the cards "so as to bring within reach of students objects that are often rare and costly, and throw light on the manners and customs of former times."[44]

Others, however, were vehemently opposed to such utilitarian notions of art. Jameson, in particular, argues

> In referring to the vast number of first-rate pictures now in England, scattered through many houses and galleries—in distant counties—in remote country seats—in town houses, shut up half the year—I have heard the wish expressed, that these treasures were assembled in one place—in one national gallery, easily and constantly accessible to all. I cannot say I sympathize with the wish; no: not if the object could be effected without wrong to individuals, and with advantage to the pictures themselves, would I wish this . . . God forbid that our country become so *unpoetized*. Of all the utilitarian theories of the *practical* man of this time, this is to me the most distasteful.[45]

Her attitude is certainly tinged with elitism; nonetheless, she was justified in her distaste for the utilitarian motivations of the great mercantile collectors who founded museums. Indeed, their behavior was unpoetical in the extreme. True to their nature as men who had gained their wealth and social position by trading in capital goods, they quite literally commodified their art, often buying and selling their pieces to reap tremendous profits. Furthermore, although most professed themselves shocked at the fact, several of them were not the least above price fixing and market manipulation in the pursuit of those profits.[46]

The most significant ramification of such an unpoetical attitude, however, was that message—especially of a morally improving didactic sort—was prized over aesthetic in these collections. This emphasis led to a preference for genre and literary subjects. More importantly, though, it gave rise to the peculiarly nineteenth-century phenomenon of mass reproduction of fine art. Throughout history, artists often produced two and three copies of their work, but not on the scale that it was done in the nineteenth century. Collectors ordered copies of oil paintings owned by others as casually as one might order a copy of a book—at least until a few collectors realized the market value of exclusivity and insisted on business-like contracts that spelled it out. Furthermore, the same improvements in printing technology that also made mass literacy possible caused reproduction of pictures by engraving to expand rapidly, disseminating fine art into middle-class households—and often leading collectors to select pieces with an eye to how well they would sell as reproductions.[47]

This capacity for mass reproduction gave nineteenth century art collecting unprecedented potential to reify social values into cultural capital. In this context, Jameson's plea for the individual genius of the collector can be read as a discourse of resistance—a resistance that becomes particularly suggestive in light of Bal's claim that, in addition to establishing the collector's position in history, collecting also establishes gender identity. For Jameson's simply assuming the authority of an art critic challenged social norms for her gender. Indeed, how unusual her accomplishment was can be read in Frank Herrmann's admiring claim, "The three women who dominated the nineteenth-century collecting scene because of their remarkable intellectual capacity, their scholarship and their fantastic energy were Lady Eastlake, Mrs. Jameson and Lady Charlotte Schreiber."[48]

In fact, "remarkable" and "fantastic" seem too mild a pair of adjectives to apply to any of these formidable women. Lady Elizabeth Eastlake, *nee* Rigby, was born into a cultured and intellectual Norwich family with ties to the Martineaus, among others.[49] A stay in Heidelberg with her mother gave Elizabeth Rigby both the contacts and fluency in German that allowed her to become "the first woman to review for the Quarterly [and contribute] significantly through her essays on art and translations of German art criticism to the growth of English art historical scholarship."[50] All this occurred before she was taken in to dinner by Sir Charles Eastlake, the future director of the National Gallery, at a party, where the guests also included Turner, Landseer, and Mrs. Jameson. The couple were married in 1849.[51]

After her marriage, Lady Eastlake happily adapted to the conventional role as Sir Charles' helpmeet—both domestically and intellectually. Not only was she a "stimulating and knowledgeable catalyst" to her husband's work, but "there can be little doubt it was she who made possible the annual search for new paintings on the Continent."[52] She learned to use the self-effacement dictated by such conventionality to her own advantage, however. For instance, she used "the conventions of book reviewing anonymity to . . . be . . . thoroughly dismissive of Ruskin's aspirations to be the definitive moralist of modern British painting"[53]—casually unintimidated by the fact that Ruskin was the preeminent critic of the day.

The biography of Anna Jameson followed quite the opposite trajectory. Instead of gradually turning the socially conventional roles of wife and mother to her advantage, she embraced the role of an outsider, beginning with her first novel, *Diary of an Ennuyee* (1825), in which she invents "her own female version of the world-weary Byronic outsider."[54] "A purportedly autobiographical although anonymous account of a love-lorn maiden who dies after wandering around Italy," the novel cost Jameson popularity with readers who were disappointed to find the writer "alive, well, and heart-whole."[55]

Mrs. Jameson (the "Mrs." was largely honorific; the alcoholic Mr. Jameson left her for the Americas, and, on dying, left her penniless) went on to a career as a distinguished art historian, her reputation earned by *Public Galleries* (1842) and *Companion to the Most Celebrated Private Galleries of London* (1844), in the preface of which she launched a scathing attack on the conventional female taste of the day, asking

> What have we now for the grandeur and the grace of the heroic and ideal in art? . . . I do not hesitate to say, that the false, the frivolous taste of women, has had a permanently injurious effect on art and artists, and that their better education in this respect is likely to do much good. There is an immeasurable difference between the mere liking for pretty pictures, the love of novelty and variety, and the feeling and comprehension of the fine arts, their true aim and high significance; still the *capacity* to discriminate as well as to feel is given to many, and I would raise such from love to knowledge.[56]

Jameson's attitude toward other women should scarcely be judged by a single quote. Nonetheless, such an overt attack on her own gender seems to reinforce Nancy K. Miller's distinction between an extraordinary woman and ideal one—as well as suggesting a certain adversarial relationship between the two. Similarly, Henry Layard's description of Lady Charlotte as "an extraordinary woman, and her character a remarkable one—in some ways resembling Mme. de Stael in the union of feminine and masculine qualities,"[57] characterizes his cousin in terms of difference and violation, rather than perfection and ideals.

Arguably, Jameson's apparent hostility to other women is ameliorated by the fact that she was an active feminist, lobbying to have art schools opened to women and being the first to sign a petition to Parliament to allow married women to control their own earnings.[58] Furthermore, she was also more than willing to recognize the extraordinary in other women. Her entry on Joshua Reynolds' portrait of Mrs. Siddons as the tragic muse is a case in point:

> It has been said that when Mrs. Siddons went to sit to Sir Joshua for this picture, the attitude first sketched was different; that as he paused in his work, she turned round to gaze upon a picture which hung opposite, and placed herself in the attitude we see before us; and that Sir Joshua instantly seized the felicitous and characteristic action and look, and fixed them on his canvas . . .
>
> Mrs. Siddons' own account is somewhat different, and no-one who knew her strict habits of accuracy will doubt its literal truth. She says, "When I attended him for the first sitting, after more gratifying encomiums than I can now repeat, he took me by the hand, saying 'Ascend your undisputed throne, and graciously bestow upon me some good idea of the Tragic Muse.' I walked up the steps and instantly seated myself in the attitude in which the Tragic Muse now appears. This idea satisfied him so well, that without one moment's hesitation, he determined not to alter it."[59]

The reversal of power structures in this episode speaks for itself. In the conventional telling of the story, Mrs. Siddons is nothing but the object of the artist's gaze, and the finished portrait is solely the product of Sir Joshua's recognizing and capturing the felicity of the pose. In Mrs. Siddons' retelling, however, she is the one who creates the aesthetic effect, and Sir Joshua's role is simply to capture her vision without alteration. Despite her dismissal of women's taste in general, Mrs. Jameson has no doubt that in this case, Mrs. Siddons' version is the "literal truth."

As Ann Eatwell suggests in her essay, "Private Pleasure, Public Beneficence," Lady Charlotte was forced to negotiate similar boundaries between conventionality and assertiveness in her career as a collector. In fact, the art community may well have marginalized woman collectors more than woman art critics, for Eatwell suggests several contributory factors that are unique to the activity of collecting. First, the figure of the collector was still a suspect one, "not wholly approved of" in polite society. Thus, becoming a collector represented a double unseemliness for a genteel woman, for, not only was it a trespass on masculine territory, but it was also risking identification "as an outsider and an eccentric."[60] Second, collecting, in the nineteenth-century atmosphere that stressed the evangelical "call to seriousness,"[61] still smacked of conspicuous consumption, allowing women to be "condemned for extravagance and slavishly following fashion."[62] Third, women collectors were largely excluded from support structures, such as the Collector's Club (later the Fine Arts Club). Even such a sterling candidate for membership as Mrs. Bury Palliser, the sister of Joseph Marryat, the nineteenth century's foremost expert on porcelain, as well as a significant collector in her own right, met with significant resistance. Mrs. Palliser could have no more shining endorsement than that provided by her brother in his preface to the second edition of his *History of Pottery and Porcelain, Medieval and Modern*:

> In the preparation of this edition, I have had the signal advantage of a coadjutor in my sister, Mrs. Palliser, the author of the translation of M. Laberte's "Handbook of Medieaeval Art," by whose assistance and supervision as Editor I have accomplished the task, which my distant residence from London, and avocations elsewhere, would otherwise have made it impossible for me to have done by my own efforts.[63]

Nonetheless, when it came to her joining the Collector's Club, "a decision was postponed until the following year, when ladies were admitted as honorary members for the season only." Similarly, although both Schreibers were actively involved with the club from 1860 until at least 1867, it was Charles, not Lady Charlotte, who was the member—a fact that did nothing to diminish Lady Charlotte's responsibility as a hostess for the dinner parties the couple gave for club members.[64]

Eatwell claims that women collectors reacted to such marginalization by establishing informal networks among themselves, pointing out that

> From the evidence of Lady Charlotte's journals, the meeting of like-minded ladies to discuss art objects, ask for assistance or exchange or sell ceramic pieces would appear to be a not uncommon occurrence ... By the late 1870s, Lady Charlotte was regarded as something of an expert ... and her journal records the advice she gave to ladies

and the errands she would run for them at home and abroad . . . She may have purchased items on her ladies' behalf; and she took under her wing the more inexperienced, as her relationship with Mrs. Bloomfield Moore demonstrated.[65]

Such networks may well have provided an important support structure for many women, including Lady Charlotte; nonetheless, her relationship with Mrs. Moore demonstrates an ambivalence about the abilities of her own sex that is similar to, if not as scathing as, Jameson's comments about women's taste. Lady Charlotte did certainly assist Mrs. Moore in her purchases and maintained a life-long acquaintance with her. However, a certain underlying condescension for Mrs. Moore, whether because she was an American or because she was an inexperienced collector, is evident even in the first passage that mentions her:

> Met there an American lady, Mrs. Moore, who is staying at our Hotel, and who said she was buying curiosities for a Museum, for which her husband had bequeathed a sum of £2000. She has little knowledge, and I do not think her selection will be a very interesting one.[66]

When Lady Charlotte did help Mrs. Moore with her purchases, the gentle denigration in her voice becomes more obvious, in notes such as "After dinner we went to Mrs. Moore's rooms, where there was an amusing scene with Sarlin, from whom she has made large purchases."[67] Within the month, however, Mrs. Moore was proving somewhat of an annoyance:

> Called on the Bisschops early, to show them some of our recent purchases, etc. Mrs. Moore went with us and engaged them to come to dinner in the evening. She afterwards accompanied us to Dirksen's, which was rather unlucky for us. We had set apart this day for winding up all our purchases at The Hague, and visiting the remaining shops, but the whole morning was consumed with one thing or other. Among these interruptions was a scene between Mrs. Moore and Sarlin.[68]

Mrs. Moore was not the only woman to fall afoul of Lady Charlotte's critical eye. Lady Sykes, who "delighted [Lady Charlotte] with an account of the ceramic and other treasures she had found carefully packed away, in her new home,"[69] was considerably less delightful when she rented the Schreibers' house. Lady Charlotte sounds like many a disgruntled subletter when she complains, "She has greatly altered our arrangements in the rooms etc., to her taste. I cannot say I think she has improved it."[70]

Despite Lady Charlotte's pen often seeming as sharp as her eye, her patronizing attitude toward Mrs. Moore can be largely excused by simply accepting that part of the fun of being an acknowledged connoisseur is being able to disdain others' taste. Furthermore, there are other, better examples of her networking with like-minded women. Her involvement with selling needlework done by Turkish refugees provides a stellar case in point. In 1878, Lady Charlotte and Charles Schreiber made a visit to her daughter Enid, whose husband, Henry Layard, had been appointed ambassador to Constantinople. The situation in Turkey was very unsettled, for

> an Anglo-Turkish Convention was signed . . . [that] provided that if any attempt should be made at any future time by Russia to take possession of any further territories of the Sultan in Asia, England engaged to join the Sultan in defending them by force of arms. In return the Sultan promised to introduce necessary reforms into the Government, and assigned the island of Cyprus to England.[71]

Lady Charlotte's reaction to the country's plight was immediate and articulate—albeit rife with the paternalism of a colonial empire builder: "Poor devoted country, how will its sad history end? The Turks are so much the best of the population, if they could only be decently governed, but Russian intrigue will never leave them alone."[72] Yet, as a woman who could not even vote, she had no way to act on these feelings in the public arena. The private sphere, however, was another matter altogether. Within the year, she had become involved in selling needlework done by Turkish refugees to the English. It was an activity ideally suited to her formidable skills as activist, connoisseur, socialite, and entrepreneur. Her primary market consisted of wealthy women who would use the needlework in decorating their houses, such as "Lady Bolsover [who] wanted pieces for furnishing at Welbeck, for the Prince of Wales' visit next week."[73] Her associates in the venture were other like-minded women, including one Mrs. Hanson, who in 1880 wrote "saying she must give up the Turkish Refugee Work. This was a matter of great regret, both on the account of art and that of humanity . . . Of course I write as strongly as I can to have it continued and put on a permanent footing."[74] Lady Charlotte continued her admirable efforts in selling the needlework until at least 1884, when "A decorator, Mr. Godwin, bought some for Oscar Wilde's house."[75]

Collecting china and presenting it to the nation provided a similar means for Lady Charlotte to inscribe herself into public cultural discourse in a socially appropriate way. Although the collection was presented as a memorial to her husband, Lady Charlotte's diary entries on the subject make it clear that there was also a certain component of self-assertion in the act. In fact, her first entry begins with the words "my desire," reading "My desire has long been that our valuable, I might say unique, collection of English china and enamels should be the property of the nation. I wish to offer it as a tribute to my dear husband's memory." It is not until the next day that she claims "The idea is not a new one with me, indeed years ago, my darling used to say what a pleasure it would be to collect national objects for the benefit of the country."[76]

The point here is not to determine "whose idea" presenting the collection "really" was. Instead, it is to foreground the hybridic nature of Lady Charlotte's desire. The use of Bal's term is deliberate, for Lady Charlotte's self-assertion in assembling and donating the collection can be seen as occupying a liminal space between public and private that is given iconic representation in the twin portraits of Lady Charlotte and Charles Schreiber that hang above the collection today, in a museum named for the quintessentially hybridic marital partnership of a queen who ruled in the public sphere and obeyed in the private sphere. Such hybridic assertion is also similar to the common textual strategy of women couching the essential self-assertion of their autobiography in a biography of another.[77] Or, as Eatwell sums it up neatly,

> It would be wrong to think that Lady Charlotte acted entirely selflessly. She liked to be seen to have done well, if not to have been the best at anything she undertook. The wide scope and the quality of the collection is testimony to that wish and to its fulfillment in her lifetime. It is material evidence of the expertise, knowledge, energy, commitment and stamina of the greatest of the nineteenth-century lady collectors, Lady Charlotte Schreiber.[78]

The balance of such a view stands in sharp contrast to Werner Muensterberger's Freudian "diagnosis" of Lady Charlotte:

> This lonely, defensively rigid girl had turned into an impressively astute woman, energetic, single-minded, and often better informed

than her suppliers. Her resolute stance sounds like an echo of early fights for survival, and the residue of a childhood with two younger, mentally deficient brothers. There had been constant friction, mainly with her alcoholic stepfather . . . I see her mode of action as an attempt to prove her dominance vis à vis her stepfather, and also to enhance her self-esteem. At its simplest, it can be a fleeting impulse, like bringing home a souvenir. At its most committed, it assumes the proportions of a kind of aggression with masculine potential, if not dominance or an all-consuming, sensuous activity surpassing rational ends.[79]

Granted, as a fairly doctrinaire Freudian, Muensterberger sees all collecting as a form of compensation "closely allied with moodiness and depressive leanings."[80] Nonetheless, diagnosing her aggression as having "masculine potential"—as though that were some kind of illness requiring treatment—not to mention allying it with "sensuous activity" that "surpasses rational ends" is beyond sexist. This is not to claim that, in her relationship with other collectors, Lady Charlotte was not aggressive and competitive in the extreme. But, as is clear from the rueful admiration in Duveen's anecdote,[81] far from being perceived as a character flaw, it was a trait prized by her peers.

Despite its offensive sexism, what genuinely limits Muensterberger's argument is his reading Lady Charlotte's impulse to collect in purely private, Freudian terms rather than seeing it, as Bal does, as opening up a crucial nexus between private, Freudian fetishization and public, Marxist fetishization. Benjamin, too, sees this intersection between private and public as important to understanding collecting. In particular, he argues that the collector has a unique ability to resist the repressive influence of tradition, which "puts the past in order, not just chronologically but first of all systematically in that it separates the positive from the negative, the orthodox from the heretical."[82] In this systematization of judgment, tradition stands in stark opposition to

The collector's passion, [which] is not only unsystematic but borders on the chaotic, not so much because it is a passion as because it is not primarily kindled by the quality of the object—something that is classifiable—but is inflamed by its "genuineness," its uniqueness, something that defies any systematic classification.[83]

According to Arendt, Benjamin saw the key to the collector's ability to resist the constraints of tradition in the fact that collecting an object redeemed it from "the drudgery of usefulness."[84] Baudrillard phrases this in slightly different terms, characterizing collecting as divesting an object of its function and making it relative to a subject.[85] Regardless of which characterization one prefers, this divestment of the socially constructed meaning of an object's "use" value allowed collectors such as Lady Charlotte to create an important countering discourse to the one reified in the endless Victorian reproductions of signifying aesthetic objects. Indeed, these collections are nothing less than semiotic systems. However, the location of these semiotic systems between public and private gives their signs a crucial multivalence, making them capable of inscribing contradictory public and private meanings at the same time.

China collecting is a case in point. Maurice Jonas's approving 1907 entry on china collecting makes it clear that china collecting was perceived as an appropriate semiotic system for ladies:

> This is a hobby that ladies should cultivate: the exquisite Chelsea and Dresden figures seem to be made especially for the delicate fingers of women to handle . . . Women, as a rule, have little taste for collecting books, prints or pictures, but it is a fact that they evince quite an attachment to their ordinary china services.[86]

Both Benjamin's and Baudrillard's discussions suggest, however, that women who were collecting domestic objects were, despite the opinions of the approving Jonas, actually mounting an assault, not only on the tradition of collecting, but also on the tradition that the collected objects represented. In liberating domestic objects, such as china, from their usefulness as objects—a usefulness which was closely allied to traditional female roles—women collectors can be seen as liberating themselves from the roles those objects symbolized. Furthermore, in collecting such modest "domestic" objects, women collectors can be seen as liberating the tradition of collecting from its role in inscribing historical values into the larger cultural discourse.

This latter assault on tradition can be quite clearly read in one particular group of objects from Lady Charlotte's collection: figurines that miniaturized the scale of history, literature, and myth into a form that could be contained in a domestic cabinet and handled by even the delicate fingers of refined ladies—creating an unexpected exemplar of Benjamin's delightful characterization of the collector as "motivated by dangerous though domesticated passions."[87] The Bow fig-

Fig. 1. General Wolfe, Schreiber Collection, No. 54.
©V&A Images/Victoria and Albert Museum

ure of General Wolfe (Fig. 1)[88] is a good example of such miniaturization. General Wolfe was a military hero, as was the Marquis of Granby, depicted in a matching statuette. The two figurines were "probably made to commemorate the victories over the French in 1759 at

Quebec and Minden, in which the respective generals were engaged."[89] Copied from contemporary portraits, the generals are por-
trayed with all the expected military accouterments: musket, cannon,
grenades, a sword, and an axe, as well as the sprays of laurel due a vic-
tor. Yet the effect of the two pieces can only be described as effemi-
nate or childlike: both generals have the cupid-bow lips and arched
eyebrows of china dolls.

A similar miniaturization of myth can be seen in the Chelsea figures of Hercules and Omphale[90] and Leda and the Swan.[91] Hercules
and Omphale look to be more shepherd and shepherdess than
hero and nymph, despite the presence of Hercules' identifying
club. Leda is described in the catalogue as "seated on a tree-stump,
slightly draped in a pink mantle, looking down with a gesture of surprise at the swan by her side."[92] One hand may evince surprise, but
the other, rather than attempting to repel the swan—who is gazing
up at her with the decidedly unintimidating adoration of a puppy
begging food—seems to be stroking its back. Any other hint of the
brutal rape that underlies the story was safely miniaturized away
when "[a]n attendant nymph in the original composition [was] replaced by the figure of Cupid."[93]

It is not surprising that Leda was adapted from a painting by
Francois Boucher; Rococo painters were favorite sources for china
figurines. Indeed, the shelves of the Schreiber Collection are a riot
of genre scenes between shepherds and shepherdesses with coy titles such as *"Le Noeud de Cravatte,"*[94] *"Pensent-ils au Raisin?*[95] and "The
Music Lesson"[96] (Fig. 2). In addition, grander, tragic narratives are
also miniaturized in porcelain figurines. Lady Charlotte's collection
boasts Derby figures of King Lear[97] and Garrick as Richard III.[98]

Superficially, the narrative emphasis in the Rococo and Shake-
spearean subjects appears very similar to the preference for narrative exhibited by the great bourgeois collectors, who prized genre
scenes and subjects taken from literature for their usefulness in in-
structing the lower classes both morally and culturally. However,
there is in fact an aesthetic distancing in the porcelain figurines that
sharply distinguishes them from genre paintings. Genre pictures derived their instructive value from their relation to reality; their
avowed purpose was to allow viewers to see themselves as they really
were.[99] In contrast, not only are the porcelain genre scenes in fact
copies of works of art, not reality, but they are copies of French
works of art—their difference signaled in their very titles, which are

Fig. 2. The Music Lesson, Schreiber Collection, No. 197.
©V&A Images/Victoria and Albert Museum

in a foreign language. Moreover, the subjects from Shakespeare are portraits of actors playing roles, again emphasizing the artificiality of the figurine, rather than its reality.

This preference for distancing and artificiality may also explain the large number of allegorical figures found in the collection. A fa-

Fig. 3. Allegory of Minerva Crowning Constancy, Schreiber Collection, No. 422.
©V&A Images/Victoria and Albert Museum

vorite subject is the four seasons; however, the four elements also make their appearance,[100] as well as the four (!) continents.[101] A pair of little girls, presumably from either the Seven Liberal Arts or the Nine Muses, represent Painting and Astronomy.[102] In the most extended allegory, a Minerva crowns Constancy, while on the obverse of the piece, Hercules kills the Hydra (Fig. 3).[103]

The miniaturization of these allegories is even more obvious than that of the literary and mythological subjects. Minerva is only distinguishable from a *putto* by her toy helmet and shield (complete with a miniature Gorgon's head), and Hercules is represented as a child as well. Even allowing for the vagaries of taste over time, the

Fig. 4. Lord Chatham, Schreiber Collection, No. 306.
©V&A Images/Victoria and Albert Museum

overall effect of such abrupt inconsistencies of scale is to make the figurine a sort of grotesque—perhaps none more so than the statuette of Lord Chatham casually bestowing his colonial blessing on an alligator and a Sambo-esque figure intended to represent a Native American woman (Fig. 4).[104]

Fig. 5. Derby Vase, Schreiber Collection, No. 372.
©V&A Images/Victoria and Albert Museum

In addition to these disconcertingly miniaturized allegories, Lady
Charlotte's collection includes several actual grotesques, including a
pair of dwarves,[105] exhibited in the same case as

Three figures of monkeys, copied from Meissen figures belonging to a set known as the "*Affenkapelle*" . . . Two are dressed as men, and one as a woman in costume of the period. Both the former are standing: one wearing a cocked hat, a yellow short-sleeved tunic, and purple breeches, is playing a pipe and a side drum; the other, clothed in a green and purple cap, loose white shirt, and purple breeches, carries two draped kettle-drums slung on his shoulders. The female wears a lace cap tied with ribbons and a flowered Watteau dress over a yellow bodice and skirt; she is seated in a folding chair, singing from a music-book open on her knees.[106]

Yet a third class of grotesques in Lady Charlotte's collection derive their grotesquerie from hybridization, rather than from scale or content. In this they are most closely related to objects such as the coral Daphne from earlier collectors' *Wunderkammers*. Just as those objects bridged the gap between the natural and the created, many of the porcelain hybrids bridge the gap between decorative and functional. A painted mug or plate is clearly a functional object, while a figurine is purely decorative. However, objects such as the Derby vase (Fig. 5)[107] are impossible to categorize as functional or decorative at first—or even second—glance. Certainly, the vase's basic form seems functional, but the decoration has taken over the piece, so that the form of the vase is obscured beneath:

three white caryatid figures ending downwards in lions' paws, which rest on a moulded circular pedestal painted with trophies of arms *en grisaille*. Wreaths of flowers painted in colours are festooned round the body and across the figures. The high domed covers are decorated with gilt pierced rococo scrolls and surmounted by a bouquet of flowers.[108]

Other hybrids disguise their function by masquerading as another object. A box and cover,[109] for example, are designed and colored to be so close to nature that they were described in the Chelsea sale catalogue as "Four fine APPLES for desart [*sic*]."[110] In the same case stands, according to another sale catalogue, "A very fine tureen, in the form of a RABBIT BIG AS LIFE" (Fig. 6).[111]

The grotesque was an important concept for Benjamin, who saw it as "the highest escalation of what is sensually imaginable . . . an expression of the teeming health of a time."[112] Needless to say, Benjamin's claim creates a central difficulty for anyone attempting to

Fig. 6. Rabbit-Shaped Tureen, Schreiber Collection, No. 151.
©V&A Images/Victoria and Albert Museum

discuss the Schreiber collection. For, although it does not take much of a feminist leap to see Lady Charlotte and her fellow collectors as possessing the "dangerous but domesticated passions" of Benjamin's collector, it seems a stretch, to say the least, to see them as exemplars of the teeming sensual health of the High Victorians.

Benjamin's argument, however, can be reconciled with a discussion of Lady Charlotte when one considers that the grotesque is a liminal object. Therefore, the grotesque can be said to give concrete form to the crucially ill-defined space that Bal terms hybrid. When this concrete form is also an allegorical figure, interpretation itself is called into question. For an allegory is a form that depends on distinction—specifically between tenor and vehicle, real and idea. A grotesque allegory is thus a contradiction in terms, a concrete denial of the very notion of being able to abstract metaphorical meaning from discourse.

Daniel Miller sees a similar resistance to interpretation as inherent in the nature of objects themselves. In a theory that resembles Chomsky's generative grammar, Miller claims that individuals in society both read and write objects, construing their "social appropriateness" and using them to generate new forms.[113] What is important about the process Miller describes is the flexibility of meanings that can pertain to objects. This flexibility is not obvious, for humans are biased toward seeing the meaning of objects as inherently more absolute than that of linguistic systems—in Miller's felicitous phrasing "an implied innocence of facticity."[114] In fact, quite the opposite is true and "[t]he artefact's affinity to the unconscious also allows it to play an important role in marking different forms of social reality, and allowing these and the perspectives arising from different social positions to exist concurrently without coming into overt conflict."[115]

Dianne Macleod advances a similar argument about the ambivalent signification of even the genre pictures beloved of the Victorians, claiming that the conventional idea that a picture's iconography is a "communicable code" or "neutral marker" from which an informed viewer can read the absolute "truth" of the artist's meaning is an oversimplification. Indeed, she claims many Victorian genre pictures that seem to reinforce social authority simultaneously offer a subtle critique of the authority they seem to be reinforcing. For example, William Witherington's *The Hop Garden* seems to be an idyllic genre picture of children enjoying themselves in the country. However, the children are in fact migrant laborers imported from London, and the play captured on the canvas is only a moment's respite from their customary hard work. [116] Interestingly, Macleod claims that the collectors themselves sometimes offered similar critiques of authority when they were discussing their paintings. She cites the example of John Sheepshanks telling ribald stories as he showed his collection to the prime minister, Lord Palmerston—characterizing those stories as Bakhtinian "slurs directed at the governing social and cultural order—the buffoon-king, the addlepated queen, and the defective lover."[117]

A subtler, and arguably more directly relevant, social critique can be found in the writing of the great connoisseur of porcelain, Joseph Marryat. The primary purpose of his magisterial *History of Pottery and Porcelain* was to be "useful to the collector in enabling him to ascertain the nature of the specimens he possesses, and what are considered the most desirable in forming a collection,"[118] an intention that certainly seems to reinforce conventional systems of authority and value. However, Marryat's secondary purpose, to substantiate his claim that "The Plastic or Ceramic Art is deserving of our attention, as being one of those first cultivated by every nation of the world. Its productions, though in modern times restricted to domestic use, were employed by the ancients for higher and nobler purposes,"[119] introduces the same contrast between ancient and modern society that was central to much nineteenth-century social resistance. Although such nostalgia may at first glance seem to be a conservative, rather than liberal, discourse, Debra Mancoff, among others, has pointed out how such looking backward to the "higher and nobler" lives of the ancients—in particular King Arthur and other medieval heroes—was an important countering discourse to capitalism and materialism.[120]

In order to illustrate these higher and nobler lives, Marryat spices his catalogue with anecdotes—often, although not exclusively, in footnotes. For example, he bolsters the rather straightforward point that Majolica is supposed to have been introduced into Italy while it was at war with the Muslims in the twelfth century by adding

> It is related by Sismondi, that the zeal of the Pisans against the Infidels urged them to undertake the deliverance of the Tyrrhene Sea from the Mussulman corsairs. A king of Majorca, named Nazaredeck, by his atrocious acts of piracy spread terror along the coasts of France and Italy. It was computed that 20,000 Christians were confined in his dungeons. In the year 1113 the citizens of Pisa were exhorted, on the festival of Easter, by their archbishop, in the name of the God of the Christians, to undertake the deliverance of their brethren who were groaning in the prisons of the Infidels . . . Religious enthusiasm was soon kindled in the minds of all present, and every man capable of bearing arms took up the cross . . .[121]

As in Lady Charlotte's *Mabinogion*, Marryat's footnotes are often more fun than the text itself, as they range from the history of Jacqueline, the Countess of Hainault, to the informative definition:

> Pax—an ecclesiastical instrument of ancient use in the Roman Catholic Church, which the priest kissed first, then the clerk, and lastly the people who assisted at the service, one after another . . . The term is derived from the divine salutation "Pax vobiscum." The

custom of kissing it was in compliance with the apostolic injunction of "Salute one another with a holy kiss," which, in the early ages of the Church, was literally practiced, but was discontinued in after times.[122]

Lady Charlotte provided few such narrative glimpses in her china catalogues—an interesting contrast to her copious notes on the *Mabinogion*. Arguably, this can be attributed to her advanced age and failing eyesight, as well as to the fact that those catalogues were edited and revised by a professional curator. However, there are traces of the old Lady Charlotte's eye for the telling detail in the catalogues of her other collections. For example, in her catalogue of fans and fan leaves, she concludes her citation of a 1733 advertisement of fan no. 7 with the brisk comment, "The advertiser proceeds with some uncomplimentary remarks about rivals in his trade, which are hardly worth transcribing."[123] She also takes particular pains with no. 142, the "New Opera Fan for 1797," a wonderful artifact that provides a seating chart of the opera house, presumably so operagoers could identify one another while they were watching the performance. Not only does Lady Charlotte provide a complete two-page list of the seat holders on the fan, but she also carefully cross-references the entry with no. 143, Miss Lewis' Fan, pointing out that "At the top of the obverse is the representation of an opera ticket on which is written Mifs Lewis Pit Box No. 20, which corresponds with the inscription in the plan of the Opera House 1797."[124] Moreover, Lady Charlotte's preface to the catalogue of her playing cards makes it clear that she perceives this same ability to "throw light on the manners and customs of former times" to be the primary significance of her collection. Such "little records of the past," she claims, "Like the engraved fans of which I published two volumes, . . . illustrate the changes of fashion, and the fleeting sentiments of the period at which they were published."[125]

It is tempting to extract from that last comment a Benjaminian argument that the object provides a locus for the collector's dialectical encounter with the past. However, terms like "records," "published," and "throw light," imply a systematization that would be anathema to Benjamin. Nonetheless, to a nineteenth-century woman collector of domestic objects, such systematization might create a significant, but very different, dialectic. For, as has already been suggested, domestic objects reinforce nineteenth-century societal expectations about women both metaphorically and metonymically.

China, for example, metaphorically reinforces a woman's presumed daintiness, delicacy, and fragility, while metonymically, it is associated with an affection for feeding or nurturing one's family.[126] Yet, even as the objects in such a collection appear to be reinforcing the female collector's conventional femininity, the collector herself can use her collection to trespass on the traditionally male intellectual territories of systematization and categorization—all the while decorously disguising her activities as a form of suitably feminine collecting.

In keeping with her admittedly ambitious, competitive nature, Lady Charlotte may be a rarity not so much because she practiced such systematization, but rather because she gave it written form, first in her collector's journals, then, more formally, by preparing her catalogues. Perhaps her most significant gesture, however, was her donating the collection to a museum. Such a donation can be read in Lacanian terms as a final rupture that allowed her to seize control of the paternal symbolic. More importantly, however, it was an act of framing.

The importance of the frame was first noted by Gombrich in *The Sense of Order* (1979). Miller expands Gombrich's argument, claiming

> What is crucial to this argument, if extended a little beyond Gombrich's own assessment, is that the frame's anonymous and modest presence belies its significance for the appreciation of the work of art. It might be suggested that it is only through the presence of the frame that we recognize the work of art for what it is, perceiving it and responding to it in the appropriate way. In short, it is the frame rather than the picture which establishes the mode of appreciation we know as art.[127]

Pearce points out that collecting is a similar act of framing, claiming "The kind of object collected is not important: what matters is the reframing of the object within the collection, as an act of formal admission from one state to another."[128] Moving the collection to a museum, she argues, is a second act of framing, in which the object is "marked" as art. Part of that marking includes the collector's act of self-definition being transformed into a larger sort of societal definition, in which judgment or taste, rather than self, is defined. Borrowing Thompson's categorization of objects into "rubbish," "transients," and "durables," Pearce points out that a museum's importance is directly related to the importance of the role it plays in maintaining this categorization. The purpose of a museum is to house only durable objects. However, since as soon as an object is placed in a museum, it is, by definition, a durable, it is the museum that ultimately determines which objects are placed in which category.[129]

Interestingly, Pearce sees in this final framing a rupture that is very similar to Benjamin's concept of redeeming the object from its usefulness. For Pearce argues that it is the act of removing the object from economic circulation that permanently establishes the object as "art." Specifically, she characterizes the museum as an "other-world" in which objects attain special value precisely because they have been removed from the commodity marketplace.[130]

In fact, however, the result of the rupture described by Pearce is antithetical to that described by Benjamin. Indeed, Benjamin argues quite vehemently that "the phenomenon of collecting loses its meaning as it loses its personal owner. Even though public collections may be less objectionable socially and more useful academically than private collections, the objects get their due only in the latter."[131] In contrast, as is perhaps natural for a professional curator, Pearce sees objects as finally getting their due only when they are reinscribed into the larger cultural discourse.

However it is not only objects that are reinscribed into the larger cultural discourse with the donation of a collection. It is the collector herself—in this case, Lady Charlotte, along, of course, with her husband. Significantly, in reinscribing herself thus, Lady Charlotte also inserts herself in the broader cultural code. The result is a paradoxical one. On the one hand, this reinscription, according to Pearce's logic, fixes her meaning as a "durable," a person of discernment and taste. Yet, codes as well as objects are capable of a singular multivalence. Indeed, in reinserting herself in the broader semiotic code, Lady Charlotte transforms both herself and her collections into signifiers that others can resituate in order to create new public and private meanings. The next chapter will explore exactly how such new meanings were created with the textual collection Lady Charlotte called the *Mabinogion*.

4

Covering the Earth
with Leather

IN ALL THE DISCUSSIONS OF WHETHER OR NOT LADY CHARLOTTE WAS writing for children, one simple fact is consistently omitted: There is a children's version of the *Mabinogion*. Called *The Boy's Mabinogion*, it was edited from Lady Charlotte's translation by the American Sidney Lanier and published in 1881, when Lady Charlotte had long since abandoned her Welsh interests and was busy cataloguing her collections and selling Turkish embroidery. Although Lanier left about 80 percent of Lady Charlotte's text completely intact, he cut material, rearranged the stories, and provided a new introduction and notes. Such reworking seems to provide somewhat summary evidence that Lady Charlotte was in fact writing for adults. More importantly, however, Lanier's text also provides a significant opportunity to observe how the code Lady Charlotte created in her *Mabinogion* was resituated to both to a very different context, the unreconstructed South in America, and to a very different audience, children. The difference created by this dual resituation is significant: If Lady Charlotte's translation established the *Mabinogion* as cultural capital, Lanier entered that capital into circulation, both in the larger American educational discourse as well as quite literally in the marketplace.

Indeed, the marketplace was the destination Lanier unabashedly intended for his *Boy's Mabinogion*. A perennially impoverished poet and musician, Lanier made no pretense that *The Boy's Mabinogion* and its companion pieces in his *Boy's Library of Legend and Chivalry* were anything but "pot-boilers" whose purpose was to put bread on table.[1] They were also the closest thing he had to publishing success in the course of his brief, romantic life.

Gently raised in an idyllic and idealized childhood in Macon, Georgia, Lanier was prevented from fulfilling his plan to go to Heidelberg to study philosophy and literature by the outbreak of the Civil War. He served bravely—even dashingly—in the signal corps during the war. As was the case with many, the first half of his army career seemed largely to consist of playing the flute—at which he excelled—and courting ladies in Norfolk, where he was posted. Eventually, he became a blockade runner—as was Rhett Butler. However, in a gesture one cannot imagine his fictional counterpart making, when Lanier was captured running a blockade, he refused to don a British uniform and claim immunity as a British citizen—as was the custom among Southern soldiers. Instead, he was taken to a federal prison camp in 1864, where he contracted the tuberculosis that would end his life at thirty-nine.

The story of his delivery from captivity is as romantic as that of his capture: As Lanier was being transported in the hold of a ship with other prisoners, a female acquaintance, traveling in first class, heard a man playing the flute. When she asked him to play, the man said his playing was nothing compared to one of the prisoners being held below. When the woman was taken down to meet this other flautist, she recognized Lanier, who was insensate and near death. He was removed to a first-class cabin to recover, and when the other prisoners finally heard him playing his flute, they all cheered. Upon the intercession of the woman friend, Lanier regained his freedom in a prisoner exchange.[2]

It was a happier tale than many; nonetheless, Lanier regained his freedom only to live the rest of his life dogged by poverty and ill-health. Indeed, Aubrey Starke, Lanier's chief biographer, has characterized Lanier as embodying the Reconstruction of the South in the failed reconstruction of his own fortunes.[3] However, another metaphor seems to characterize Lanier's life equally well: The delicate Southern youth who longed to breathe the rarefied air of German idealism at Heidelberg instead found himself thrust rudely into the most material of worlds, where money and the demands of his body became the dominant forces that governed his intellect.

Such tension between idealism and materialism is also of central importance in considering the ideal of chivalry underlying *The Boy's Mabinogion*. Like many Southerners, Lanier associated an imagined chivalric past with the antebellum way of life destroyed by the Civil War. This association was strengthened in Lanier's case by the fact that chivalry was a large part of his childhood. As there were no public schools in Macon, Lanier spent his childhood in a tight knit relationship with his siblings that Starke described as not "in the strictest sense of the word, wholesome."[4] Lanier's relationship with these siblings was elaborately courtly, modeled on the manly friendship among knights in the case of his brother, Clifford, and courtly devotion to women in the case of his sister, Gertrude.[5] Lanier also reinforced these chivalric relations with his siblings by organizing bands of his childhood friends into Arthurian clubs where they paraded with wooden weapons and homemade armor.

Lanier's childhood behavior was not as unusual as it might seem today; long before the war, Southerners had developed an obsession with Walter Scott and things medieval, which led them to build faux castles and to stage tournaments. However, in the wake of the war, this obsession turned into something far less savory: the "White Knights" of the Ku Klux Klan, who justified their unconscionable activities in the name of "Chivalry, Humanity, Mercy, and Patriotism."[6] Although some of Lanier's dialect poems do give expression to the frustrated anger of the white Southerner during Reconstruction, there is no evidence Lanier so much as sympathized with either the aims or the activities of the Ku Klux Klan. In fact, he spent a great deal of his adult life in such northern cities as Baltimore and New York. Nonetheless, this coding of chivalry as a countering discourse to perceived Northern aggression was characteristic of many, more reactionary Southerners during Reconstruction, as well as afterward.

At the same time, however, chivalry and King Arthur were developing into important elements in the discourse that justified and reinforced the American capitalist culture that Southerners saw as eradicating their way of life. Alan Lupack, among others, has commented on how unexpected the popularity of a king as a cultural symbol is in a democratic society. However, in nineteenth-century America, King Arthur was quickly converted from an aristocratic ideal into a moral exemplar of muscular capitalism. By stressing the virtues of self-reliance and accomplishment in King Arthur's knights, Americans turned the chivalric tales of the Round Table into parables of individual accomplishment and social advancement, whose heroes were divinely chosen for their inherent personal qualities rather than their rank—a knighthood of the spirit, so to speak, rather than of birth.[7] This moral and moralizing use of King Arthur culminated in formal children's chivalric societies that greatly resembled the informal society that Lanier created for himself. Most notable among these societies was the boys' club known as the Knights of King Arthur, established by William Byron Forbush in 1893 to promote "chivalry, courtesy, deference to womanhood, recognition of the *noblesse oblige,* and Christian daring." Faintly absurd to our modern sensibilities, these clubs, who called their adult advisors "Merlins" and rewarded chivalric behavior by allowing boys to sit in the "Siege Perilous," were claimed by Forbush to be the largest fraternal organization for boys in the world. In addition, they were in a large part the model for the Boy Scouts.[8]

Lanier's *Boy's Mabinogion* resituates Lady Charlotte's text within both of these new discourses about King Arthur. The book's position within the second of these discourses is evident from the very title page of the work, which commodifies the text by providing an explicit system of judgment with which to approach it. The result is that the cultural value of the piece is no longer dependent upon an external context that guides the reader. Instead, the system is inscribed in the text itself—in a form of take-out cultural discourse, if you will.

This inscription of interpretation can easily be read by comparing the two title pages of the books:

The Mabinogion
From the *Llyfr Coch o Hergest,* and other ancient Welsh manuscripts, with an English translation and notes, by Lady Charlotte E. Guest.

Knightly Legends of Wales, or *The Boy's Mabinogion*
Being the earliest Welsh Tales of King Arthur in the famous
Red Book of Hergest
Edited for boys with an introduction by Sidney Lanier
Editor of "The Boy's Froissart" and "The Boy's King Arthur."

Lady Charlotte's title is so deceptively simple one might overlook the fact that it reifies a group of disparate texts into a work known as *The Mabinogion*. With equally deceptive simplicity, the title also establishes an external system of value by inscribing Lady Charlotte's rank. However, the title offers few other keys to interpretation. Without an external source such as a working knowledge of Welsh, or at least a Welsh dictionary, it is impossible to interpret even the title itself.

Lanier's title, in contrast, is a miniature course in how to interpret both the title and the text. The title itself identifies what a *Mabinogion* is: a knightly legend from Wales. This identification also directs the reader's interpretation: the stories of the *Mabinogion* are meant to be read as knightly legends. This is not a trivial imposition of interpretation; indeed, many of the tales, including all four branches of the Mabinogi, seem more naturally suited to be read as myth. Moreover, Lanier's subtitles provide additional guidance. The tales' importance is validated by their relationship to King Arthur and the fact they come from a "famous" book. They are further guaranteed by their superlative nature, being the earliest (Welsh) Arthurian tales. In addition, the text has been "Edited for boys"[9]—a phrase that guarantees systems of judgment based on both gender and age. The overall result of establishing these systems of judgment within the text itself is that its cultural value is self-contained. Therefore, the reader (or his parents) is able to purchase cultural capital by purchasing the book, just as he would any other commodity, rather than deriving his cultural capital from social sources, such as formal education.

This commodification of the cultural value of the text in turn leads to the commodification of its editor as a final guarantee of quality. The message is clear. If you want guidance in amassing cultural capital, purchase Sidney Lanier.[10] Reciprocally, the commodification of the text's cultural value is reinforced by the book's status as part of a larger collection edited by Lanier. Illustrated by Alfred Fredericks, *The Boy's Mabinogion* was third in a series that began with *The Boy's Froissart* and continued with *The Boy's King Arthur,*[11] both illustrated by Alfred Kappes. *The Boy's Percy* was published in 1882, after Lanier's untimely death in 1881. Among his papers were unfinished plans for at least two more books, *The Boy's Gesta Romanorum* and *The Boy's Monstrelet.*[12] The term "Boy's Library," used to describe the entire collection, reinforces the books' status as chattel or movable personal goods and implies that purchasing them would allow parents to "furnish" their children with literacy.[13]

Because Lanier was quite literally dying when he was working on the *Mabinogion*, it is impossible to tell to what degree he intended to incorporate corresponding systems of judgment into the rest of the text as well. In the published version, Lanier's changes to Lady Charlotte's text are fairly straightforward. He cuts scenes that he considers indelicate for young readers—references to sex, largely,

and, perhaps less obviously, references to pregnancy.[14] More telling-
ly, however, he substantially alters the focus of at least two stories by
changing their names from "Math the Son of Mathonwy" and "Manawyddan the Son of Llyr" to "The Origin of the Owl" and "Manawydden and the Mouse," respectively. These new titles provide an
additional system of value to guide the reader's interpretation, suggesting that the stories be read as fairy tales rather than as the epics
suggested by the patronymic titles.

"The Origin of the Owl" is also the story Lanier bowdlerizes the
most, beginning as it does with a king who can only rule with his
feet in the lap of a virgin, the subsequent rape of that virgin, and
the failure of her proposed successor, Arianrod, to prove she has
the main qualification for the position. Most critics attempt to explain this admittedly confusing section as either the remnants of a
tale of a druidic *geis* or a version of the impotence of the Fisher King.
Lanier doesn't bother with any explanations; he simply gives up and
excises the first seven pages of the story, beginning it instead with
Math discovering Dylan—the son to whom Arianrod gave birth instead of proving her virginity—miraculously in a closet at the foot of
his bed.

What is much more congenial about the story to Lanier is "the
dainty composition of the maiden Blodeuwedd, who was constructed
by magic out of certain flowers in order to be a bride for Gwyddion."[15] In fact, so congenial is Blodeuwedd's dainty composition
that Lanier excises her frank sexual betrayal of her husband, replacing it with the simple parenthetical summary, "Now Blodeuwedd, in
spite of her descent from the flowers, was at heart a wicked woman,
and so she began to plot with Gronw Pebyr how they might slay the
valiant Llew Llaw Gyffes, and enjoy his possessions."[16] This excision
is much more than simple evidence of Lanier's prudishness, however. It also inscribes two important idealizing discourses in his treatment of chivalry that run consistently counter to the commodification of the books themselves.

The first of these discourses is his nearly obsessive idealization of
women, which Lanier himself summarized in a speech on women's
suffrage:

> As voters we could not love you, for you would be no whit different
> from men, and men do not love men. As lawyers, as ministers, as
> physicians, we can not possibly love you; we ourselves are all these,
> and we want something *beside* ourselves; we want two in one, and not

one in two. . . . The question is simple: will you rule our votes, or rule our voters? At the ballot-box, you can control the votes; at home, you can control the voters.[17]

Obviously, much of this discourse derives from medieval notions of courtly love. However, Lanier's view of love was much broader and more heterodox than that. In Starke's words, love was, for Lanier, nothing less than "the organic idea of moral order"[18]—or, as Lanier put it more poetically, "Love is the only rope thrown out by Heaven to us who have fallen overboard into life."[19]

Given his idealization of love and women, it is natural that Lanier would root Blodeuwedd's betrayal in something other than a corruption of either. It is equally natural that the materialistic motivation he ascribes to her is consistent with his hatred of Trade—a word he capitalizes, as though it were a demonic entity. Lanier's reviling of trade is the second idealizing discourse evident in his treatment of chivalry—one that counters the cultural commodification of his children's books much more obviously than his idealization of love. Indeed, trade was a subject that could rouse him to nearly prophetic cadences.

> Trade has now had possession of the civilized world for four hundred years; it controls all things, it interprets the Bible, it guides our national & almost all our individual life with its maxims; & its oppressions upon the moral existence of man have come to be ten thousand times more grievous than the worst tyrannies of the Feudal system ever were. Thus in the reversals of time, it is *now* the *gentleman* who must arise & overthrow Trade. That chivalry which every man has, in some degree, in his heart; which does not depend upon birth but which is a revelation from God of justice, of fair dealings, of scorn of mean advantage . . . it is this which must in these latter days organize its insurrections & burn up every one of the cunning moral castles from which Trade sends out its forays upon the conscience of modern Society.[20]

This opposition of chivalry and mercantilism is much more characteristic of nineteenth-century Arthurian discourse in England than in America. Nonetheless, Lanier's characterization of chivalry is distinctly American in its description of chivalry as an innate, rather than a socially constructed quality. Paradoxically, however, this quintessentially American valorization of the individual calls into question American values, for Lanier places this individual chivalry squarely in the service of overthrowing, not reinforcing, capitalist society.

There is a similar subversiveness in Lanier's aesthetic discourse. At first glance, it seems conventional enough when Lanier calls the reader's attention to the "Oriental luxuriance" of the tales in his introduction to *The Boy's Mabinogion*, offering as an example the picture of King Arthur "reclining upon green rushes, with a cushion of red satin under his elbow, Guenever and her ladies grouped at the other end of the hall, mantles of flame-colored satin, gilded bows, gold-headed arrows winged with peacock feathers, gold-banded garments, shoes of variegated leather . . . and the like."[21] His claim that some of the Welsh tales have an even "greater sense of foreignness, of a wholly different cultus, than even Chinese or other antipodal tales"[22] is another very conventional mapping of the Welsh as Other. In fact, Lanier begins to sound very much like Matthew Arnold when he rearranges the order in which Lady Charlotte placed the stories, pairing "Kilhwch and Olwen" with "The Lady and the Fountain" "in order to bring these two classes into striking contrast, and to show how much a foreign admixture [of the kind seen in "The Lady and the Fountain"] might smooth down the grotesque ruggedness of its Welsh original ["Kilhwch and Olwen"] . . . which is almost hideous in many of its huge fancies and distortions."[23]

Lanier begins to sound much less like Arnold, however, when he attempts to characterize the English regard for Law, which he claims makes their aesthetic superior to the Oriental luxuriance of the Celts:

It would be going far beyond proper bounds to discuss here how this . . . underlying perception of the artistic necessity of law and order has quietly reigned . . . [over] . . . the whole of English development . . . I have thought this consideration particularly forcible at the present moment in our own country, where the making of statutes increases in exact proportion to the decrease in the popular esteem for them. Daily and endlessly our Legislatures multiply laws and murder Law. But—may I not add, if only as one of those utterances which a boy sometimes profitably remembers, though at first dimly understood—the love of Law beyond all laws would seem to be particularly vital in a republic; being a principle so comprehensive, that at one extreme . . . it flowers into that sense of proportion, of the due relation of all parts of the universe to the whole, which is the artist's largest perception of beauty, and is the main outfit of genius in constructing Mabinogion . . . while at the other extreme . . . the same love of Law is at once the root of decorous behavior on the part of the private citizen, and of large statesmanship on the part of the public official.[24]

Arnold, after all, believed the English genius was for rhetoric, not law—language conditioned by its social context, not an abstract concept. Lady Charlotte exhibited a similar belief in the importance of the relationship between the Welsh language and its context when she examined place names as proof of the Welsh tales' antiquity—reading meaning, not just in the social context of the language, but in the landscape itself. In contrast, Lanier's only response to the Welsh language is to offer a detailed pronunciation guide. Granted, part of this difference obviously reflects the difference in his intended audience. However, this pronunciation guide demonstrates the same dual meaning of the word "abstraction" as his characterization of the Law. Both are, obviously, conceptual in nature; however, both can be removed—abstracted—from their context so that they become a form of personal property.

There is a paradoxical progressiveness to this transformation of concepts into personal property. For in turning chivalry, the law, and Welsh pronunciation into attributes than can be acquired, Lanier also makes it possible for his readers to aspire to be like Arthur. This emphasis on evolving toward Arthur, rather devolving from Arthur is another significant difference between Lanier's discourse about the *Mabinogion* and Lady Charlotte's. They agree that stories like "Kilhwch and Olwen" are older; however, Lady Charlotte refers to them as "purer" while Lanier refers to them as "ruder." Lady Charlotte sees civilization in terms of "ornament" whose addition "corrupts" a pure text. Lanier sees civilization as an application of law that refines wilder flights of fancy. The differences are telling. Lanier's point of view is progressive and idealizing, Lady Charlotte's, retrospective and historicizing. The overall result is to change King Arthur into a goal that can be achieved, rather than a symbol of a lost past.

This contrast between retrospection and progressiveness is supremely evident in the changes Lanier makes to "The Dream of Rhonabwy." They are not large changes and they are logical ones when dealing with young readers. Nonetheless, they significantly affect how one reads the story. In the original version of the story, several legendary Welsh kings make brief appearances along with Arthur. Lanier cuts these passages, as well as a long, later list of knights, leaving only the appearance of Adaon, the son of the legendary bard Taliesin. The result is to abstract the figure of Arthur from the context of Welsh history and instead situate him in the realm of art.

Even more significantly, Lanier cuts Arthur's reaction on seeing Rhonabwy and his companions:

> "And where, Iddawc, didst thou find these little men?"
> "I found them, lord, up yonder on the road."
> Then the Emperor smiled.
> "Lord," said Iddawc, "wherefore dost thou laugh?"
> "Iddawc," replied Arthur, "I laugh not; but it pitieth me that men of such stature as these should have this island in their keeping, after the men that guarded it of yore."[25]

The antiprogressive resonance of Arthur's dismay at the stature of the men who now run England needs no explication. Interestingly, Lanier also cuts the passage that immediately follows, in which Iddawc shows Rhonabwy the stone in Arthur's ring and tells him the stone is the only reason he will remember what happened to him. Lanier does not, however, cut the mention of the stone in the tale's envoi:

> And this tale is called the Dream of Rhonabwy. And this is the reason that no one knows the dream without a book, neither bard nor gifted seer, because of the various colors that were upon the horses, and the many wondrous colors of the arms and the panoply, and of the precious scarfs, and of the virtue-bearing stones.[26]

Elsewhere in the text, Lanier proves himself supremely unconcerned by the inconsistencies created by his cuts. Nonetheless, leaving the final mention of the "virtue-bearing stones" while cutting the first one does substantially alter the relationship between the reader and the text. Like the Law, like Welsh pronunciation, the stones have been abstracted from their context. Now that they are no longer explicitly associated with either Rhonabwy or Arthur, their only function can be to offer the reader unmediated access to the story. Their being abstracted from their context also reverses the relationship between the book and the bard or seer. If we know the stone is the key to the vision, the book is a devolved repository of knowledge, a substitute because bards and seers no longer have access to the stone. Without knowing the stone is the key to the vision, the passage simply seems to claim that the bard or seer is helpless without books.

The effect of this second interpretation is to demystify learning in much the same way that Lanier's offering his reader a system of judgment on the title page does. Rather than being something that can only be transmitted by the initiated, knowledge is available to anyone who is able to acquire it. It is a notion of learning that Lanier reiterates when he urges his readers to commit to memory excerpts from the Welsh Triads, claiming,

> It would be difficult to find more wisdom in fewer words, or loftier thought in simpler terms; and any young reader of *The Mabinogion* will have done a good day's work if he will commit these words so thoroughly that they will say themselves over to him, day by day, as a noble and fruitful formula, alike stimulating in every line of life, from the ploughman's to the president's.[27]

That the book's role in this process is simply as a means of conveying knowledge is made clear in Lanier's footnote to the tale of Taliesin—by far the longest footnote in the work. After quoting Lady Charlotte's biography of Taliesin, Lanier adds,

> Hereby hangs a little Welsh story, which has always seemed to me of great significance. A certain Einigan Gawr saw three rays of light, on which were inscribed all knowledge and science. And he took three rods of mountain-ash, and inscribed all the sciences upon them, as it should seem in imitation of the three rays of light. And those who saw them deified the rods, which so grieved Einigan, that he broke the rods, and died.[28]

Lanier's message in this passage is a subtly subversive one, especially in the context of the introduction's overt didacticism, for the Welsh tale of Einigan Gawr clearly urges the reader against privileging such contemporary counterparts to the rods as teachers, schools, and even books for young readers.

The subversive implications of this approach to knowledge are worked out even more thoroughly in Lanier's article "The Legend of St. Leonor." In that article, Lanier relates the old Armorican legend of St. Leonor, who, seeking to establish a monastery in the untamed wilderness, saw a bird carrying a grain of wheat in his beak. Taking it as a sign, he followed the bird to a clearing where he saw the remains of wheat growing and decided to found his monastery

there. However, the land was untillable and St. Leonor's sixty disci-
ples begged the saint to change his mind. Instead, however, when
the monks went out to plough the next morning, twelve stags appeared from the forest and allowed themselves to be yoked to the
plows until the field was fully cultivated.

Lanier's reading of this legend is as follows:

> Of course, the twelve stags did not appear from the forest and
> plough; and yet the story is true. The thing which actually happened
> was that the Bishop Leonor, by his intelligence, foresight, practical
> wisdom, and faithful perseverance, remade it good, arable soil . . .
> the people have related it in terms of poetry . . . But notice again that
> these are not silly, poetic licenses; they are not merely a child's em-
> bellishments of a story; the bird and the stags are *not* real; but they
> *are* true . . . they mean the powers of Nature. They mean . . . that if a
> man go forth, sure of his mission, fervently loving his fellow-men,
> working for their benefit; if he adhere to his mission through good
> and evil report . . . presently he will succeed, for the powers of Na-
> ture will come forth out of the recesses of the universe and offer
> themselves as draught-animals to his plow . . . We have seen steam
> come and plow the desert seas, for Fulton; we have seen lightning
> come and plow the wastes of space for Franklin and Morse.[29]

There is much that is quintessentially American about Lanier's
reading—well beyond his references to Fulton, Franklin, and Morse.
St. Leonor's intelligence, foresight, practical wisdom, and faithful
perseverance are all key qualities of American rugged individualism,
while the privileging of the populace as those who can correctly
judge and articulate the truth of the tale reflects the basic tenets of
democracy. Even the story of turning the wilderness into arable land
is a peculiarly American parable.

What makes Lanier's reading uniquely his own, however, is his
suggesting, in a peculiarly antiquarian twist, that Leonor had actually found the remains of a Gallo-Roman farm, and that the stags
were in fact feral cattle that the monks retrained.[30] This suggestion
creates a second parable, which counters the parable of nature rising to aid the extraordinary man with a story of the extraordinary
man taking the knowledge of previous cultures and putting it to his
own use. Both nature, thus, and culture put themselves in the service of the extraordinary man's vision.

This notion of the extraordinary man reshaping the remains of
the past for his own purposes is crucial to understanding the sub-

versiveness of Lanier's vision. In her work on the "First Families" of Virginia, Susan Miller has shown how informally schooled writers turning such textual remains to private use by copying them into commonplace books was in fact a countering discourse to the textual hierarchies imposed by mass public education.[31] In Lanier's situation, where such mass education was inextricably bound up with the larger political and economic discourse imposed on the South by the North, his resistance to formal education can be seen as a resistance to the larger cultural discourse of Reconstruction that is very similar to that embodied in his idealized view of chivalry.

This idea is reinforced by Lanier's scholarly career—which was unorthodox, to say the least. Unable to obtain any formal teaching positions, Lanier began to give lectures to society ladies in Baltimore under the aegis of his friend Mrs. Edgworth Bird. Such was the popularity of these lectures that the fledgling Johns Hopkins University, which had previously refused Lanier a position as a professor, asked him to expand the "Bird Lectures" into a series of public lectures, which finally evolved into a university course for advanced students.

Even given the relative informality of teaching qualifications in the nineteenth century, Lanier's was an audacious assault on conventional educational hierarchies. Furthermore, his unconventionality was not limited to his definition of an instructor; he substantially expanded the definition of a student as well. He continued to teach women and adults long after he received a formal university appointment—at one point proposing to President Gilman that Johns Hopkins run "Schools for Grown People"—making him in the view of Kemp Malone "one of the fathers of academic adult education in America."[32]

The content of the courses Lanier taught was arguably as unorthodox as both his career trajectory and his intended audience. For example, in his last series of lectures,[33] collected as *The English Novel*, Lanier proposes an ersatz-Darwinian theory of the evolution of human personality, which he characterizes as the "sacred difference . . . by virtue of which I am I and you are you, this marvelous separation which we express by the terms 'personal identity,' 'selfhood,' 'me.'"[34] Lanier's theory is that the nature of personality has evolved over time so that

> whereas in the time of Aeschylus the common man was simply a creature of the State, like a modern corporation with rights and powers

strictly limited by the State's charter, now he is . . . a king as to every minutest particle of his individuality so long as that kinghood does not cross the kinghood of his fellow . . . [35]

This change in the nature of man is reflected by a change in man's system of signification. Originally, because people's speech was naturally rhythmical and monosyllabic, they spoke in poetry. However, poetry is governed by strict rules derived from a scientific analysis of music. (Lanier explicates these rules in *The Science of English Verse.*) The rigidity of these rules eventually began to limit poetry from adequately expressing the infinite variations of the evolutionarily developed modern personality. Therefore, prose evolved as a more flexible signifying system.

Admittedly, Lanier's ideas make the wilder fancies of nineteenth-century philology look reasonable. However, even this peculiar theory reflects the stubbornness with which he insisted on the subjectivity of judgment and meaning. For, unlike the "heavy," "unwieldy" words of philologists like Muller, which owe their materiality to objective, external referents, Lanier's language evolves from within human nature. And, although that language does have a material basis, even that basis is quite literally grounded in the subject as well, for, according to Lanier, the rigid rules of poetry ultimately derive from human physiology. He offers blank verse as proof of this last idea, arguing,

> the very breath of every man necessarily divides off his words into rhythmic periods: the average rate of a man's breath being seventeen to twenty respirations in a minute. Taking the faster rate as the more probable one in speaking, the man would, from the periodic necessity of refilling the lungs, divide his words into twenty groups, equal in time, every minute, and if these syllables were equally pronounced at (say) about the rate of two hundred a minute, we should have ten syllables in each group, each ten syllables occupying . . . the time of one breath.[36]

This same insistence on the subjectivity of language and knowledge is expressed more gently and delightfully in the one fairy tale Lanier wrote for children, "The Story of a Proverb."[37] A proverb, of course, is an absolute form of knowledge, a miniature piece of wisdom literature. However, absolute judgment is problematized in the story's very first line:

Once upon a time,—if my memory serves me correctly, it was in the year 6 7/8,—His Intensely-Serene-and-Altogether Perfectly-Astounding Highness the King of Nimporte was reclining in his royal palace. The casual observer (though it must be said that casual observers were as rigidly excluded from the palace of Nimporte as if they had been tramps) might easily have noticed that his majesty was displeased.[38]

The fairy tale kingdom's name is a none-too-subtle play on the French *N'importe* or "it doesn't matter"—one of the few felicitous opportunities for Lanier to exercise what was often an unwieldy and heavy-handed taste for puns and punning. That name reinforces the kingdom's allegorical identification as a realm of the imagination, in which outside verification—both in the form of the casual observer and in the form of the narrator with a shaky memory—is rigidly excluded.

That same exclusion of externally imposed judgment is also the central metaphor of the plot, in which the king stubs his toe as he makes his way barefoot to greet his new bride and sets his counselors a seemingly impossible task: They must cover the world with leather in three days or their lives will be forfeit. The grand vizier, the king's chief advisor, can think of no better reaction to this outrageous request than to ask another person for advice, his wife. The only advice she can offer is "to pluck out his beard, to tear up his garments, and to make his will," and the vizier is in the course of doing this when "a footman ushered in a young man of very sickly complexion, attired in the seediest possible manner," who offers the vizier a solution to his problem.

The central conceit of the story is that "To him who wears a shoe, it is as if the whole earth was covered with leather,"[39] an epigram whose application to the subjective value of knowledge needs no explication. And indeed the young man does present the king with a pair of shoes. However, the vizier and other advisors violently resist the young man's solution—even when their heads are literally on the block. The vizier's reaction is particularly vehement: "'I do not like it; I cannot understand it; I think the part of wisdom is always to reject the unintelligible; I therefore advise your majesty to refuse it,' said the grand vizier, who was really so piqued, that he would much rather have been beheaded than live to see the triumph of the young person whom he had kicked down both pairs of stairs."[40]

The entire story, thus, is a metaphor for the failure of received forms of judgment. That it can also be read as a metaphor for Lanier's didactic position as a children's author can be inferred from the fact the hero is simply described as a "young person" (a word pronounced by the citizens of Nimporte, Lanier informs his readers helpfully, like the French *personne*, or nobody).[41] However, on the final page, the hero is identified as a poet as well. With this final identification, Lanier establishes a conspiracy of poet and child against the socially sanctioned systems of judgment represented by the king's counselors—a conspiracy whose main weapon is the freedom and resituability of knowledge embodied in the symbol of the shoe.

The Boy's Mabinogion is best read as a similar conspiracy. To extend Lanier's metaphor a—well-shod—step further, Lady Charlotte sized the medieval Welsh stories into the *Mabinogion* according to her own needs. By resizing the *Mabinogion* for children, Lanier demonstrates how the work that Lady Charlotte had cobbled together from scraps of other texts could indeed prove rugged enough for a trip across an ocean, if not all the way around the world.

Conclusion:
The Carrier Bag Theory
of Fiction

LADY CHARLOTTE'S LIFE, AS HER BIOGRAPHERS RARELY FAIL TO POINT out, spanned nearly the entire nineteenth century. Born at the height of Napoleon's powers, she lived to witness not only the birth of the British Empire, but also the beginnings of its dissolution. More importantly, her life spanned more than just the years of the nineteenth century. She also traveled the whole of Europe and through much of the Middle East, while sending at least one son as far afield as India. She rubbed elbows with figures ranging from Disraeli to the Rebecca Rioters to Edward Lear to the King of Italy. It is this scope of her life that led Revel Guest and Angela John to subtitle their book "A Biography of the Nineteenth Century"—a phrase that is particularly felicitous because it can either refer to a life that took place during the nineteenth century or a biography that describes the nineteenth century. This study has attempted to examine the parallel ambiguity between Lady Charlotte's roles as psychological and historically conditioned subjects in her own texts—in particular by examining the nexus between self-construction and the inscription of cultural discourse that Mieke Bal has described as "hybridity."

Significantly, Bal suggests that both narrative and collecting—two important facets of Lady Charlotte's life—are loci where such hybridity can be explored. Ursula K. Le Guin has suggested this relationship between collecting and narrative as well—in a narrative that is itself a hybrid between fiction and criticism. In "The Carrier Bag Theory of Fiction," she argues that teleological narratives that construct a subject through a linear series of adventures are a masculinist form of narrative that only evolved when hunters went out to catch animals and returned with stories of their adventures. She contrasts this to the "carrier bag" idea of narration practiced by the female gatherers, claiming that the novel's "proper, fitting shape" is "that of a sack, a bag. A book holds words. Words hold things. They bear meanings. A novel is a medicine bundle, holding things in a particular, powerful relation to one another and to us."[1]

Le Guin's hunters and gatherers are, of course, as much of a mythic construct as F. Max Muller's Aryans or the earlier antiquarians' preadamites. However, her myth also suggests a critical approach to literature—an approach that I have attempted to address through more formal critical means in this study. This approach—especially its articulation in mythic terms—creates a particularly felicitous counterpoint to that of the antiquarians among whom Lady Charlotte moved. For Le Guin's mythologizing heuristic is a deliberate reversal of standard "objective" critical practices. Conversely, among nineteenth-century antiquarians, mythic approaches to intellectual inquiry evolved into these same "objective" standards that we now accept as the norm. History, in particular, "was to acquire powerful human appeal as the intellectual mechanism whereby time could be measured and evaluated. The transition from myth to history was an uncomfortable and often painful process which involved very centrally the questioning of assumptions about universality and permanence."[2]

The transitional nature of the antiquarians' intellectual context is evident in their uneasy positioning between Le Guin's hunters and gatherers. Antiquarians were closer to gatherers than hunters in their emphasis on a collection—or gathering—of facts sparingly diluted with theory. Nonetheless, antiquarianism acquired a strong teleological thrust largely from the idea of culture paralleling the larger progress of history—a thrust evident in everything from the prefix "pre-" in "preadamite" to Scott's theory of literary devolution.

Given Le Guin's insistent gendering of her argument, it is tempting to see Lady Charlotte's *Mabinogion* as closer to a "gatherer's" work than that of other antiquarians. However, Le Guin herself would dismiss such a reading as over-schematizing. Instead, it is far more satisfying simply to enjoy the "particular, powerful relations" Lady Charlotte creates without worrying about categorizing them—taking pleasure, for example, in the touch of the ironmonger's wife that unselfconsciously surfaces on her note on the spear of Gwres the son of Rheged, which was "overlaid with fine silver":

The words in the original are "Gwedy latteinu ac aryant coeth," being lattened over with refined silver. Latten, or laton, was a mixed metal of the colour of brass, and was much employed in the fourteenth century for monumental effigies. For this and many other purposes it was prepared in the form of plate, and hence its name seems occasionally to have been used to express a plate or coating of metal generally, as in this particular instance of silver.

It may be remarked, that the term "latten" is still technically applied to the thinnest manufactured iron plate.[3]

This "carrier bag" approach to narrative is even more helpful in reading Lady Charlotte's autobiography. All of Lady Charlotte's biographers have attempted to organize the facts of her existence by categorizing them. As the critical work of Sidonie Smith suggests as much as Le Guin's does, it is far more useful to read Lady Charlotte's autobiography as another medicine bundle, responsible, not for organizing its elements, but for holding them in a "particular, powerful relation to one another and to us."

Indeed, Lady Charlotte's journals are quite literally a medicine bundle, jammed with clippings, sketches, and dried flowers. The yellowed program tucked next to Lady Charlotte's description of the *tableaux vivants* at which the queen of the Netherlands "received [Lady Charlotte] very kindly and enquired why [she] had never been to see her in [her] former frequent visits,"[4] creates a particular power that vastly exceeds either text or souvenir alone. More importantly, that power is transferable and renewable, for it possesses an infinite capacity to create new relations with new readers of the text—a capacity that Le Guin foregrounds by reminding her reader that the carrier bag was first invented for holding food. Words cannot express the extraordinary energy generated by rediscovering the original relationship between the dried lily of the valley leaf tucked in the flyleaf and Lady Charlotte's entry describing Charles Schreiber picking it for her. And the persistent enigma of the mass card from Lourdes in the staunchly Protestant Lady Charlotte's diary remains an untapped source of intellectual energy as vast and impenetrable as the Alaskan wilderness.

Moreover, this transferability and renewability does not stop with the text's reader. It also extends to writers, such as Sidney Lanier, who generate further aesthetic discourse by forging new relations both among the elements in the medicine bundle and between old and new text. Indeed, Susan Pearce has gone so far as to character-ize collecting as a form of language which is both immediate to the collector and resituable to other contexts. Baudrillard, in contrast, argues against such resituability, claiming that objects are "too dis-continuous" for a collection to be articulated as a real dialectical structure, leading to his final conclusion that "he who [collects] can never entirely shake off an air of impoverishment and depleted hu-manity."[5] What is telling about Baudrillard's argument, however, is his use of the word "dialectical," which assumes a teleological notion of narrative. If one contents oneself simply with Le Guin's "rela-tions" instead, a collection's linguistic and narrative energy can feed humanity rather than deplete it.

And this nourishment is crucial, for the relations generated by Le Guin's medicine bundle can extend to the historical moment in which the text was created. As a result, collecting can be seen as nothing less than an alternate way of reading history. Reading this way, however, requires an important reversal in conventional ap-proaches to the subject and its historical context. Instead of reading the subject as a part of a larger, overarching historical system, Le Guin's approach suggests that instead we need to examine history and culture from the perspective of the "peculiar, powerful rela-tions" forged by a subject's experiences. Indeed, Le Guin's myth im-plies any attempt to reorganize these elements according to a larger system of logic would in fact collapse the particular power the rela-tions generate—an inference that is consistent with Benjamin's de-scription of the collected object being a sort of *Urphänomen*, "a con-crete thing to be discovered in the world of appearances in which 'significance' . . . and appearance, word and thing, idea and experi-ence would coincide."[6] History must be read in a proclamation of-fering £500 and 40 guineas reward (plus pardon unless you were the one who "*secretly* and *feloniously* set *fire* to a Stack of Wheat Straw in the Stack-yard of Thomas Woodroffe"[7]), sealed in red wax and mailed to Lady Charlotte's stepfather Mr. Pegus, not in an abstract concept known as the "Swing Riots."

We read history to educate ourselves—in Santayana's words, to avoid being condemned to repeat it. The correctness of our ap-proach to reading is thus of paramount importance. Le Guin is not the only one who propounds reading history in terms of the relations that produce and are produced by it; indeed, Francis Ponge goes further, claiming, "When man becomes proud to be not just the site where ideas and feelings are produced, but also the cross-road where they divide and mingle, he will be ready to be saved."[8] I scarcely propose to offer Lady Charlotte as a savior for mankind. Nonetheless, her life is a spectacular example of such a crossroads, where we can practice exactly this kind of reading in the hopes of saving ourselves.

Notes

Introduction: The Despotism of Fact

1. Michel Foucault, *The Archaeology of Knowledge* (New York: Pantheon, 1972), 236.

2. An accusation that is not completely specious. The merits of the cases for and against Lady Charlotte will be examined in chapter 2 of this study.

3. Judith Johnston, "Victorian Appropriations: Lady Charlotte Guest Translates *The Mabinogion*," *Studies in Medievalism* 11 (2001): 150.

4. Ibid., 154.

5. Matthew Arnold, *On the Study of Celtic Literature and on Translating Homer* (New York: MacMillan, 1904), 76.

6. Ibid., 87.

7. Ibid., 118.

8. Jacques Derrida, "Before the Law," in *Acts of Literature* (New York: Routledge, 1992). See especially page 198. See also Foucault, *The Archaeology of Knowledge*.

9. Walter Benjamin. "Edward Fuchs: Collector and Historian," in *The Essential Frankfurt School Reader*, ed. Andrew Arato and Eike Gebhardt (New York: Continuum, 1982). See also "Unpacking my Library," in *Illuminations*, ed. Hannah Arendt (New York: Schoken Books, 1968).

10. Arendt, *Illuminations*, 11.

11. Susan M. Pearce, *Museums, Objects, and Collections: A Cultural Study* (London: Leicester University Press, 1992), 24.

12. Arendt, *Illuminations*, 44.

13. Ann Eatwell, "Private Pleasure, Public Beneficence: Lady Charlotte Schreiber and Ceramic Collecting," in Orr, *Women in the Victorian Art World* (New York: Manchester University Press, 1995), 126.

14. Bernard Rackham, ed. *Catalogue of the English Porcelain, Earthenware, Enamels and Glass Collected by Charles Schreiber Esq. M.P. and The Lady Charlotte Elizabeth Schreiber* (London: Victoria and Albert Museum Department of Ceramics, 1928), 28 (no. 151).

15. Mieke Bal, "Telling Objects," in *The Cultures of Collecting*, ed. John Elsner and Roger Cardinal (Cambridge, MA: Harvard University Press), 111.

16. Lady Charlotte Guest, *Extracts from her Journal, 1833–1852* (London: J. Murray, 1950), 14.

17. Sidonie Smith and Julia Watson, *Reading Autobiography: A Guide for Interpreting Life Narratives* (Minneapolis: University of Minnesota Press, 2001).

18. Sidonie Smith and Julia Watson, eds., *Getting a Life: Everyday Uses of Autobiography* (Minneapolis: University of Minnesota Press, 1996), 14.

19. Smith and Watson, *Getting a Life*, 16.

20. Susan Miller, *Assuming the Positions: Cultural Pedagogy and the Politics of Commonplace Writing* (Pittsburgh: University of Pittsburgh Press, 1998), 32.

21. Interestingly, it is these diaries that may have brought Lady Charlotte the scholarly respect that she is so grudgingly granted for her translation of the *Mabinogion*, for her china diaries are still a standard reference source for china collectors today.

22. Revel Guest and Angela V. John, *Lady Charlotte: A Biography of the Nineteenth Century* (London: Weidenfeld and Nicolson, 1989), 217.

23. Ibid.

24. Bal, "Telling Objects," 98.

25. Ibid., 111.

26. Jean Baudrillard. "The System of Collecting," in *The Cultures of Collecting*, ed. John Elsner and Roger Cardinal (Cambridge, MA: Harvard University Press), 24.

27. Ibid.

1. Mrs. Ellis's Wives of England

1. Guest and John, *Lady Charlotte*, 3.

2. Carolyn G. Heilbrun, "Non-Autobiographies of 'Privileged' Women: England and America," in *Life/Lines: Theorizing Women's Autobiography*, eds. Bella Brodzki and Celeste Schenck (Ithaca: Cornell University Press, 1988), 63.

3. Guest and John, *Lady Charlotte*, xx.

4. Guest, *Extracts from her Journal, 1833–1852*, 89.

5. See Bella Brodzki and Celeste Schenck, *Life/Lines*, esp. Mary G. Mason, "The Other Voice," and Nancy K. Miller, "Writing Fictions."

6. See Nancy K. Miller, "Writing Fictions: Women's Autobiography in France," in *Life/Lines: Theorizing Women's Autobiography*, eds. Bella Brodzki and Celeste Schenck (Ithaca: Cornell University Press, 1988), esp. pp. 47 and 58.

7. Sidonie Smith has, in fact, pointed out the theoretical importance of such co-authors in any consideration of autobiography. See *Reading Autobiography*, esp. p. 50 and chapter 7.

8. Guest, *Extracts from her Journal, 1833–1852*, 71.

9. Guest and John, *Lady Charlotte*, 4.

10. Ibid., 5.

11. Ibid., 6.

12. Ibid., 9.

13. Ibid., 16–17.

14. Ibid., 17.

15. Ibid., 4.

16. Guest, *Extracts from her Journal, 1833–1852*, 89.

17. Guest and John, *Lady Charlotte*, 12.

18. Ibid., 13.

19. Ibid., 14.

20. Ibid., 284.

21. Ibid., 21.

22. Ibid., 39.

23. Ibid., 19.

24. Ibid.

25. Ibid.

26. Miller, "Writing Fictions," 55.

27. Ibid., 50.

28. Philippe Lejeune, *On Autobiography* (Minneapolis: University of Minnesota Press, 1989), 172.

29. Guest and John, *Lady Charlotte*, 19–20.

30. The district was the reason for Lady Charlotte's referring to her husband as "Merthyr," both personally and in her diaries.

31. Guest and John, *Lady Charlotte*, xx.

32. Journal 6, 1827–28, Papers of Lady Charlotte Guest, National Library of Wales.

33. Journal 6, 1827–28, Papers, p. 83. (Note dated December 2, 1832.)

34. Journal 6, 1827–28, Papers, p. 167.

35. Journal 7, 1827–29, Papers, p. 139.

36. Journal 6, 1827–28, Papers, p. 92.

37. Journal 7, 1827–29, Papers, p. 179.

38. Smith and Watson, *Getting a Life*, 14.

39. Miller, *Assuming the Positions*, 22.

40. Ibid., 31.

41. Ibid., 32.

42. Extracts relating to the history of the Bertie family, n.d. (However, the cover is signed C.E. Bertie, suggesting a date before her marriage.) Papers.

43. Extracts, n.d., Papers.

44. Ibid.

45. Ibid.

46. Ibid.

47. Miscellaneous Extracts and Notes on Oriental Subjects, 1828–30, Papers.

48. Notes on Oriental Subjects, 1828–30, Papers.

49. The "Oriental Notes" provide one other example of the satisfyingly circular interplay of texts that is the experience of reading Lady Charlotte's journals. In her 1833 journal, signed on the flyleaf CE Guest, with the penciled annotation beneath it, "Read with great interest by B.V. Duncammon, youngest dau: of CE Guest, 1895," there are two inserted pieces of paper. One is the 1856 coverage of Ivor's coming of age party by the *Weymouth Journal;* the other is a copy of a translation of a sonnet by Luigi Tausillo, signed CE Bertie, Feb. 3, 1832 and copied and signed CE Schreiber Canford 3 January 1877, apparently at one of her daughters' request. The original fair copy of this translation is among the "Oriental Notes."

50. Dianne Sachko Macleod, "Cross-Cultural Cross-Dressing," in *Orientalism Transposed: The Impact of the Colonies on British Culture*, eds. Julie Codell and Dianne Sachko Macleod (Brookfield, VT: Ashgate Publishing, 1998).

51. Guest and John, *Lady Charlotte*, xx.

52. Guest, *Extracts from her Journal, 1833–1852*, 14.

53. Journal 10, 1835–37, Papers, pp. 126–27.

54. Journal 10, 1835–37, Papers, p. 127.

55. Guest, *Extracts from her Journal, 1833–1852,* 14.

56. Celeste Schenck, "All of a Piece: Women's Poetry and Autobiography," in *Life/Lines: Theorizing Women's Autobiography,* eds. Bella Brodzki and Celeste Schenck (Ithaca: Cornell University Press, 1988), 291.

57. W. J. T. Mitchell, qtd. in Smith and Watson, *Reading Autobiography,* 20–21.

58. Sarah Stickney Ellis, *The Wives of England: Their Relative Duties, Domestic Influence, and Social Obligations* (London: The London Prtg. and Pub. Co., Ltd. 1853 [?]), 115.

59. Ibid., 126.

60. Ibid., 127.

61. Ibid., 136.

62. Ibid., 137.

63. More, Hannah, *Coelebs in Search of a Wife. With a New Introduction by Mary Waldron* (Bristol [England]): Thoemmes Press, 1995), viii.

64. Ibid., 67.

65. Guest and John, *Lady Charlotte,* 32.

66. Ibid., 31.

67. Guest, *Extracts from her Journal, 1833–1852,* 88-89.

68. These personas are, in order, Wife and Mother, Educator of the People, Society Lady, Intellectual in Wales, Businesswoman, Lady of the Manor, and Head of the Works.

69. Guest and John, *Lady Charlotte,* 34–35.

70. Ibid., 38.

71. Ibid., 152.

72. Ibid.

73. Guest, *Extracts from her Journal, 1833–1852,* 16–17.

74. Ibid., 66.

75. Ibid., 77.

76. Loose paper in Journal 12, 1841–44, Papers.

77. Guest, *Extracts from her Journal, 1833–1852,* 56–57.

78. The Rebecca Rioters were later romanticized by no less a person than Dylan Thomas, in a sketch for a screenplay called *Rebecca's Daughters.*

79. Guest and John, *Lady Charlotte,* 59.

80. Ibid., 57.

81. Ibid., 99.

82. Ibid., 103.

83. Ibid.

84. Ibid., 100.

85. Ibid., 101.

86. Guest, *Extracts from her Journal, 1833–1852,* 63.

87. Ibid., 63–64.

88. Ibid., 64.

89. Ibid., 65.

90. Guest and John, *Lady Charlotte,* 216.

91. Ibid., 65.

92. Ibid., 67.

93. Ibid., 71. What appear to be two preliminary sketches of these buildings, in Lady Charlotte's hand, can be found tucked into Journal 15.

94. Ibid., 67.

95. Ibid., 70.

96. Walter Benjamin, "Edward Fuchs: Collector and Historian," in *The Essential Frankfurt School Reader*, eds. Andrew Arato and Eike Gebhardt (New York: Continuum, 1982), 230.

97. Ibid., 245.

98. Ibid.

99. Guest, *Extracts from her Journal, 1833–1852*, 211.

100. Lady Charlotte Schreiber. *Extracts from her Journal, 1853–1891* (London: J. Murray, 1952), 127.

101. Guest and John, *Lady Charlotte*, 19.

102. See "Edward Fuchs" for a full exposition of this argument, as well as chapter 3 of this study.

103. Guest, *Extracts from her Journal, 1833–1852*, 200.

104. Ibid., 199.

105. Ibid., 185, 225–26.

106. Ibid., 206.

107. Ibid.

108. Ibid., 241.

109. Ibid.

110. Guest and John, *Lady Charlotte*, 81.

111. Ibid., 47.

112. Ibid.

113. Ibid.

114. Leonore Davidoff, *The Best Circles: Women and Society in Victorian England* (Totowa, NJ: Rowman and Littlefield, 1973).

115. Guest and John, *Lady Charlotte*, 79.

116. Ibid., 82.

117. Ibid., 80.

118. Guest, *Extracts from her Journal, 1833–1852*, 27–28.

119. Ibid., 121.

120. Ibid., 123.

121. Ibid., 124.

122. Smith and Watson, *Reading Autobiography*, 59.

123. Ibid., 60

124. Ibid., 61

125. Guest, *Extracts from her Journal, 1833–1852*, 249–50.

126. Sir John's opinion (*Lady Charlotte* 91). Lady Charlotte claimed to be "overpowered with compliments" on her debut (*Extracts* 145).

127. Guest and John, *Lady Charlotte*, 128.

128. See Judith Johnston's "Victorian Appropriations: Lady Charlotte Guest Translates *The Mabinogion,*" discussed in chapter 2 of this study.

129. Guest and John, *Lady Charlotte*, 86.

130. Ibid., 103.

131. Bella Brodzki, "Mothers, Displacement, and Language in the Autobiographies of Nathalie Sarraute and Christa Wolf," in *Life/Lines: Theorizing Women's Autobiography*, eds. Bella Brodzki and Celeste Schenk (Ithaca: Cornell University Press, 1988), 246.

132. Guest and John, *Lady Charlotte*, 41.

133. A tale that, while never substantiated, sounds at least plausible for the head-strong and rank-conscious Lady Charlotte.

134. Guest and John, *Lady Charlotte*, 42.

135. Guest, *Extracts from her Journal, 1833–1852*, 113–14.

136. Ibid., 255.

137. Ibid., 256.

138. Ibid., 258.

139. Ibid., 259.

140. Ibid., 263.

141. Ibid., 264.

142. Journal 15, November 21, 1851, Papers.

143. Journal 15, 1851–53, Papers, p. 254.

144. Loose Paper in Journal 15, 1851–53, Papers.

145. Guest, *Extracts from her Journal, 1833–1852*, 302.

146. Schreiber, *Extracts from her Journal, 1853–1891*, 1.

147. Guest and John, *Lady Charlotte*, 175.

148. Ibid., 181.

149. Schreiber, *Extracts from her Journal, 1853–1891*, 25.

150. Ibid., 5.

151. Ibid.

152. Loose photocopied pages in Journal 15, July 18, 1853, Papers.

153. Schreiber, *Extracts from her Journal, 1853–1891*, 19.

154. Journal 15, July 18, 1853, Papers.

155. Ibid.

156. Ibid.

157. Interestingly, Wales, too, is allowed his chance to weigh in on the events of the coal strike. The collection also preserves the coal reports from 1851 to 1853, sent first to Sir John and then to Lady Charlotte by Thomas E. Wales, Nicholas Wood, [George] Martin, and John Evans. A letter, unsigned but apparently in Wales's handwriting, is enclosed in the volume. It begins, "Considerable interest having been excited by the recent strike at Dowlais & some misapprehension still continuing to exist on the subject, it may not be out of place to offer, at the present moment, a short statement of the real facts of the case" and concludes "It is to be hoped that the spirit of firmness & forbearance, with which [the strikers] were met, will lead them to conclude that their claims were resisted solely upon principles of justice and sound reason." The Augustan dispassion of this entry – ranging from its careful passives, its understanding that the writer is possessed of the "real facts," and its invoking of the principles of justice and sound reason—cannot be overemphasized, and stands in clear contrast to Lady Charlotte's evocative and often emotional prose. The rhetorical difference between the two writers, however, does not mean that Lady Charlotte relied any less on reason or was any less firm in her resolve to act reasonably and justly.

158. Loose photocopied pages in Journal 15, July 21, 1853, Papers.

159. Journal 15, July 21, 1853, Papers.

160. Journal 15, May 3, 1853, Papers.

161. Journal 15, 1851–53, Papers. Currently, this list is inserted between the entries for September 22–25, 1851, but as it is a loose sheet, it could easily date from the 1853 entries in the same journal instead.

162. Schreiber, *Extracts from her Journal, 1853-1891*, 1.

163. Ibid., 10.

164. Ibid.

165. Ibid.

166. Ibid., 17–18.

167. Ibid., 26.

168. Guest and John, *Lady Charlotte*, 186.

169. Schreiber, *Extracts from her Journal, 1853–1891*, 26.

170. Ibid., 46.

171. Lady Charlotte suffered at least three documented miscarriages while married to Schreiber, but never bore a child with him.

172. Guest and John, *Lady Charlotte*, 225.

173. It must be admitted that, in contrast, Montague Guest's version of the diaries comprises a thousand pages of text, all dating to Lady Charlotte's second marriage, but these journals are a separate case, for they are largely devoted to her china collecting.

174. Journal 15, April 14, 1853, Papers, pp. 310–11.

175. Journal 16, May 13–14, 1854, Papers, pp. 184–85.

176. Schreiber, *Extracts from her Journal, 1853–1891*, 45.

177. Ibid.

178. Ibid., 46.

179. Ibid.

180. Ibid., 54.

181. Ibid., 55.

182. Ibid., 56.

183. Ibid.

184. Ibid., 57.

185. Guest and John, *Lady Charlotte*, 197.

186. Ibid., 188.

187. Ibid., 187.

188. Schreiber, *Extracts from her Journal, 1853–1891*, 51.

189. Guest and John, *Lady Charlotte*, 199.

190. Schreiber, *Extracts from her Journal, 1853–1891*, 53–54.

191. Ibid., 43.

192. Ibid., 2.

193. Ibid., 93.

194. Ibid., 101.

195. Ibid., 102.

196. Ibid., 27.

197. Ibid., 62.

198. Ibid., 69.

199. At the same time that Schreiber was flirting with politics, the couple was also flirting with the role of Bohemian intellectuals. In 1857, Lady Charlotte made the acquaintance of Tennyson, who "talked a great deal about Welsh literature, and I, who have forgotten all the little I ever knew about that and everything else, felt quite ashamed at my own ignorance." She also made the acquaintance of Edward Lear, who "sang a great many of his compositions to Tennyson's words. They are mostly very pretty things, but he has no voice, and, on the whole, it is rather painful to listen to him" *(Extracts* 72). Lear returned the favor by commenting, "I

find all that quiet part of the Island spoiling fast . . . Guests, Schreibers . . . and myriads more buzzing everywhere" *(Lady Charlotte* 201). The acquaintance with Tennyson led to further acquaintances with such pre-Raphaelites as Holman Hunt and Dante Gabriel Rossetti. An elderly, twice-widowed Lady Charlotte even dined with Oscar Wilde *(Lady Charlotte* 248). Yet, it is not insulting Lady Charlotte to say that she was neither an artist nor a Bohemian by temperament or inclination. When she at last chose a second intellectual career, it was as a connoisseur and collector.

200. Schreiber, *Extracts from her Journal, 1853–1891*, 67.

201. Ibid., 106.

202. Ibid., 105.

203. Journal 17, January 1, 1856, Papers.

204. Journal 18, February 16, 1859, Papers.

205. Journal 18, January 1, 1863, Papers.

206. Journal 19, 1869–72, Papers, p. 51.

207. "Demidoff, Anatole, Prince, Duc of San Donato (1813–70), Russian diplomat, m. Princess Mathilde, dau. of King Jerome Bonaparte; on divorcing her he was in disgrace at the Imperial Court, and devoted the rest of his life to collecting works of art." [Footnote Bessborough's]

208. "Scheffer, Ary (1795–1858), French painter of Dutch extraction. The picture of Francesca da Rimini is in the Wallace Collection." [Footnote Bessborough's]

209. "Bonington, Richard Parkes (1801–28). This picture is also in the Wallace Collection." [Footnote Bessborough's]

210. Lady Charlotte Schreiber, *Lady Charlotte Schreiber's Journals: Confidences of a Collector of Ceramics and Antiques.* (London: John Lane, The Bodley Head, 1911), vol. 1, 74.

211. Ibid., 79–80.

212. Schreiber, *Extracts from her Journal, 1853–1891*, 117–18.

213. Schreiber, *Confidences*, vol. 1, 85–86.

214. Ibid., 75.

215. Porcelain in particular, but Lady Charlotte also collected objects ranging from gemstones to screens to fans to snuffboxes.

216. Schreiber, *Confidences*, vol. 1, 158.

217. All three of her biographers tell a version of the anecdote.

218. Schreiber, *Confidences*, vol. 1, xxvi.

219. Werner Muensterberger, *Collecting: The Unruly Passion* (Princeton: Princeton University Press, 1994), 240.

220. Ibid.

221. Ibid., 13.

222. Jean Baudrillard, "The System of Collecting," 7–8.

223. It must be noted that she was by no means unique in this privileging of economic records as a personal diary. Both Betty Jane Wylie and Philippe LeJeune have pointed out the close relationship between business records and personal diaries. In *Reading Between the Lines,* Wylie demonstrates how many women's journals began as simple notations of the death or birth of a child in a record of household expenses. LeJeune goes so far as to claim that the essential difference between memoir, which he considers an aristocratic, eighteenth-century form, and autobi-

ography, which he considers a bourgeois, nineteenth-century form, is the close connection with business and business records of the latter.

224. Quoted in Jacques Derrida, "White Mythology: Metaphor in the Text of Philosophy," in *Margins of Philosophy* (Chicago: University of Chicago Press, 1982), 216.

225. Mieke Bal, "Telling Objects."

226. Schreiber, *Confidences*, vol. 2, 484.

227. Ibid., 485.

228. Ibid.

229. Schreiber's initial foray was made in February of 1873; the Schreibers' trip together and the subsequent contested purchase took place on either April 9 of that year, according to the text, or on April 8, according to Lady Charlotte's summary time table.

230. Schreiber, *Confidences*, vol. 2, 486.

231. Ibid.

232. Ibid., 487.

233. Ibid.

234. Ibid.

235. Indeed, a superficial (although by no means necessarily untrue) psychologizing reading would see their shared passion as a substitute for the child the couple could never have.

236. Schreiber, *Extracts from her Journal, 1853–1891*, 166.

237. Ibid., 167.

238. Ibid., 184.

239. Ibid., 170.

240. Ibid.

241. Journal 27, March 28, 1884, Papers.

242. Schreiber, *Extracts from her Journal, 1853–1891*, 180.

243. Ibid., 181.

244. Ibid., 183. It must, however, be pointed out that Lady Charlotte gave only the collection of English china to the nation. The collections of European porcelain remained in family hands.

245. Schreiber, *Extracts from her Journal, 1853–1891*, 182.

246. Chapter 3 of this study provides a more detailed discussion of the impulse underlying this donation.

247. Schreiber, *Extracts from her Journal, 1853–1891*, 186.

248. Ibid., 187–88.

249. Ibid., 192.

250. Ibid., 190–91.

251. Ibid., 194.

252. Ibid., 204.

253. Ibid., 186.

254. Ibid., 194.

255. Ibid., 185.

256. Ibid., 195.

257. Ibid., 200–201.

258. Ibid., 204.

259. Ibid., 199.

260. Ibid., 205.

2. Rhonabwy's Virtue-bearing Stones

1. Guest and John, *Lady Charlotte*, 101.
2. Ibid., 97.
3. Ibid., 96.
4. Ibid., 101.
5. Jeffrey Gantz, *The Mabinogion* (London: Penguin, 1976), 31.
6. Lady Charlotte Guest, *The Mabinogion* (London: Dent (Everyman), 1906), 1.
7. Gantz, *Mabinogion*, 29.
8. Ibid.
9. Proinsias Mac Cana, qtd. in Gantz, *Mabinogion*, 14–15.
10. Guest, *Mabinogion*, 48.
11. Ibid., 45.
12. Ibid., 67.
13. Ibid., 83.
14. Ibid., 97.
15. Jacques Derrida, "The Law of Genre," in *Acts of Literature*, ed. Derek Attridge (New York: Routledge, 1992), 230.
16. Ibid.
17. Guest, *Mabinogion*, 1.
18. Ibid., 31.
19. R. L. Thomson, ed. *Pwyll Pendeuic Dyuet : The First of the Four Branches of the Mabinogi / Edited from the White Book of Rhydderch with Variants from the Red Book of Hergest* (Dublin: Dublin Institute for Advanced Studies, 1957), xvii.
20. Gantz, *Mabinogion*, 32.
21. Although Terry Gilliam, at least, seems to come closer to the former theory.
22. See Debra Mancoff, *The Return of King Arthur* (New York: Harry N. Abrams, 1995), esp. pp. 24–31.
23. Qtd. in Richard Dorson, *The British Folklorists*, (London: Routledge, 1968), 76.
24. Dorson, *The British Folklorists*, 77.
25. If she did in fact believe this to be true, Lady Charlotte was not alone in this error: William Owen Pughe also referred to the tales as "Mabinogion or Juvenilities" *(Lady Charlotte*, 98).
26. Guest and John, *Lady Charlotte*, 98.
27. Gantz, *Mabinogion*, 49.
28. Ibid., 51.
29. Donna R. White, "The Crimes of Lady Charlotte Guest," *Proceedings of the Harvard Celtic Colloquium* 15 (1995), 245.
30. Ibid., 246.
31. Ibid., 247.
32. Rachel Bromwich also investigates what debt Lady Charlotte might owe to the earlier translations of William Own Pughe, but concludes, "She used Pughe's Dictionary, but her translation clearly owes nothing to his, and in the several pieces of *Pwyll* and *Math* that I have compared, it is in several instances more accurate than his. And she began her undertaking, not with the *Mabinogi* tales which Pughe had already published, but with the three Arthurian romances, of which Pughe's translation existed at this date only in manuscript" (Bromwich 12).

33. Guest and John, *Lady Charlotte*, 102.

34. Ibid., 108.

35. Ibid.

36. Ibid., 108–9.

37. White, "Crimes of Lady Charlotte Guest," 245.

38. Rachel Bromwich, "*The Mabinogion* and Lady Charlotte Guest," in *The Mabinogi: A Book of Essays*, ed. C. W. Sullivan III (New York: Garland, 1996), 15.

39. Guest and John, *Lady Charlotte*, 113.

40. White, "Crimes of Lady Charlotte Guest," 243.

41. Rev. T. Price (Carnhuanawc) to Lady Charlotte Guest, March 13, 1843, Papers.

42. David Rhys Phillips, *Lady Charlotte Guest and the Mabinogion; Some Notes on the Work and its Translator, with Extracts from her Journals* (Carmathen: Spurrell, 1921), 8–9.

43. Phillips, *Lady Charlotte Guest and the Mabinogion*, 14.

44. There is also an unpublished translation of a Welsh version of a French *chanson de geste*, "The Companionship of Amlyn and Amic," which Lady Charlotte rejects in her introduction as being "obviously of foreign extraction." She does claim, however, to have "translated and examined" it (9), a claim borne out by the existence of the manuscript. Arguably, this fact lends at least tangential substance to her claim to have translated the *Mabinogion* as well.

45. Guest and John, *Lady Charlotte*, 110.

46. Judith Johnston, "Victorian Appropriations: Lady Charlotte Guest Translates *The Mabinogion*," *Studies in Medievalism* 11 (2001), 145.

47. Ibid., 154.

48. Ibid., 160.

49. Guest, *Mabinogion*, 16.

50. Gwyn Jones and Thomas Jones, *The Mabinogion* (London: Dent, 1948), 6.

51. Gantz, *Mabinogion*, 49.

52. Although it is difficult to judge how much of this perception may be the effect of nineteenth-century prose on the twentieth-century ear, rather that a deliberate stylistic gesture on Lady Charlotte's part.

53. Jones & Jones, *Mabinogion*, x.

54. Ibid., xii.

55. Ibid., xix.

56. Ibid., xxi.

57. Guest and John, *Lady Charlotte*, 100.

58. Roger S. Loomis, "Pioneers in Arthurian Scholarship," *Bulletin Bibliographique de la Société Internationale Arthurienne*, 16 (1964), 105.

59. Guest, *Mabinogion*, 100.

60. Ibid., 309–10.

61. Ibid., 9–10.

62. Gantz, *Mabinogion*, 20.

63. Robert Ackerman, *The Myth and Ritual School: J.G. Frazer and the Cambridge Ritualists* (New York: Garland, 1991), 2.

64. Jacques Derrida, "White Mythology," 210.

65. Ibid.

66. Ackerman, *Myth and Ritual School*, 27.

67. In which Jean-Luc Picard is stranded on a planet with an alien, whose only means of linguistic communication is by referring to a story, which is known to all his species, but to no one else. The alien, thus, can only abstract by citing an episode in the epic: for example, in order to say "I am sad," he says "Shaka when the walls fell." Since Picard has no knowledge of the narrative to which the alien refers, and the alien has no meta-language to describe that narrative, Picard must first decipher the citations, then cite the Epic of Gilgamesh to respond. The episode eventually degenerates in "Me Gilgamesh, you Enkidu" pointing and grunting—albeit in orotund RSC vowels; however the initial linguistic problem is fascinating.

68. Guest's professed "solid reading" when she began to study Welsh (Guest and John, *Lady Charlotte*, 99).

69. James Cowles Prichard, *The Eastern Origin of the Celtic Nations, Proved by a Comparison of their Dialects with the Sanskrit, Greek, Latin and Teutonic Languages* (London: Houston and Wright, 1857), 1–2.

70. Ibid., 5. Even in this weighty and "scientific" approach to the origins of people and languages, there is an eerie anticipation of the twentieth-century location of this event in the mind. Prichard posits four basic relationships that can be discovered when comparing two languages: (1) Similarity in vocabulary, without similarity in grammar; (2) Similarity in grammatical structure without similarity in vocabulary; (3) Cognate languages, which demonstrate similarities in both; and (4) "a fourth relation" that:

> exists between languages in which neither of the connecting characters above described can be discerned: when there is neither analogy of grammatical structure, nor any correspondence in words sufficient to indicate a particular affinity. Such languages are not of the same family, and they generally belong to nations remote from each other in descent, and often in physical characters. But even among languages thus discovered, a few common or resembling words may often be found. These resemblances are sometimes casual, or the result of mere accident: in other instances they are perhaps too striking and too numerous to be ascribed to chance of coincidence. Such are the phenomena of connexion which M. Klaproth hypothetically terms *antediluvian* . . . (Prichard 11–12).

Although Prichard's preferred explanation for this divergence in language derives from the Book of Genesis, the post-modernist mind is drawn perhaps to a more primal myth. The mapping of Prichard's system of relationships onto Jakobson's metaphoric and metonymic axes is irresistible, and the antediluvian, despite the dotty attractions of the mythic lands of Atlantis and Lemuria, which, significantly, enjoyed a vogue in the nineteenth century, maps itself much more easily onto Kristeva's *chora*.

71. Prichard, *Eastern Origin*, 233–34.

72. W. J. Gruffydd, "Folklore and Myth in the Mabinogion" (Lecture) (Cardiff: University of Wales, 1958), 8.

73. Stuart Piggott, *Ancient Britons and the Antiquarian Imagination: Ideas from the Renaissance to the Regency* (London: Thames & Hudson, 1989), 40–42.

74. Ibid., 45–46.

75. Ibid.

76. Arnold, *On the Study of Celtic Literature*, 74.

77. Ibid., 76.

78. Ibid., 118.

79. Ibid., 87.

80. Ibid., 89.

81. Avrom Fleishman, *The English Historical Novel: Walter Scott to Virginia Woolf* (Baltimore: Johns Hopkins, 1971), 43.

82. Guest, *Mabinogion*, 8–9.

83. Philippa Levine, *The Amateur and the Professional: Antiquarians, Historians, and Archaeologists in Victorian England, 1838–1886* (Cambridge: Cambridge University Press, 1986), 3.

84. Piggott, *Ancient Britons*, 150.

85. Levine, *Amateur and the Professional*, 70.

86. Ibid., 71.

87. Ibid., 15.

88. Qtd. in Levine, *Amateur and the Professional*, 74.

89. H. N. Humphries, *Stories by an Archaeologist and his Friends* (London, 1856) qtd. in Levine 73.

90. Levine, *Amateur and the Professional*, 73.

91. Guest, *Mabinogion*, 386.

92. Ibid., 308.

93. Ibid., 330.

94. Ibid., 9.

95. Levine, *Amateur and the Professional*, 40.

96. Loomis, "Pioneers in Arthurian Scholarship," 103.

97. Guest, *Mabinogion*, 404.

98. Ibid., 422.

99. See chapter 3, esp. the discussion of Muensterberger.

100. Piggott, *Ancient Britons*, 151.

101. Vladimir Propp, "Morphology of the Folktale," *International Journal of American Linguistics*, 24, no. 4 (1958): 18.

102. Ibid., 20.

103. Claude Levi-Strauss, "Structure and Form: Reflections on a Work by Vladimir Propp," in *Theory and History of Folklore*, Vladimir Propp (Minneapolis: University of Minnesota Press, 1993), 179.

104. Levi-Strauss, "Structure and Form," 180. Italics Levi-Strauss.

105. Benjamin, "Edward Fuchs: Collector and Historian," 228.

106. Claude Levi-Strauss, *Structural Anthropology* (New York: Basic Books, 1963), 21.

107. Derrida, "Before the Law," 198.

108. Foucault, *Archaeology of Knowledge*, 138.

109. Ibid., 139.

110. Ibid.

111. Ibid., 140.

112. Foucault, "The Discourse on Language," in *The Archaeology of Knowledge*, 221.

113. Gantz, *Mabinogion*, 177.

114. Guest, *Mabinogion*, 336.

115. Ibid., 337.

116. Ibid., 341.

117. Ibid., 138.

118. Ibid.

119. Ibid., 139.

120. Ibid., 150.

121. Mark Girouard, *The Return to Camelot: Chivalry and the English Gentleman* (New Haven: Yale University Press, 1981), 184.

122. Mancoff, *Return of King Arthur*, 32–33.

123. Kenelm Henry Digby, *The Broadstone of Honour, or Rules for the Gentlemen of England* (London, 1823), 188.

124. Mancoff, *Return of King Arthur*, 39.

125. Ibid., 43 ff., 51.

126. This issue will be discussed at length in chapter 4.

127. An alteration from Maclise's original plan, which had called for the woman to be clothed in a medieval Saxon cloak. See Mancoff, *Return of King Arthur*, 40.

128. Mancoff, *Return of King Arthur*, 40.

129. Girouard, *Return to Camelot*, 181.

130. Guest, *Mabinogion*, 353.

131. Guest and John, *Lady Charlotte*, 117.

132. Guest, *Mabinogion*, 316–17.

133. Ibid., 353.

134. Ibid., 355.

135. Ibid., 382–90.

136. Ibid., 390.

3. Dangerous but Domesticated Passions

1. Guest and John, *Lady Charlotte*, 195.

2. Frank Herrmann, *The English as Collectors: A Documentary Sourcebook* (New Castle, DE: Oak Knoll, 1999), 44.

3. Muensterberger, *Collecting*, 3.

4. Walter Benjamin, *The Arcades Project* (Cambridge, MA: Bellknap Press, 1999), 205.

5. Walter Benjamin, "Edward Fuchs," 235.

6. Ibid., 207.

7. Pearce, *Museums, Objects, and Collections*, 24.

8. Ibid.

9. Ibid., 29.

10. Ibid., 26.

11. Ibid., 27.

12. Ibid., 38.

13. Ibid., 69.

14. Ibid., 72.

15. Ibid.

16. Ibid., 73.

17. Ibid., 82.

18. Ibid., 83.

19. Ibid., 81.
20. Ibid., 84.
21. Ibid., 85.
22. Ibid., 88.
23. Ibid.
24. Baudrillard, "The System of Collecting," 18.
25. Ibid., 22.
26. Ibid., 24.
27. Ibid.
28. Patrick Mauries, *Cabinets of Curiosities* (London: Thames and Hudson, 2002), 12.
29. Ibid., 25.
30. Ibid., 34.
31. Ibid., 91.
32. Bal, "Telling Objects," 110.
33. Ibid., 114.
34. Ibid.
35. Mauries, *Cabinets of Curiosities*, 185.
36. Ibid., 193, quoting Daston and Park.
37. Mauries, *Cabinets of Curiosities*, 194.
38. Herrmann, *The English as Collectors*, 210.
39. Ibid., 309.
40. Ibid., 308.
41. Ibid., 310.
42. Ibid., 311.
43. See Macleod, *Art and the Victorian Middle Class*, for an excellent discussion of this issue.
44. Lady Charlotte Schreiber, *Playing Cards, Volume I. English and Scottish, Dutch and Flemish* (London: J. Murray, 1892), preface.
45. Anna Jameson, *Companion to the Most Celebrated Private Galleries of Art in London* (London: Saunders and Otley, Conduit Street, 1844), xxxiii–iv.
46. See MacLeod, *Art and the Victorian Middle Class*, for an excellent resume of these activities.
47. Ibid., esp. pp. 68–72.
48. Herrmann, *The English as Collectors*, 329.
49. Clarissa Campbell Orr, "The Corinne Complex: Gender, Genius, and National Character," in *Women in the Victorian Art World*, ed. C. C. Orr (New York: Manchester University Press, 1995), 102.
50. Ibid., 89.
51. Herrmann, *The English as Collectors*, 307.
52. Ibid.
53. Clarissa Campbell Orr, introduction to *Women in the Victorian Art World* (New York: Manchester University Press, 1995), 19.
54. Ibid., 16.
55. Katherine Patterson, "Anna Jameson, Harriet Martineau, and their Friends," *The Victorian Women Writers' Letters Project* (University of British Columbia, Retrieved: July 22, 2003), <http://edocs.lib.sfu.ca/projects/VWWLP/Anna-Brownell-Jameson.htm>

56. Jameson , *Companion to Celebrated Private Galleries*, xxxix–xxxx.

57. A. Henry Layard, qtd. in Orr, "Corinne," 90.

58. Geraldine MacPherson, "Memoir of Mrs. Jameson," in *Sacred and Legendary Art, Part I*, Anna Jameson and Estelle M. Hurll (Boston: Houghton, 1904. Reprinted Kessinger Publishing), xxvii.

59. Jameson, *Companion to Celebrated Private Galleries*, 279–81.

60. Eatwell, "Private Pleasure," 126.

61. Orr, introduction, 3.

62. Eatwell, "Private Pleasure," 128.

63. Joseph Marryat, *A History of Pottery and Porcelain, Medieval and Modern* (London: J. Murray, 1868), xiv.

64. Eatwell, "Private Pleasure," 132.

65. Ibid., 132–33.

66. Schreiber, *Confidences*, vol. 2, 306.

67. Ibid., 314.

68. Ibid., 316.

69. Schreiber, *Extracts from her Journal, 1853–1891*, 130.

70. Ibid., 133.

71. Ibid., 145.

72. Ibid., 155.

73. Ibid., 177.

74. Schreiber, *Confidences*, vol. 2, 332.

75. Schreiber, *Extracts from her Journal, 1853-1891*, 184.

76. Ibid., 182.

77. See Mary G. Mason's "The Other Voice," discussed in chapter 1 of this study.

78. Eatwell, "Private Pleasure," 142.

79. Muensterberger, *Collecting*, 240.

80. Ibid., 4.

81. See chapter 1.

82. Arendt, introduction, 44.

83. Ibid.

84. Ibid., 42.

85. Baudrillard, "The System of Collecting," 7.

86. Maurice Jonas, qtd. in Eatwell, "Private Pleasure," 126.

87. Benjamin, "Edward Fuchs," 241.

88. Rackham, *Catalogue of English Porcelain*, no. 54.

89. Ibid., 18.

90. Ibid., no. 120.

91. Ibid., no. 134.

92. Ibid., 36.

93. Ibid.

94. Ibid., no. 352.

95. Ibid., no. 355.

96. Ibid., no. 197.

97. Ibid., no. 287.

98. Ibid., no. 342.

99. Macleod, *Art and the Victorian Middle Class*, 59 ff.

100. Rackham, *Catalogue of English Porcelain*, no. 743.

101. Ibid., no. 86.

102. Ibid., no. 135.

103. Ibid., no. 422.

104. Ibid., no. 306.

105. Ibid., no. 131.

106. Ibid., 36.

107. Ibid., no. 372.

108. Ibid., 76.

109. Ibid., no. 152.

110. Ibid., 38.

111. Ibid., 28, no. 151.

112. Benjamin, "Edward Fuchs," 237.

113. Daniel Miller, *Material Culture and Mass Consumption* (Oxford: Basil Black-well, 1987), 104.

114. Ibid., 106.

115. Ibid., 108.

116. Macleod, *Art and the Victorian Middle Class*, 62–64.

117. Ibid., 64–65.

118. Marryat, *A History of Pottery and Porcelain*, xii.

119. Ibid., xv.

120. Mancoff, *The Return of Arthur*, esp. 38–39.

121. Marryat, *A History of Pottery and Porcelain*, 14.

122. Ibid., 28–29.

123. Lady Charlotte Schreiber, *Fans and Fan Leaves: English* (London: J. Murray, 1888), no. 7.

124. Ibid., no. 143.

125. Lady Charlotte Schreiber, *Playing Cards, Vol. I, English and Scottish, Dutch and Flemish* (London: J. Murray, 1892), preface.

126. Joshua Wilner has also suggested "a more or less standing association of china with feminine virginity" (personal communication, August 22, 2003).

127. Miller, *Material Culture*, 100–101.

128. Pearce, *Museums, Objects, and Collections*, 52.

129. Ibid., 34.

130. Ibid., 33.

131. Benjamin, "Unpacking my Library," 67.

4. Covering the Earth with Leather

1. Aubrey Harrison Starke, *Sidney Lanier: A Biographical and Critical Study* (New York: Russell & Russell, 1964), 379.

2. Ibid., 68–69.

3. Ibid., 448.

4. Ibid., 12.

5. Ibid., 11.

6. Kymberly Pinder, "Class, Race, and Arthurian Narratives in San Francisco in the 1870s," in *King Arthur's Modern Return*, ed. Debra Mancoff (New York: Garland Publishing, 1998), 109.

7. Alan Lupack, "The Figure of King Arthur in America," in *King Arthur's Modern Return,* ed. Debra Mancoff (New York: Garland Publishing, 1998), esp. p. 125.

8. Jeanne Fox-Friedman, "The Chivalric Order for Children," in *King Arthur's Modern Return,* ed. Debra Mancoff (New York: Garland Publishing, 1998), 149.

9. The phrase is likely to resonate peculiarly to the modern ear, giving rise to the logical question, would Lanier have edited the texts differently for girls? The answer is at least a qualified yes: there is evidence that in the first flush of success of *The Boy's Froissart,* Lanier had planned writing an entire separate children's library aimed at girls.

10. This last did not work as well as Lanier might have hoped. Although the sales of *The Boy's Froissart* were brisk, and *The Boy's King Arthur* sold 12,900 copies by 1900, *The Boys' Mabinogion* only sold 5,500 copies, and *The Boy's Percy* 3,300 (Starke 380).

11. By far the most popular book in the series, it is the only one than can still be found in reprint editions.

12. Admittedly undertaken for money, *The Boy's Library* represents almost Lanier's entire output for children. His other children's works are a few poems, including the reasonably well-known "Christmas in Elfland"; an article on King Arthur; and a short story, called "The Story of a Proverb," which will be discussed below.

13. Interestingly, Lanier planned, but never completed, a similar series of classic texts prepared especially for the nonexpert adult reader—anticipating Norton Critical Editions by nearly a century (Starke 329).

14. Donna White,"Sidney Lanier and *The Boy's Mabinogion,*" chapter 1 in A *Century of Welsh Myth in Children's Literature* (Westport, CT: Greenwood Press, 1998). White amusingly points out that apparently Lanier's delicacy extended even to concealing the pregnancy of the mouse in "Manawydden the Son of Mathonwy."

15. Sidney Lanier, *The Boy's Mabinogion* (New York: Scribner's, 1920), xvi. This is an error on Lanier's part. Blodeuwedd is destined as a bride for Llew Llaw Gyffes, on whose behalf Gwyddion labors.

16. Ibid., 214.

17. Starke, *Sidney Lanier,* 138.

18. Ibid., 518.

19. Ibid., 94.

20. Sidney Lanier, letter to Logan E. Bleckley Nov. 15, 1874, in *The Centennial Edition of the Works of Sidney Lanier,* ed. Charles R. Anderson (Baltimore: Johns Hopkins Press, 1945), vol. 9, 121–22.

21. Lanier, *Boy's Mabinogion,* xv.

22. Ibid., vi.

23. Ibid.

24. Ibid., xi.

25. Guest, *Mabinogion,* 139.

26. Lanier, *Boy's Mabinogion,* 168.

27. Ibid., xii–xiii.

28. Ibid., 341.

29. Sidney Lanier, "The Legend of St. Leonor," in *The Centennial Edition of the Works of Sidney Lanier,* vol. 2, 249–50.

30. Ibid., 248–49.

31. Miller, *Assuming the Positions*.

32. Kemp Malone, introduction to *The Centennial Edition of the Works of Sidney Lanier*, vol. 3, viii.

33. *The English Novel* was the last series of lectures, given while Lanier was dying. In addition, he gave the Bird lectures, which subsequently evolved into *The Science of English Verse*, and a series of lectures at the Peabody Institute, which, combined with a series of Johns Hopkins lectures on the same topic, became *Shakspere and his Forerunners*. Lanier was continually dogged by illness at this time; nonetheless, the scope of his ambition for these lectures (which was never carried out) is truly extraordinary, even when it was reduced to forty lectures from the originally planned eighty. Lanier proposed to give twenty-four lectures: On the Technic of English Verse (5), The Early English Sonnet (5), The Less-Known Writers between Surrey and Shakspere (5), The Pronunciation of English in Shakspere's Time (2), Music and Musical Instruments in Shakespere's Time (2), Domestic Life in Shakespere's Time (2), And Shakespere's Relation to our Novels and Common Speech (3). Six colleagues would give sixteen additional lectures on related topics (Kemp x).

34. Sidney Lanier, *The English Novel*, in *The Centennial Edition of the Works of Sidney Lanier*, Vol. 4, 6.

35. Ibid., 7.

36. Ibid., 20.

37. Lanier actually wrote two "Stories of a Proverb." The first one was intended for children and published in *St. Nicholas Magazine* in May 1877. That story is discussed here. The second story, intended for adults and published in *Lippincott's Magazine*, was far less successful.

38. Sidney Lanier, "The Story of a Proverb," in *The Centennial Edition of the Works of Sidney Lanier*, vol. 6, 324.

39. Ibid., 330.

40. Ibid., 329.

41. Ibid., 327.

Conclusion: The Carrier Bag Theory of Fiction

1. Ursula K. Le Guin, "The Carrier Bag Theory of Fiction," in *The Ecocriticism Reader*, eds. Cheryll Glotfelty & Harold Fromm (Athens: University of Georgia Press), 153.

2. Levine, *Amateur and the Professional*, 3.

3. Guest, *Mabinogion*, 349.

4. Journal 21, March 14, 1874, Papers.

5. Baudrillard, "The System of Collecting," 24.

6. Arendt, introduction, 12.

7. Loose paper inserted in flyleaf of Journal 12, 1841–44, Papers.

8. Qtd. in William Rueckert, "Literature and Ecology," in *The Ecocriticism Reader*, 105.

Bibliography

PRIMARY SOURCES

Cust, Lionel, comp. *Catalogue of the Collection of Fans and Fan-Leaves Presented to the Trustees of the British Museum by the Lady Charlotte Schreiber.* London: Longmans, 1893.

Guest, Lady Charlotte. Collected Papers. National Library of Wales, Aberystwyth. Deposited by Dowager Lady Wimborne.

———. *Extracts from her Journal, 1833–1852.* Edited by The Earl of Bessborough. London: J. Murray, 1950.

———, ed. and trans. *The Mabinogion. From the Llyfr Coch o Hergest, and Other Ancient Welsh Manuscripts, with an English Translation and Notes, by Lady Charlotte E. Guest.* London: Longmans, 1849.

———, trans. *The Mabinogion.* London: Dent (Everyman), 1906.

Lanier, Sidney. *Knightly Legends of Wales or The Boy's Mabinogion.* New York: Scribner's, 1920.

———. *The Centennial Edition of the Works of Sidney Lanier.* Edited by Charles R. Anderson. 10 vols. Baltimore: Johns Hopkins Press, 1945.

O'Donoghue, Freeman M., comp. *Catalogue of the Collection of Playing Cards Bequeathed to the Trustees of the British Museum by Lady Charlotte Schreiber.* London: Longmans, 1901.

Rackham, Bernard, ed. *Catalogue of the English Porcelain, Earthenware, Enamels and Glass Collected by Charles Schreiber Esq. M.P. and The Lady Charlotte Elizabeth Schreiber and Presented to the Museum in 1884.* London: Victoria and Albert Museum Department of Ceramics, under the authority of the Board of Education, 1928.

Schreiber, Lady Charlotte. *Extracts from her Journal, 1853–1891.* Edited by The Earl of Bessborough. London: J. Murray, 1952.

———. *Fans and Fan Leaves. English. Collected and Described by Lady C. Schreiber.* London: J. Murray, 1888.

———. *Fans and Fan Leaves. Foreign. Collected and Described by Lady Charlotte Schreiber.* London: J. Murray, 1890.

———. *Lady Charlotte Schreiber's Journals: Confidences of a Collector of Ceramics and Antiques.* Edited by Montague Guest. 2 vols. London: John Lane, The Bodley Head, 1911.

————. *Playing Cards of Various Ages and Countries / Selected from the Collection of Lady Charlotte Schreiber.* 3 vols. London: J. Murray, 1892–95.

————. *Schreiber Collection. Catalogue of English Porcelain, Earthenware, Enamels, etc., collected by Charles Schreiber and the Lady Charlotte Elizabeth Schreiber, and Presented to the South Kensington Museum in 1884.* London: H. M. Stationery Office, 1885.

SECONDARY SOURCES

On Lady Charlotte Guest Schreiber

Bromwich, Rachel. "*The Mabinogion* and Lady Charlotte Guest." In *The Mabinogi: A Book of Essays,* edited by C. W. Sullivan III, 3–18. New York: Garland Publishing, 1996.

Eatwell, Ann. "Private Pleasure, Public Beneficence: Lady Charlotte Schreiber and Ceramic Collecting." In Orr, *Women in the Victorian Art World,* 125–45.

Fraser, Maxwell. "Lady Llanover and Lady Charlotte Guest." *The Anglo-Welsh Review* 13 (1963): 36–43.

Guest, Revel, and Angela V. John. *Lady Charlotte: A Biography of the Nineteenth Century.* London: Weidenfeld and Nicolson, 1989. (Tempus Publishing. Stroud, Gloucestire, England, 2007.)

Johnston, Judith. "Victorian Appropriations: Lady Charlotte Guest Translates *The Mabinogion.*" *Studies in Medievalism* 11 (2001): 145–66.

Loomis, Roger S. "Pioneers in Arthurian Scholarship." *Bulletin Bibliographique de la Société Internationale Arthurienne* 16 (1964): 95–106.

Meinhold, George D. "The Idylls of the King and the Mabinogion." *Tennyson Research Bulletin* 1 (1969): 61–63.

Phillips, David Rhys. *Lady Charlotte Guest and the Mabinogion; Some Notes on the Work and its Translator, with Extracts from her Journals.* Carmathen: Spurrell, 1921.

White, Donna R. "The Crimes of Lady Charlotte Guest." *Proceedings of the Harvard Celtic Colloquium* 15 (1995): 242–49.

Wood, Juliette. "A Welsh Triad." In *Women and Tradition: A Neglected Group of Folklorists,* edited by Carmen Blacker and Hilda Ellis Davidson, 259–76. Durham, NC: Carolina, 2000.

On Sidney Lanier

DeVoto, Marya. "The Hero as Editor: Sidney Lanier's Medievalism and the Science of Manhood." *Studies in Medievalism* 9 (1997): 148–70.

Lupack, Alan. "Beyond the Model: Howard Pyle's Arthurian Books." In *The Arthurian Yearbook,* edited by Keith Busby, 215–34. New York: Garland Publishing, 1991.

Parks, Edd Winfield. *Sidney Lanier: The Man, the Poet, the Critic.* Athens: University of Georgia Press, 1968.

Starke, Aubrey Harrison. *Sidney Lanier: A Biographical and Critical Study.* New York: Russell & Russell, 1964.

White, Donna R. "Sidney Lanier and *The Boy's Mabinogion.*" Chapter 1 in A *Century of Welsh Myth in Children's Literature.* Westport, CT: Greenwood Press, 1998.

Other

Ackerman, Robert. *The Myth and Ritual School: J.G. Frazer and the Cambridge Ritualists,* New York: Garland Publishing, 1991.

Anderson, Bonnie S. and Judith P. Zinsser. *A History of their Own.* New York: Harper & Row, 1989.

Arendt, Hannah. Introduction. In *Illuminations,* by Walter Benjamin, 1–55. New York: Schoken Books, 1968.

Arnold, Matthew. *On the Study of Celtic Literature and on Translating Homer.* New York: MacMillan, 1904.

Bal, Mieke. "Telling Objects: A Narrative Perspective on Collecting." In Elsner and Cardinal, *The Cultures of Collecting,* 97–115.

Baudrillard, Jean. "The System of Collecting." In Elsner and Cardinal, *The Cultures of Collecting,* 7–24.

Benjamin, Walter. *The Arcades Project.* Translated by Howard Eiland and Kevin McLaughlin. Cambridge, MA: Bellknap Press of Harvard University Press, 1999.

———. "Edward Fuchs: Collector and Historian." In *The Essential Frankfurt School Reader,* edited by Andrew Arato and Eike Gebhardt, 225–53. New York: Continuum, 1982.

———. *Illuminations.* Edited and with an Introduction by Hannah Arendt. New York: Schoken Books, 1968. See esp. chapter 1, "Unpacking my Library," and chapter 2, "The Task of the Translator."

Brodzki, Bella. "Mothers, Displacement, and Language in the Autobiographies of Nathalie Sarraute and Christa Wolf." In Brodzki and Schenck, *Life/Lines: Theorizing Women's Autobiography,* 243-259.

Brodzki, Bella, and Celeste Schenck, eds. *Life/Lines: Theorizing Women's Autobiography.* Ithaca: Cornell University Press, 1988.

Butler, Judith. *Gender Trouble: Feminism and the Subversion of Identity.* New York: Routledge, 1999.

Codell, Julie F., and Dianne Sachko Macleod, eds. *Orientalism Transposed: The Impact of the Colonies on British Culture.* Brookfield, VT: Ashgate Publishing, 1998.

Crane, Mary Thomas. *Framing Authority: Sayings, Self and Society in Sixteenth-Century England.* Princeton: Princeton University Press, 1993.

Darling, Richard L. *The Rise of Children's Book Reviewing in America, 1865–1881.* New York: R. R. Bowker, 1968.

Davidoff, Leonore. *The Best Circles: Women and Society in Victorian England.* Totowa, NJ: Rowman and Littlefield, 1973.

Derrida, Jacques. *Acts of Literature.* Edited by Derek Attridge. New York: Routledge, 1992. See esp. chapter 5, "Before the Law," and chapter 6, "The Law of Genre."

———. "White Mythology: Metaphor in the Text of Philosophy." In *Margins of Philosophy.* Translated by Alan Bass, 207–71. Chicago: University of Chicago Press, 1982.

Dorson, Richard M. *The British Folklorists: A History.* London: Routledge & Kegan Paul, 1968.

Eastlake, Elizabeth Rigby, Lady. *Journals and Correspondence of Lady Eastlake: Edited by her Nephew, Charles Eastlake Smith; with Facsims. of her Drawings and a Portrait.* London: J. Murray, 1895.

Ellis, Sarah Stickney. *The Wives of England: Their Relative Duties, Domestic Influence, and Social Obligations.* London: The London Printing and Publishing Company, Ltd., 1853(?)

Elsner, John, and Roger Cardinal. *The Cultures of Collecting.* Cambridge, MA: Harvard University Press, 1994.

Fleishman, Avrom. *The English Historical Novel: Walter Scott to Virginia Woolf.* Baltimore: Johns Hopkins Press, 1971.

Foucault, Michel. *The Archaeology of Knowledge & The Discourse on Language.* Translated by A. M. Sheridan Smith. New York: Pantheon, 1972.

Fox-Friedman, Jeanne. "The Chivalric Order for Children: Arthur's Return in Late Nineteenth- and Early Twentieth-century America." In Mancoff, *King Arthur's Modern Return,* 137–58.

Gantz, Jeffrey, ed. *The Mabinogion.* London: Penguin, 1976.

Gilbert, Sandra M., and Susan Gubar. *The Madwoman in the Attic: The Woman Writer and the Nineteenth-Century Literary Imagination.* New Haven: Yale University Press, 1979.

Gilmore, Leigh. *Autobiographics: A Feminist Theory of Women's Self-Representation.* Ithaca: Cornell University Press, 1994.

Girouard, Mark. *The Return to Camelot: Chivalry and the English Gentleman.* New Haven: Yale University Press, 1981.

Glotfelty, Cheryll and Harold Fromm, eds. *The Ecocriticism Reader.* Athens: University of Georgia Press, 1996.

Gruffydd, W. J. "Folklore and Myth in the Mabinogion" (lecture). Cardiff: University of Wales, 1958.

Havens, Earle. *Commonplace Books: A History of Manuscripts and Printed Books from Antiquity to the Twentieth Century.* New Haven: Beinecke Rare Book and Manuscript Library. Distributed by University Press of New England, ca. 2001.

Heilbrun, Carolyn G. "Non-Autobiographies of 'Privileged' Women: England and America." In Brodzki and Schenck, *Life/Lines: Theorizing Women's Autobiography,* 62–76.

Herder, Johann Gottfried. *Volkslieder: Stimme der Volker in Liedern.* 2 vols. Leipzig: Weygandsche Buchhandlung, 1778–79.

Herrmann, Frank. *The English as Collectors: A Documentary Sourcebook.* New Castle, DE: Oak Knoll, 1999.

Jameson, Anna. *Companion to the Most Celebrated Private Galleries of Art in London.* London: Sunders and Otley, 1844.

——. *Essays upon Art, and Notices of the Collection of Works of the Old Masters at the Lyceum Gallery, 563 Broadway.* New York: G. F. Nesbitt, 1849.

——. *Handbook to the Public Galleries of Art in and near London.* London: J. Murray, 1842.

Jameson, Anna, and Estelle M. Hurll. *Sacred and Legendary Art.* 2 vols. Boston: Houghton Mifflin, 1904. Reprint, Cambridge, MA: Kessinger, 2006.

Jones, Gwyn, and Thomas Jones, eds. *The Mabinogion.* London: Dent, 1957.

Kamnetsky, Christa. *The Brothers Grimm & their Critics: Folktales and the Quest for Meaning.* Athens: Ohio University Press, 1992.

Kristeva, Julia. "Revolution in Poetic Language." In *The Kristeva Reader*, edited by Toril Moi, 89–138. New York: Columbia University Press, 1986.

Langland, Elizabeth. *Nobody's Angels: Middle-Class Women and Domestic Ideology in Victorian Culture*. Ithaca: Cornell University Press, 1995.

Le Guin, Ursula K. "The Carrier Bag Theory of Fiction." In Glotfelty and Fromm, *The Ecocriticism Reader*, 149–54.

Leighton, Angela, ed. *Victorian Women Poets: A Critical Reader*. Cambridge, MA: Blackwell, 1996.

Lejeune, Philippe. *On Autobiography*. Translated by Katherine Leary. Minneapolis: University of Minnesota Press, 1989.

Levine, Lawrence. *Highbrow/Lowbrow: The Emergence of Cultural Hierarchy in America*. Cambridge, MA: Harvard University Press, 1988.

Levine, Philippa. *The Amateur and the Professional: Antiquarians, Historians, and Archaeologists in Victorian England, 1838–1886*. Cambridge: Cambridge University Press, 1986.

Levi-Strauss, Claude. *Structural Anthropology*. Translated by Claire Jacobson and Brooke Grundfest Schoepf. New York: Basic Books, 1963.

———. "Structure and Form: Reflections on a Work by Vladimir Propp." In Propp, *Theory and History of Folklore*, 167–88.

Lilly Library, Duke University. Art Reference Database. http://www.lib.duke.edu/lilly/artlibry/dah/jamesona.htm (accessed July 22, 2003).

Locke, John. *A New Method of Making Common-Place Books*. London: Greenwood, 1706.

Lupack, Alan. "Arthurian Youth Groups in America: The Americanization of Knighthood." In B. T. Lupack, *Adapting the Arthurian Legends for Children*, 197–216.

———. "The Figure of King Arthur in America." In Mancoff, *King Arthur's Modern Return*, 121–36.

Lupack, Alan, and Barbara Tepa Lupack. *King Arthur in America*. Rochester, NY: D. S. Brewer, 1999.

Lupack, Barbara Tepa, ed. *Adapting the Arthurian Legends for Children: Essays on Arthurian Juvenilia*. New York: Palgrave Macmillan, 2004.

Lynch, Andrew. "*Le Morte D'Arthur* for Children: Malory's Third Tradition." In B. T. Lupack, *Adapting the Arthurian Legends for Children*, 1–50.

Macleod, Dianne Sachko. *Art and the Victorian Middle Class: Money and the Making of Cultural Identity*. New York: Cambridge University Press, 1996.

———. "Art Collecting and Victorian Middle-Class Taste." *Art History* 10, no. 2 (1987): 320–50.

Macpherson, C.B. *The Political Theory of Possessive Individualism: Hobbes to Locke*. Oxford: Clarendon Press, 1962.

Mancoff, Debra N. *The Return of King Arthur: The Legend through Victorian Eyes*. New York: Harry N. Abrams, 1995.

———, ed. *King Arthur's Modern Return*. New York: Garland Publishing, 1998.

Marryat, Joseph. *A History of Pottery and Porcelain, Medieval and Modern*. London: J. Murray, 1868.

Mason, Mary G. "The Other Voice." In Brodzki and Schenck, *Life/Lines: Theorizing Women's Autobiography*, 19–44.

Mauries, Patrick. *Cabinets of Curiosities*. London: Thames and Hudson, 2002.

Miller, Daniel. *Material Culture and Mass Consumption*. Oxford: Basil Blackwell, 1987.

Miller, Nancy K. "Writing Fictions: Women's Autobiography in France." In Brodzki and Schenck, *Life/Lines: Theorizing Women's Autobiography*, 45–46.

Miller, Susan. *Assuming the Positions: Cultural Pedagogy and the Politics of Commonplace Writing*. Pittsburgh: University of Pittsburgh Press, 1998.

More, Hannah. *Coelebs in Search of a Wife*. Edited and with a new introduction by Mary Waldron. Bristol: Thoemmes Press, 1995.

Muensterberger, Werner. *Collecting: An Unruly Passion*. Princeton: Princeton University Press, 1994.

Orr, Clarissa Campbell. "The Corinne Complex: Gender, Genius, and National Character." In Orr, *Women in the Victorian Art World*, 89–106.

———, ed. *Women in the Victorian Art World*. New York: Manchester University Press, 1995.

Paradiz, Valerie. *Clever Maids: The Secret History of the Grimm Fairy Tales*. New York: Basic Books, 2005.

Patterson, Katherine. "Anna Jameson, Harriet Martineau, and their Friends." *The Victorian Women Writers' Letters Project*. Dept. of English, University of British Columbia. http://edocs.lib.sfu.ca/projects/VWWLP/Anna-Brownell-Jameson.htm (accessed July 22, 2003).

———. *The "Anna Jameson and her Friends Database": Mapping Anna Jameson's Associative Links with the Victorian Intellectual Community*. Simon Fraser University. http://texttechnology.mcmaster.ca/patterson.html (accessed July 22, 2003).

Pearce, Susan M. *Museums, Objects, and Collections: A Cultural Study*. London: Leicester University Press, 1992.

Perkins, Joan. *Victorian Women*. London: J. Murray, 1993.

Peterson, Linda H. *Traditions of Victorian Women's Autobiography: The Poetics and Politics of Life Writing*. Charlottesville: University Press of Virginia, 1999.

———. *Victorian Autobiography: The Tradition of Self-Interpretation*. New Haven: Yale University Press, 1986.

Piggott, Stuart. *Ancient Britons and the Antiquarian Imagination: Ideas from the Renaissance to the Regency*. London: Thames & Hudson, 1989.

Pinder, Kymberly N. "Class, Race, and Arthurian Narratives in San Francisco in the 1870s." In Mancoff, *King Arthur's Modern Return*, 99–120.

Prichard, James Cowles. *The Eastern Origin of the Celtic Nations, Proved by a Comparison of their Dialects with the Sanskrit, Greek, Latin and Teutonic Languages*. London: Houston and Wright, 1857.

Propp, Vladimir. "Morphology of the Folktale." Translated by Laurence Scott. *International Journal of American Linguistics*, 24, no. 4 (1958): 1–134.

———. *Theory and History of Folklore*. Translated by Ariadna Y. Martin and Richard P. Martin. Minneapolis: University of Minnesota Press, 1993.

Rhys, John and J. Gwenogvryn Evans, eds. *The Text of the Mabinogion and other Welsh Tales from the Red Book of Hergest*. Oxford: Clarendon Press, 1887.

Richmond, Velma Bourgeois. *Chaucer as Children's Literature: Retellings from the Victorian and Edwardian Eras.* Jefferson, NC: McFarland and Co., 2004.

Schenck, Celeste. "All of a Piece: Women's Poetry and Autobiography." In Brodzki and Schenck, *Life/Lines: Theorizing Women's Autobiography*, 281–305.

Schiller, Friedrich von. *Über naïve und sentimentalische Dichtung.* Stuttgart: Reclam, 1966.

Scott, Sir Walter. *The Lady of the Lake.* Project Gutenberg Etext #3011. Release Date: January, 2002. Date last updated: November 3, 2004. http://www.gutenberg.org/catalog/world/readfile?fk_files=3466 (accessed February 6, 2006).

Smith, Sidonie. *A Poetics of Women's Autobiography: Marginality and the Fictions of Self-Representation.* Bloomington: Indiana University Press, 1987.

Smith, Sidonie, and Julia Watson, eds. *De/Colonizing the Subject: The Politics of Gender in Women's Autobiography.* Minneapolis: University of Minnesota Press, 1992.

———. *Getting a Life: Everyday Uses of Autobiography.* Minneapolis: University of Minnesota Press, 1996.

———. *Reading Autobiography: A Guide for Interpreting Life Narratives.* Minneapolis: University of Minnesota Press, 2001.

———. *Women, Autobiography, Theory: A Reader.* Madison: University of Wisconsin Press, 1998.

Tatar, Maria. *The Hard Facts of the Grimms' Fairy Tales.* 2nd ed. Princeton: Princeton University Press, 2003.

———. *Off with their Heads! Fairy Tales and the Culture of Childhood.* Princeton: Princeton University Press, 1992.

Thomson, R. L., ed. *Pwyll Pendeuic Dyuet: The First of the Four Branches of the Mabinogi / Edited from the White Book of Rhydderch with Variants from the Red Book of Hergest.* Dublin: Dublin Institute for Advanced Studies, 1957.

Vicinus, Martha. *A Widening Sphere: Changing Roles of Victorian Women.* Bloomington: Indiana University Press, 1977.

Warner, Marina. *From the Beast to the Blonde: On Fairy Tales and their Tellers.* New York: Farrar, Strauss, and Giroux, 1994.

Wylie, Betty Jane. *Reading Between the Lines.* Toronto: Key Porter, 1995.

Index

Page numbers in **bold** refer to illustrations